1.辽宁省社会科学规划基金项目“语言学英语期刊学术论文各语步中模糊限制语研究（ZX20160634）”

2.大连理工大学人才引进基金二期“中国英语专业学生毕业论文文献引用能力研究”（DUT18RC）

学术语篇中模糊限制语的篇章建构功能研究

A Discourse Construction Approach to Hedging in Academic Writing

葛天爽 著

图书在版编目(CIP)数据

学术语篇中模糊限制语的篇章建构功能研究 = A Discourse Construction Approach to Hedging in Academic Writing / 葛天爽著. —苏州: 苏州大学出版社,2019.1(2019.9 重印)
ISBN 978-7-5672-2578-7

Ⅰ.①学… Ⅱ.①葛… Ⅲ.①英语-模糊语言学-研究 Ⅳ.①H31

中国版本图书馆 CIP 数据核字(2018)第 194166 号

书　　名: A Discourse Construction Approach to Hedging in Academic Writing
学术语篇中模糊限制语的篇章建构功能研究

著　　者: 葛天爽
责任编辑: 沈　琴
装帧设计: 刘　俊

出版发行: 苏州大学出版社(Soochow University Press)
社　　址: 苏州市十梓街 1 号　邮编: 215006
印　　刷: 虎彩印艺股份有限公司印装
邮购热线: 0512-67480030
销售热线: 0512-67481020

开　　本: 890 mm×1 240 mm　1/32　印张: 8.875　字数: 231 千
版　　次: 2019 年 1 月第 1 版
印　　次: 2019 年 9 月第 2 次印刷
书　　号: ISBN 978-7-5672-2578-7
定　　价: 36.00 元

苏州大学出版社网址　http://www.sudapress.com
苏州大学出版社邮箱　sdcbs@suda.edu.cn

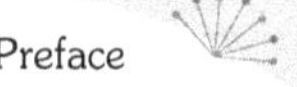

Preface

The traditional view considers academic written work as a channel to transmit information in an objective and impersonal manner without any involvement of the writer's personal opinions. Indeed, academic writing is better regarded as socially constructed 'rhetorical artifacts'. Thus, in order to avoid the appearance of over-rigid categorization in putting forth information, authors of academic papers often engage in process of negotiation or persuasion. Hedging has been considered as a salient characteristic of academic writing.

The use of hedging devices (HDs) in academic writing has recently received a lot of attention. As hedging is a prominent feature in English academic discourse, non-native speakers of English (NNS) who wish to gain academic recognition must develop proficiency in an appropriate use of hedging in their academic English writing. However, presenting information with an appropriate degree of certainty or hesitation presents a challenge for English language learners. In many studies it has been found that NNS writers do not adequately understand or do not recognize what the norms of academic writing in English.

Given this broad context, this book focuses on Chinese university level students' use of hedging in their academic written work in English. There are two central aims in this book. One aim is to investigate how Chinese students' choices of HDs are different in terms of patterns and rhetorical functions, from those of native speakers of English (NS) students. A comparison of learner corpus with native speaker corpus provides data on the

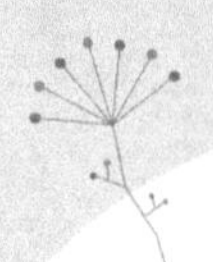

properties of interlanguage, covering lexico-grammatical patterns which are typically overused or underused, in addition to those which are misused by language learners (Barlow 2005:342). A corpus linguistic① approach in the first phase is considered as a lexical approach to the description of HDs, which focuses on co-occurrence patterns of HDs in texts.

Another aim of this current study is to examine the patterns of HDs in rhetorical structures. This provides a useful starting point for the corpus approach to genre-level discourse analysis of lexical patterns of HDs. Previous corpus studies of HDs have focused on the quantitative distribution of lexical and grammatical features, generally disregarding the language used in higher-level discourse structure and discourse organisation. The genre-level discourse analysis starts with the macrostructure of a text with a focus on larger units of text rather than only focus on lexico-grammatical patterning. However, most qualitative discourse analysis has focused on the analysis of discourse patterns in a few texts, but they have not provided tools for empirical analysis that can be applied on a large scale across a number of texts. The advantages of a corpus approach to discourse analysis for the study of HDs lie in the representativeness of a large amount of authentic text samples, and the computational tools for investigating distributional patterns across discourse contexts.

This book is structured into eight chapters. Chapter 1 introduces the research context in which the present book is set.

---

① Corpus linguistics is not just a branch of linguistics, nor a linguistic theory, but a methodology of 'doing' linguistics (e.g. Leech 1992; Biber *et al.* 1998: 3 – 4; McEnery & Wilson 2001; Meyer 2002). However, it has been argued, corpus linguistics is more than just a methodology (Leech 1991).

After a brief overview of the general notion of hedging, its background and development, it introduces the main models and approaches that form the interpretive framework of this research. The methodological approach applied in this research draws on corpus linguistic and genre-based research. Therefore, Chapter 2 focuses on corpus linguistics and genre analysis. With the corpus approach, this book focuses on lexical and grammatical features of HDs. With genre analysis approach (move analysis in the current study), a text structure view of HDs is taken. The research questions guiding the present research are listed in Chapter 3, which introduces the methodology of the study. The HDs analysed in detail are initially selected on the basis of frequency comparison between the NS and NNS corpora. Ten HDs are selected for detailed analysis: *would*, *may*, *should*, *suggest*, *seem*, *most*, *possible*, *perhaps*, *always* and *usually*. Chapters 4, 5 and 6 are a direct consequence of the selection of HDs on the basis of frequencies. These three chapters present the results of corpus analysis and move analysis, dividing the HDs into three main groups: 'modal verb HDs', 'lexical verb HDs' and 'adjective and adverb HDs'. Each of these three chapters has a structure where the first half deals with the patterns of HDs in the context of the concordance lines, and the second half looks at HDs in the rhetorical structure. In Chapters 4 to 6, analysis of concordance lines of the ten selected HDs reveal the linguistic patterns of HDs and the relationships between the particular patterns of HDs and their functions in local textual context. Corpus-based genre-level discourse analysis in the second half of these three chapters illustrates how textual features, patterns of HDs and functions of HDs are linked. Chapter 7 brings the results of the three groups

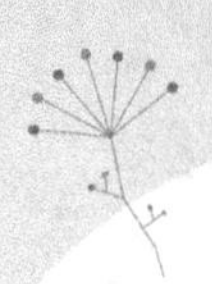

of HDs together, and discusses the relationships among patterns, functions and rhetorical structures. Moreover, how students from both the NS and the NNS groups manipulate their attitudes to the truth of statements and reflect the different rhetorical purposes of the academic writing through the use of HDs is discussed in this chapter. Finally, the main conclusions of the study are drawn in Chapter 8, outlining the contribution of the present research to the corpus theoretical approach to the study of HDs, to a corpus-based approach to genre analysis, and to a contrastive study of learner corpora.

TABLE OF CONTENTS

Chapter 1 The Attention Hedging Has Been Getting ········· 1
Introduction ········· 1
1.1 Development of the concept of hedging ········· 1
1.2 Academic writing and hedging ········· 4
1.2.1 The social nature of knowledge and academic writing ········· 5
1.2.2 HDs in academic writing across different rhetorical sections ········· 7
1.2.3 Studies on the use of HDs by L2 learners ········· 12
1.3 Grammatical forms of hedging devices ········· 15
1.4 Functions of hedging devices ········· 17
1.4.1 The politeness interpretation of hedging in academic writing ········· 18
1.4.2 Hyland's approach ········· 19
Conclusion ········· 34

Chapter 2 The Corpus Linguistics Point of View ········· 36
Introduction ········· 36
2.1 A lexical approach to the description of English ········· 37
2.2 Corpus linguistics and discourse analysis ········· 38
2.2.1 Move analysis ········· 39
2.2.2 Using a corpus-based approach to move analysis ········· 44
Conclusion ········· 48

Chapter 3 Interpreting Corpus Data ········· 50
Introduction ········· 50

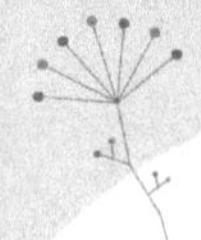

3.1 Aims of the book ······ 50
3.2 The corpora of the present study ······ 52
3.2.1 The non-native speaker corpus (NNS corpus) ······ 52
3.2.2 The native speaker corpus (NS corpus) ······ 53
3.3 Frequency ······ 55
3.3.1 Overview ······ 55
3.3.2 The selection of hedging devices in the corpus study ······ 56
Conclusion ······ 59

Chapter 4 Modal Verb Hedging ······ 60
Introduction ······ 60
4.1 Concordance analysis of *would*, *may* & *should* ······ 61
4.1.1 Meanings of *would*, *may* & *should* ······ 62
4.1.2 Discussion on the similarities and differences of co-occurrence patterns of hedging modal verbs between the NS corpus and the NNS corpus ······ 63
4.1.3 Polypragmatic functions of hedging following modal verb patterns ······ 73
4.2 Move analysis of modal verbs ······ 93
4.2.1 Modal verb hedging realisations in the Introduction sections ······ 95
4.2.2 Modal verb hedging in Discussion sections ······ 110
Conclusion ······ 125

Chapter 5 Lexical Verb Hedging with *Suggest* and *Seem* ······ 128
Introduction ······ 128
5.1 Frequency of hedging lexical verbs ······ 129
5.2 Judgment verb—*suggest* ······ 132

5.2.1 Personalised and depersonalised constructions of *suggest* ······ 134
5.2.2 'Authors' + *suggest* ······ 138
5.2.3 Compound hedges ······ 140
5.3 Evidential verb—*seem* ······ 143
5.4 Move analysis of hedging lexical verbs *suggest* and *seem* ······ 152
5.4.1 Lexical verb hedging realisation in Introduction sections ······ 158
5.4.2 Lexical verb hedging realisation in Discussion sections ······ 168
Conclusion ······ 173

Chapter 6 Adjectives and Adverbs Hedging ······ 177
Introduction ······ 177
6.1 Concordance analysis of *most*, *often*, *usually*, *perhaps* and *possible* ······ 178
6.1.1 An overview ······ 178
6.1.2 *Most* ······ 181
6.1.3 Adverbs of frequency: *often* and *usually* ······ 186
6.1.4 Hedging adverb *perhaps* ······ 195
6.1.5 Hedging determiner *most* and adjective *possible* ······ 197
6.1.6 Polypragmatic functions of hedging adverbs and adjectives ······ 204
6.2 Move analysis of adverbs and adjectives hedging ······ 205
6.2.1 Distribution of hedging adverbs and adjectives across different rhetorical sections and rhetorical move types in the NS and NNS corpora ······ 207
6.2.2 Hedging adverbs and adjectives in the move 'establishing a territory' of the Introduction sections ······ 211

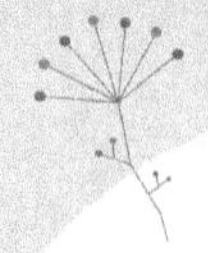

6.2.3 Hedging adverbs and adjectives in the move 'consolidating important points' of the Discussion sections ············ 217

Conclusion ·· 223

Chapter 7 Reconsidering the Role of Hedging in Academic Writing ···························· 226

Introduction ·· 226

7.1 Frequency ·· 228

7.2 Polypragmatic functions and co-occurrence patterns of HDs ·· 231

7.3 Hedging as a textual feature in academic writing ········· 236

Chapter 8 Contributions of the Book ·························· 240

8.1 The methodology of corpus study and genre study ········· 242

8.2 Implications for teaching of HDs in academic writing ·· 244

Appendices ·· 248

Bibliography ·· 250

Chapter 1

The Attention Hedging Has Been Getting

Introduction

For the study of hedging devices (HDs) in English academic writing of Chinese undergraduate students, this chapter provides both a review of relevant literature on HDs and a theoretical framework for the study. Section 1.1 traces in literature how the concept of hedging has developed over time. Such a historical overview reveals the core concept of hedging, its basic properties and characteristics. Then, in Section 1.2, some important and up-to-date studies of HDs in discourse of academic writing are reviewed, which indicate the direction of the current study. This is followed by Section 1.3, which outlines the grammatical forms and functions of HDs. A theoretical framework of HDs in academic discourse is then established for the present study by collecting information on the grammatical form of HDs and evaluating the various functions of HDs in the context of academic discourse.

1.1 Development of the concept of hedging

The development and enlargement of the concept of hedging can be divided into three stages. The first stage has a mainly linguistic

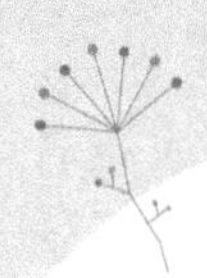

focus, in which hedge is considered as a modifier of words or phrases within a proposition, chiefly in respect of propositional content (Lakoff 1972; Brown & Levinson 1987). The second stage is mainly linguistic and pragmatic, in which hedge is seen to modify the truth-value of the whole proposition and the speaker or writer's commitment or attitude to the propositional content. In this account the focus is on the speaker-content relationship (Fraser 1975; Vande Kopple 1985). The third stage is mainly pragmatic and social, in which hedge is seen to modify the relationship between interlocutors or wider social relationships, with the focus being on interpersonal and social relationships (Markkanen & Schroder 1989, 1992).

The notion of 'hedge' and its use as a linguistic term date from a 1972 article by Lakoff entitled 'A study in meaning criteria and the logic of fuzzy concepts' (Hyland 1996b; Meyer 1997). Lakoff was not interested in the communicative value of the use of HDs but instead was mainly concerned with the logical implications of sending statements that were more or less vague in nature; therefore, his definition of HDs is purely semantic. Therefore, according to Lakoff, words or phrases like 'sort of', 'rather' and 'largely' can be regarded as HDs because they have the ability to make things fuzzier or less fuzzy.

Since the publication of Lakoff's (1972) original paper, the concept of HDs has been extended as HDs have been examined using other approaches such as Speech Acts Theory (Brown & Levinson 1987), the study of oral discourse (Holmes 1982; Hosman 1989), and, particularly, pragmatic analysis and the study of academic discourse (Butler 1990; Markkanen & Schroder 1997). Various definitions of hedging have been proposed by researchers. Zuck and Zuck (1986: 172), for instance, define HDs as 'the process whereby the author reduces the strength of what he is writing' in case the results of research turn out not to be true. In their definition, the

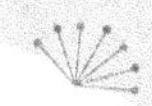

interpersonal aspect of hedging has been emphasized, which extends the original concept of hedging in language to a pragmatic use in communicative situations. Brown and Levinson (1987: 145), define HDs as 'a word, particle or phrase' modifying another linguistic unit (such as a predicate or noun), category membership or an element of an utterance, to make the modified part more vague (in terms of face value) or more precise (in terms of the speaker's own opinion). In this sense, hedging can be interpreted as a sign of politeness strategy to build up writer-reader relationship by supporting the writer's position and opinion. In other words, hedging aims at mitigating a face-threatening act (Brown & Levinson 1987). Writers leave room for opinions of readers as well as to him/herself against potential criticism in case of being proven wrong.

In later work, HDs have been treated as realizations of an interactional or communicative strategy called hedging, which takes the hedge concept far from Lakoff's original concept. Thus, Markkanen and Schroder (1989, 1992), who discuss the role of HDs in academic texts, see them as modifiers of the writer's responsibility for the truth value of the propositions expressed or as modifiers of the weightiness of the information given, or the attitude of the writer to the information. According to Markkanen and Schroder (1992), HDs can even be used to hide the writer's attitude. Markkanen and Schroder (1992) also suggest that HDs offer a possibility for textual manipulation in the sense that the reader is left in the dark as to who is responsible for the truth value of what is being expressed.

Thus, the following devices can all be regarded as HDs in academic writing: the use of modal verbs, adverbs and particles, the use of certain pronouns and avoidance of others, the use of impersonal expressions, and the use of the passive and other forms of agentless construction, even the use of certain rhetorical and stylistic devices

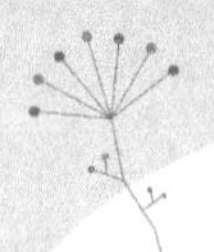

can be regarded as HDs.

Starting from a functional view of HDs, the role that might be performed by HDs in interpersonal and social relationships have been considered and debated by researchers. According to Brown and Levinson (1978, 1987), hedging can be used as a strategy to maintain social relationships and preserve face of communicators. Based on the discussion of Brown and Levinson's (1978, 1987) work, Myers (1989) argues that the use of HDs can be seen as a politeness strategy in both a positive way and a negative way. The interpersonal politeness strategy can help to build up the writer-reader relationship by supporting the writer's position. Hyland's (1998a) view of hedging was not limited to the politeness interpersonal strategy, but extended to consideration of the whole academic community. He states that HDs are 'the means by which writers can present a proposition as an opinion rather than a fact: items are only HDs in their epistemic① sense, and only when they mark uncertainty' (Hyland 1998a: 5). Hyland (1998a) argues that by using HDs in academic texts, besides showing the extent of the accuracy of writers' statements, writers also attempt to invite readers to evaluate the truth value of the proposition as individuals in order to establish an academic community (see also Hyland 1996a, 1996b).

1.2 Academic writing and hedging

The following literature review pays attention to the use of HDs in academic writing, where HDs are often examined within a corpus. This research begins with a description of characteristics of academic

① Epistemic modality, according to Coates (1983: 18), is concerned with 'the speaker's and writer's assumptions or assessment of possibilities, and in most cases, it indicates confidence in the truth of proposition expressed'.

text in which HDs are examined in the present study. Then, a literature review of previous empirical studies of HDs is presented in Sections 1.2.2 and 1.2.3. Section 1.2.2 focuses on studies which examined and compared the forms and functions of hedging across different rhetorical sections of academic texts. How L2 learners use HDs in English and the problems they encounter are discussed in Section 1.2.3.

1.2.1 The social nature of knowledge and academic writing

The majority of hedge studies are found to be concerned with academic writing, in areas such as economics (Pindi & Bloor 1986; Channell 1994), abstracts (Rounds 1982), medical papers (Salager-Meyer 1991, 1994), molecular genetics (Myers 1989), and news (Zuck & Zuck 1986, 1987). According to Hyland (1998a: 6), hedging is an 'essential element of academic argument', which other researchers have also found to be the case (Myers 1989; Hyland 1996a; Hinkel 1997) and help structure the research paper. As Hyland notes,

> In science, HDs play a critical role in gaining ratification for claims from a powerful peer group by allowing writers to present statements with appropriate accuracy, caution, and humility. HDs help negotiate the perspective from which conclusions can be accepted (Hyland 1996a: 434).

That is to say, the use of HDs is obligatory in academic writing and science articles, thus becoming one type of 'obligatory context' in which HDs occur (Hyland 1996b: 434). Clearly, functions of

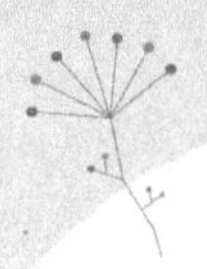

HDs in academic writing are more pragmatic than semantic①. For example, they rely more on the characteristics of contexts and the academic genre than on the semantic meaning of the HDs in question (Meyer 1997). Features of academic writing are considered below in order to show why academic writing can be a fruitful area of examination in hedging research.

Academic written genres have their own communicative purposes and distinctive structural patterns. Widdowson (1984: 220) claims that 'academic genres, like other forms of writing, require writers to consider the expected audience and anticipate their background knowledge, processing problems, and reaction to the text'. According to Hyland (1994), readers try to generalize the main thought from an academic paper, criticise the positions of the author, and evaluate the work for its importance to their own research. Academic writing is the main channel through which new research findings are communicated. The primary objective of academic writing is to present new knowledge claims and to make the strongest possible case for their acceptance by peers and for their ratification of those claims as new knowledge by the community of members of their discipline (Hyland 2000; Thompson 2001). Therefore, it may be said that academic writing is an act of argumentation, and research articles are characterized by such acts as stating, questioning, asserting, evaluating, reporting, arguing and concluding. The accomplishment of these acts in academic research writing concerns epistemic change and interpersonal relations. In securing acceptance for their new knowledge claims, writers have to alter the knowledge set of the reader according to their purpose (Hyland 2000; Thompson

① 'Pragmatic' is concerned with the use and function, while 'semantic' is focused on the meaning of propositions.

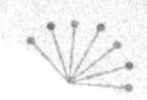

2001). During this process, disagreement, arguments and debates are expected. In the process of bidding for space for new findings within the body of existing knowledge, contributors of existing knowledge can be questioned when new work contradicts their own. In both processes, hedging language plays an important role in persuading readers and in accommodating interpersonal relations (Myers 1989; Hyland 1997).

1.2.2 HDs in academic writing across different rhetorical sections

Considering only written language, Hyland (1996b) argues that the distribution of HDs across various research article sections reflects their essentially rhetorical role in discourse. There may be different ways to divide an academic article into different sections, but the most prevalent way to introduce the organization of research articles is to divide them into 'Introduction, Method, Results and Discussion' sections. This organization has been applied by several researchers to approach the distribution of HDs (Swales 1990; Salager-Meyer 1994; Hyland 1998a). The results from these studies suggest that it is generally believed that the Introduction and Discussion sections are complex, subjective and author-centred because these two sections are where argument is emphasized and where decisions, claims and justifications are most commonly found, while Method and Results sections are believed to be rhetorically simple, objective and detached. The rhetorical features found in all sections of an academic paper are achieved through careful linguistic choices.

Both Myers (1989) and Salager-Meyer (1994) identified differences in frequency and distribution of hedging phenomena in different sections of research articles. Myers noted that the Discussion sections of research articles are heavily hedged. Salager-Meyer

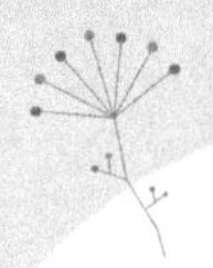

observed that hedging may also often occur in the Results and Introduction sections of medical research articles. However, Results sections are likely to be less hedged than Discussion sections, since they are considered to be less subjective than Discussion sections.

Salager-Meyer (1994) studied the use of HDs in medical English. In her study, the frequency of HDs in the different rhetorical sections of research papers (RPs) and case reports (CRs) varies. The results show that the Discussion section in the RPs and their equivalent Comment section in CRs contain the most HDs (HDs accounting for 13% and 10.7%, respectively), whereas the Methods section is the least-hedged rhetorical section in RPs and CRs (0.8% and 3.6%, respectively).

Hyland specifically chose to investigate hedging in research articles because of the important role that hedging plays in this genre. Hyland's (1998a) study provides an explanatory framework (emerging from the analysis of actual language behaviour) of the role of hedging in cell and molecular biology research articles, by clarifying the incidence and function of particular hedging expressions. The study is based on a corpus of 75,000 words taken from 26 research articles in cell and molecular biology. The results show that the Discussion sections have both the highest total frequencies of HDs and the highest density per thousand words. Hyland (ibid) also describes his pragmatic analytical framework, a polypragmatic model of hedging—as providing a functional account for the use of HDs in scientific research articles (see Section 1.4.2.2 for a detailed description). This framework combines sociological, linguistic and discourse perspectives; this means that standards of knowledge (beliefs concerning the nature of reality), plus textual representations (that is how knowledge or information is expressed linguistically in writing), and discourse community norms (norms or

expectations of the academic community), are considered in combination to clarify the use of HDs in research article writing. In other words, reality, language and audience are all necessary considerations in analysis of HDs.

Using Hyland's polypragmatic model of hedging, Varttala (2003) investigated the use of HDs in scientific texts in three different disciplines. Differences were found in hedging frequency between disciplines, between research articles (RAs) and popular scientific articles, and between different rhetorical sections. In RAs, the Discussion section is found to be the most heavily hedged section, followed by the Introduction section. In a similar study, Falahati (2005) also uses Hyland's model of hedging (Hyland 1998a) to study the forms and functions of hedging in two rhetorical sections of RAs in three different disciplines. Hedging forms and functions are unevenly distributed across different rhetorical sections. The frequency of occurrence of hedging forms in the Discussion sections of RAs is greater than in the Introduction sections. The results of this study are consistent with those of Hyland's (1998a) study of the distribution of hedging across the different rhetorical sections of biology RAs, Salager-Meyer's (1994) corresponding investigation of hedging in medical RAs, and Vassileva's (2001) study of hedging in English and Bulgarian RAs (see Vassileva 2001 for detail). In all these studies, it is found that the frequency of occurrence of hedging expression varies across different rhetorical sections of RAs.

As noted previously, the communicative purpose of academic writing is to present new knowledge claims and secure their acceptance by readers. To achieve this purpose, an academic paper typically has a distinctive structure. An academic paper is generally presented in what Swales (1990) terms an IMRD format, consisting of the Introduction section, the Method section, the Results section

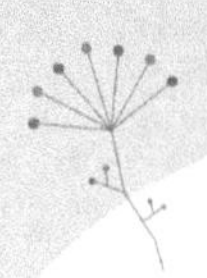

and the Discussion section. The IMRD structure remains a model recommended and required by academic papers in general. As proposed by Swales (1990), each section of the research article performs different rhetorical functions, which are reflected by differences in the distribution of HDs across individual sections of the academic paper. Each of these rhetorical sections is further divided into smaller rhetorical functions which Swales (1990) refers to as moves.

In this book, the use of hedging devices across different rhetorical sections, and across the moves in students' academic writing, the use of modals across the moves in the different sections of research articles are analysed, taking the moves identified by Swales (1990:127) as the basis. Analysis of Discussion sections of students' research papers is also based on a modified version of the model outlined by Hopkins and Dudley-Evans (1998: 118) for natural sciences in order to gain deeper insight into modal verb use in the Discussion sections of the research papers.

The rhetorical purposes of the Introduction section are traditionally explained according to Swales's three basic moves: 'establishing a territory', 'establishing a niche' and 'occupying the niche' (Swales 1990, 2004). According to Swales (1990, 2004), writers realize the first move of the Introduction section of their academic writing—'establishing a territory'—by 'claiming centrality' and/or 'making topic generalizations' and/or 'reviewing items of previous research'. The second move is usually followed by 'counter claiming' and/or 'indicating a gap in the previous research' and/or 'raising a question' and/or 'extending a finding' in order to establish a niche in the Introduction section. The third move of the Introduction sections—'occupying the niche'—is realized by 'outlining the purposes or stating the nature of the present

research' and/or 'describing present research' and/or 'indicating the structure of the research paper'. Swales explains that the function of the Introduction is 'to justify the publication of the study by showing that the author's contribution to the discipline, whilst previously established as significant and reference-worthy, is as yet incomplete' (Swales 2004: 138). It seems that when research authors are establishing a position for their work among those of other researchers, their language is cautious and diplomatic. HDs may be employed in a variety of contexts, for instance when writers are pointing out gaps or shortcomings of previous work or introduce their own research project and its importance and definiteness (Varttala 2001: 159).

Contrary to the Introduction section, the Discussion/Conclusion section moves incrementally outward. Considering the fact that the findings are foregrounded and the work of others are cited to confirm, compare and contrast with the present findings, the Discussion/Conclusion section is expected to be general and tentative rather than particular and precise. According to Hopkins and Dudley-Evans (1998), academic writers realize a number of sub-moves to realize three moves to 'consolidate important points', 'state limitations', and 'make suggestions'. These sub-moves range from providing background information to stating their results, from expressing their (un)expected outcomes to referring to previous research, and from explaining and exemplifying to making deductions/hypotheses in order to be able to consolidate important points. In addition to these strategies, they also state their limitations and make recommendations. In their attempts to realize these moves of the Discussion/Conclusion section, which is general and tentative, academic writers convey their imprecision by employing HDs to varying degrees.

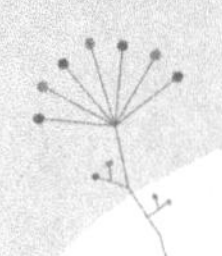

1.2.3 Studies on the use of HDs by L2 learners

To date, published studies of HDs have mainly been concerned with native speakers' use of HDs, with emphasis on grammatical, semantic or pragmatic properties of the HDs in question. Less has been published on the use of HDs by learners, especially L2 learners and the problems they experience with the use of HDs when writing in a foreign language.

Some researchers have arrived at the conclusion that NNSs state their arguments in their English academic writing in a more direct and unqualified way which distinguishes them from their native English speaking counterparts. For example, Ventola and Mauranen (1990) finds that Finnish learners writing in English tend to rely upon few expressions of epistemic modality, and exhibit less variation in hedging than native speakers of English do. In contrast, Clyne (1991) had analysed German academic writing in English. The study of Clyne (ibid), which focuses on German academic authors writing in English, has shown that German writers hedge more. This study also finds that German writers hedge more in both their native language and English than native English speakers writing in English do. Compared to L1 English writers, it is found that German writers use double and even triple number of HDs. When writing in English, they tend to follow the norms of their native German writing culture. With regard to this, it has been argued that writers' background and mother tongue transfer may affect their use of HDs (Atai & Sadr 2006; Hwang, Ze & Dyer 2010).

Researchers have found that the use of HDs in academic writing is necessary to support claims sufficiently (Cherry 1988; Myers 1989; Swales & Feak 1994). To sound native-like in a foreign language, a writer needs to use an appropriate number of hedging expressions in his or her written work, and in the style of a native

writer. Due to the internationalisation of English, English is no longer owned by Inner Circle speakers only, in Kachru's (1985) terms, and that other varieties, for example, those from the Outer Circle, also have developed their own norms. According to Kachru (1985), China belongs to the Expanding Circle, where it has no official capacity. English is considered to depend on the norms and standards of Inner Circle native speakers model of English. That is to say, British and American writers are considered as native writers and norm in the current study.

Tutors of academic writing for NNSs and their textbooks tend to overemphasise directness in writing of academic articles in English, viewing hedging as weakening the quality of writing (Bloor & Bloor 1991; Gilbert & Mulkay 1991). What is more, some textbooks have even advised writers 'to avoid hedging altogether' (e.g. Winkler & McCuen 1989, cited in Hyland 1998: 8). According to Dudley-Evans (1991), L2 students of English become so direct in their writing that their writing has been considered inappropriate and they are criticised for being offensive.

Salager-Meyer (1994) suggests that vagueness used to present information by native speakers of English is frequently overlooked by non-native speakers of English, and one reason for this might be that little guidance on this topic is available in ESL textbooks. Salager-Meyer (1994) further proposes that awareness of the need to mediate claims in academic writing should be developed in students learning to write academic English. Exercises, such as sensitization and translation exercises and rewriting exercises, can also be recommended to tutors of English for academic purposes to help students become aware of the range of HDs available and the ways in which they are used.

Another important study is conducted by Hyland and Milton

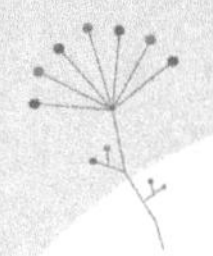

(1997), who investigated students' expression of doubt and certainty in academic writing through either hedging or boosting devices①. Using a corpus-based method, the authors compared the use of HDs and boosters in the examination scripts of Chinese students writing in English with those of British students of a similar age and educational level. Through a series of detailed analysis of the overall frequency of HDs and a range of epistemic modifiers of HDs in both NS and NNS corpora, the researchers find that both Chinese students and British students employ around 20 HDs per thousand words. However, the L2 students differ significantly from the native speakers in relying upon a narrower range of hedging and boosting items, stating stronger commitments, and showing greater problems in expressing degree of certainty.

According to some researchers (e.g. Low 1996; Hyland 2000), it seems that HDs are, to a certain degree, 'invisible' to L2 writers. However, this claim seems quite contradictory in respect to language proficiency level, contrasting with the findings of other researchers, for example, Wishnoff (2000) and Lewin (2005). Both researchers studied advanced non-native English writers; however, Lewin (2005) focused more on reading, whereas Wishnoff (2000) was interested in writing. In both cases, students were of a sufficiently high language proficiency level to be able to understand and produce both propositional content and metadiscoursal elements② of the academic text. Thus, both researchers at the end of their investigation

---

① According to Hyland (1998b: 236), boosters (e.g. definitely ..., I am sure that ..., we firmly believe ...) create an impression of certainty, conviction and assurance and they can be used to instill trust and confidence in academic papers.

② Metadiscourse embodies the idea that communication is more than just the exchange of information, goods or services, but also involves the personalities, attitudes and assumptions of those who are communicating (Hyland 2005:3).

concluded that L2 students were very conscious of HDs in reading or writing scientific texts. Šeškauskien's (2008) study focuses on the use of HDs by L2 users of English, more specifically, by Lithuanian undergraduate students majoring in English. The investigation draws on the data collected from the Lithuanian students' BA papers written according to Swales's IMRD model (Swales 1990). The findings do not support the view that L2 users of English have limited awareness of HDs in texts they are exposed to (see Low 1996; Hyland 2000). Moreover, more advanced and proficient learners of English are able to produce texts which, in terms of hedging, are comparable to those produced by experienced academics. Hyland and Milton's (1997) study examines some important differences across ability bands among NNSs, which may reveal some hedging development across different proficiency levels. The results show that higher ability students use more HDs in their essays which demonstrate greater similarity to the NS usage, while lower ability students use more boosting devices. Both higher and lower ability students prefer modal verbs as compared to the NS samples. NS students' usage, on the other hand, exhibits a greater range and frequency of adverbs, with over 55% more occurrences. However, low ability students' preference for using modal verbs is particularly noticeable.

1.3 Grammatical forms of hedging devices

Hedging is a broad term which captures a variety of forms of expression with differing hedging qualities. More specifically, there are some linguistic concepts, such as modality, which are considered to be aspects of hedging. Modality refers to a speaker's attitude toward the propositional content of his or her utterance (Simpson 1990; Horslund 2005). Since both hedging and epistemic modality are related to the nature of a writer's attitude to the proposition, it seems

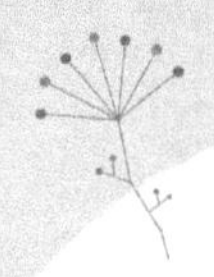

reasonable to equate hedging with epistemic modality. According to Hyland (1998a: 1 – 5) and Marco and Mercer (2004), HDs can appear as modal auxiliaries (*would*, *should*, *etc.*); epistemic adjectives (*possible*, *most*, *etc.*), adverbs (*perhaps*, *often*, *etc.*), verbs (*suggest*, *seem*, *etc.*) and nouns (*possibility*, *probability*, *etc.*); tag questions (*isn't it?*, *can't we?*, *etc.*); and if-clauses (*if true*, *if anything*, *etc.*). Another common way to hedge a statement is the use of passive voice, which enables the writers to distance themselves from their assertions by avoiding mentioning the agent. The writer thus appears objective and minimizes personal commitment as a means of self-protection.

In reference to the explanations given by Hyland (1998a: 102 – 155) and the listing of Gillett (2006), there are two forms of HDs—lexical HDs and non-lexical HDs. Lexical HDs (see examples in Table 1) account for 85% (Hyland 1998a: 104) of scientific hedging and represent the most common means of epistemic modality in English, while non-lexical HDs account for another 15% (Hyland 1998a: 141) of scientific hedging. The division of HDs into lexical and non-lexical forms is illustrated in the tables below (Table 1 and Table 2). Since strategic non-lexical HDs are extremely context-related and therefore difficult to define as separate words, they will not be considered in depth in this book.

Table 1: Lexical HDs (Hyland 1998a; Gillett 2006)

<table>
<tr><th colspan="7">Lexical HDs</th></tr>
<tr><td>Modal Auxiliaries</td><td colspan="2">Epistemic Lexical Verbs</td><td colspan="3">Epistemic Adjectives, Adverbs and Nouns</td><td>Hedging Numerical Data</td></tr>
<tr><td></td><td>Epistemic Judgement Verbs</td><td>Epistemic Evidential Verbs</td><td>Epistemic Adjectives</td><td>Epistemic Adverbs</td><td>Epistemic Nouns</td><td></td></tr>
</table>

(continued)

must/need, can/could, will/would, shall/ should, may/might	propose, suggest, believe, speculate, think, indicate ...	show, appear, seem, tend, look like ...	likely, possible, most, significant, clear, certain, ...	probably, apparently, possibly, perhaps, often, usually, ...	probability, possibility, assumption, ...	about, approximately, some, around, ...

Table 2: Strategic Non-lexical HDs (Hyland 1998a; Gillett 2006)

Strategic Non-lexical HDs		
Reference to Limited Knowledge	Reference to Limitation of Modal, Theory or Method	Reference to Experimental Limitations
Nothing is known about ...	In the context of the proposed model ...	Under these conditions ...

1.4 Functions of hedging devices

The use of HDs can be regarded as a strategy by which academic writers may indicate, for example, that they have explored the limitations of their own research process, and that they have approached their own procedures critically, meticulously indicating to the readership to what degree their accounts can be seen to correspond to reality. The interpretation, establishing a clear link between the linguistic strategy of hedging and the social nature of knowledge-making, appears to be the dominant one in literature dealing with HDs in academic writing and in communication between academic peers (Varttala 2001). These interpretations of hedging in academic writing have been worded in many ways by researchers. Two main approaches are taken towards hedging functions: they are hedging in the interpersonal politeness model and in the polypragmatic model. These two approaches are discussed below.

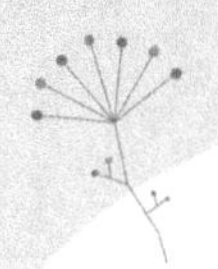

1.4.1 The politeness interpretation of hedging in academic writing

The concept of hedging as an indicator of politeness in academic discourse has become known from the work of Myers (1989) on RAs in biology. As Bloor and Bloor (1993) surmise, the use of HDs as politeness markers has always been acknowledged, but Myers was the first researcher to pay close attention to the role that politeness markers, including HDs, might play in scientific discourse. According to Myers (1989), hedging expressions may serve as mediators of negative politeness. According to Brown and Levinson (1987), negative politeness can be defined as a strategy for self-protection which adheres to or respects the other person rights and privileges in a sense of avoiding of intrusion to the other personal space in academic articles. By hedging information pertaining to those aspects of RAs that might give rise to objections, authors can mark 'a claim, or any other statement, as being provisional, pending acceptance in the literature, acceptance by the community—in other words, acceptance by the readers' (Myers 1989: 12).

Exploration of the politeness interpretation of HDs has provided new insights into the value that hedging phenomena may have in scientific RAs. According to Crompton (1997), Myers' account of HDs demonstrates that scientific discourse abides by principles of social interaction observed in all linguistic activity. In Crompton's view, people involved in scientific communication pay attention to the effects of the way in which they address the scientific community just as people addressing communities do in general.

The politeness interpretation of HDs has not been accepted by all researchers interested in the use of hedging in academic articles. The politeness approach is criticized by Hyland (1998a: 67), who proposes that portraying hedging in academic articles as a politeness

phenomenon in the sense suggested by (among others) Brown and Levinson (1978, 1987) shows less concern among the academic community for the importance of 'maintaining standards, judging merit and evaluating reputation' (Hyland 1997: 12). It also seems that one of the central problems of the politeness approach to HDs in research articles is associated with the model's emphasis on the relationship between sender and addressee, and on the concerns relating to the face needs of the two. As Hyland (1998a: 69) says, 'while the choice of linguistic form in science is undoubtedly partly determined by the writer's appreciation of a responsibility to the reader, a failure to observe "politeness" will not merely prevent individuals securing goals, but will incur social sanction.' In other words, in academic articles, hedging is not solely a matter of interpersonal politeness between writer and reader. Its employment is also determined by the requirements of the wider academic community. A disregard for indications of politeness may not only result in a face-threatening conflict between sender and addressee, but may also link to establish the author's reputation within his or her academic community. Hyland (1998a) considers hedging in academic articles as an interaction within the academic community norms concerning the confidence with which ideas are expressed and the deference due to the views of other researchers.

Given the deficiencies identified by Hyland in the politeness approach to the analysis of hedging in academic writing, an alternative means of analysis is needed. In deriving a satisfactory approach to the study of hedging in academic discourse, the work of Hyland can again be considered.

1.4.2 Hyland's approach

A model devised precisely for the analysis of hedging in

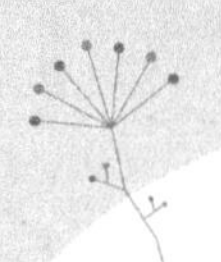

academic research articles has been established by Hyland (1998a), whose work is based on a study of HDs in a corpus of biology research articles. In the following sections, Hyland's (1998a) work are described in detail since this forms the basis of this study on HDs.

1.4.2.1 Hyland's study—an overview

This section provides an overview of Hyland's (1996a, 1998a) investigation into hedging in research articles, and an introduction to his analytical framework. A detailed explanation of this framework is provided in this section, since the current study is based on it.

Hyland specifically chose to investigate hedging in research articles because of the important role that hedging plays in the genre. Hyland (1998a:1) refers to hedging as 'any linguistic means used to indicate either a) lack of complete commitment to the truth value of an accompanying proposition, or b) a desire not to express that commitment categorically'. Hedging is regarded as one part of epistemic modality.

Hyland's study (1998a) seeks to identify the major hedging devices (HDs) used in cell and molecular biology articles, determine their distribution across different rhetorical sections, explore their pragmatic functions, and briefly compare the overall findings with other forms of academic writing.

The data for Hyland's study was obtained from two sources: a large computer data base of published academic writing and research articles selected from a number of leading scientific journals in the field of cell and molecular biology consisting of 75,000 words. The large computer database consists of three corpora: the JDEST science corpus (Jiao Da English for Science and Technology), and the academic sections of the Brown University and Lancaster/Oslo-Bergen (LOB) corpora. The collection of cell and molecular biology research articles was named the Journal Corpus. The computer database is

used to provide an overview of lexical markers of hedging in an extensive set of written academic texts, as it is by no means clear in the literature which of the various ways of expressing hedging are typical in academic discourse.

A list of high frequency items used to express hedging was compiled by reference to published studies of hedging or related notions in computer corpora, principally Holmes (1988) and Kennedy (1987) (Hyland did not append the list in his study). Both of these writers used the Journal sections of the Brown and LOB corpora, Holmes to determine the relative frequency of items expressing epistemic modality, and Kennedy to determine the devices used to refer to temporal frequency. Kennedy's research appeared useful as many adverbs such as *often*, *usually* and *generally* are also found to be used to hedge and express probability. Holmes's work indicates the likelihood of encountering epistemic verbs in academic discourse which are used to express tentativeness, such as *appear*, *assume* and *suggest*.

The next stage in Hyland's study was to determine how often each of the words or phrases identified in the list appeared in the Journal Corpus. Following this, a detailed study was made of the journal corpus using the information gained from the above investigations. Every word or phrase expressing a hedging function in the RAs was noted. The judgments rested on close contextual investigations and estimations concerning whether the devices performed hedging functions. Hyland then carried out semi-structured interviews to provide access to insider interpretations, to test and refine the categorisation, and to validate particular interpretations. In addition, two 'scientist informants' were also used to help with analysing the extracts discussed in his book (Hyland 1998a: 162). Quantitative analysis was taken to reveal both the frequency of the principle lexical

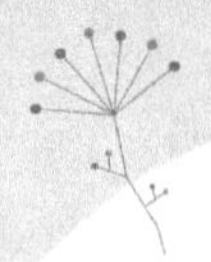

forms of hedging and their distribution. Analyses of the three corpora in the computer data-base were also made to determine the frequency and distribution of lexical HDs in more general contexts for comparison. Then, oral interviews were conducted and discourse analyses were carried out which sought to account for pragmatic choice and demonstrate the linguistic features of hedging in the Journal Corpus performed in particular contexts.

In the category of modal auxiliaries, Hyland (1998a) ran a frequency analysis of each modal verb used to express hedging in various corpora. Hyland figured out that the clearest differences occured between the uses of *would* and *may* in Butler's study and the Journal Corpus (see Hyland 1998a), which altered their rankings. In Butler's study of modal verbs, *would* ranked 1st, followed by *may*, while in the Journal Corpus, *may* occupied the 1st place followed by *would*. Hyland then discussed individual modals in turn in the closer context of the Journal Corpus. Hyland approached the modal verbs in two different ways: semantic and syntactic. Taking *would* as an example, semantically, a common use of epistemic *would* in academic writing is as the hypothetical variant of *will*, a marker of prediction (Coates 1983; Perkins 1983; Leech 1987). Syntactically, examples of *would* frequently co-occur with verbs (the most frequent co-occurring verb is *be*, followed by *appear* and *suggest*). Hyland listed several examples of *would* as a marker of prediction with the construction of '*would* + verb' taken from the Journal Corpus in his study. See the following examples taken from Hyland's (1998a: 112 – 113) study.

a) ... if the haemoglobin in the root were mainly at the tip, it *would* have a local concentration 100-fold or greater than originally deduced. (D1:638)

b) From this discussion, then, it *would appear* that some of the

changes in amino acid concentrations ... (E2:732)

A problem in Hyland's study is that he did not describe exactly how he approached HDs semantically and syntactically. It is difficult to find information on how Hyland obtained his examples listed in his book. Also, there is no information about how many examples Hyland analysed in his study. In Hyland's book, he reports that the Journal Corpus yielded 395 instances of modal verbs, of which 257 were used epistemically, the most frequent being *would*, *may* and *could* which accounted for 76.6% of the total (Hyland 1998a: 107). In the analysis of each most frequent hedging modal verb, Hyland generally used arguments like 'it is noticeable that *be* frequently co-occurs with *must* in the corpus' (1998a: 109), or 'the majority of examples of *would* are active, and one of the most frequent co-occurring main verbs is *be*' (1998a: 112) to summarise the co-occurrence patterns without giving any statistical information.

In the current study, a contextualized view of selected hedging items is provided, so that readers can see hedging devices in real texts and see what patterns of lexis, grammar and meaning surround them. Unlike Hyland's (1998a) study, this research does not merely focus on identifying the forms and functions of HDs. As mentioned above, the two main purposes of this study are: (1) to compare the frequency information between the NS corpus and the NNS corpus and to investigate the collocational behaviour of selected HDs used by NS and NNS students of English; (2) to identify and evaluate the linguistic features of selected HDs in moves and sections in order to find out how selected HDs contribute to the rhetorical functions of different rhetoric move types in two corpora.

According to Hyland (1998a), HDs can have different meanings that are specific to particular writers and readers, and to particular contexts. Having proposed that various functions of hedging in academic writing cannot be fully interpreted from a linguistic point of view, such as epistemic modality, Hyland (1996a) attempted to establish a taxonomy for scientific HDs from a social, pragmatic and discoursal point of view. Hyland (1996a) created a fuzzy category model for HDs, which permitted more than a single unequivocal pragmatic interpretation of HDs and permitted overlap of usage. Instead of approaching hedging within a rigid interpretive model such as the politeness theory, Hyland begins from the basic observation that HDs not only have different semantic interpretations, but also serve various polypragmatic functions in different contexts (Hyland 1998a). Hyland notes that HDs are useful for reaching a number of different pragmatic goals. HDs are treated in a sociopragmatic way in Hyland's approach. In his approach, he states that members of different discourse communities may use HDs in different ways. In this approach, hedging constitutes a 'polypragmatic' strategy. Hyland has established a polypragmatic model of hedging. He proposes that particular linguistic forms cannot necessarily be interpreted in specific ways, but a given form may be seen to fulfil a range of functions. Prototype Theory proposes that we have a broad picture in our minds of what a chair is; and we extend this picture by metaphor and analogy when trying to decide if any given thing that we are sitting on counts. Taylor (1995) developed prototype theory within the field of sociolinguistics and one finding of the theory is that different social groups tend to have quite different prototypes in mind when classifying something.

1.4.2.2 Hyland's analytical framework

Hyland (1998a) described his pragmatic analytical framework (see Figure 1) as providing a functional account for the use of HDs in scientific research articles. According to Hyland (1998a), his data revealed two major functions of hedging in research article writing,

which he has called content-oriented and reader-oriented (as shown in Figure 1). Both are regarded as acknowledging the role readers play in accepting knowledge, since hedging shows the writer's awareness of the possibility of readers' response to claims. Writers are therefore making assumptions about the nature of reality (content-oriented) and the acceptability of a statement to an audience (reader-oriented). Claims that ignore these conditions are unlikely to be accepted. Content-oriented HDs comprise accuracy type HDs and writer-oriented HDs. Accuracy type HDs enable the writer to present claims that reflect precision regarding the phenomena being described, while writer-oriented HDs serve to protect the writer against professional damage that may result from bald propositions. Reader-oriented HDs express the writer's acknowledgement of the reader's role in ratifying claims. In Hyland's model, accuracy-oriented hedges are further divided into attribute hedges and reliability hedges. However, this study focuses on the three general motivations of hedging, writer-oriented, reader-oriented and proposition-oriented.

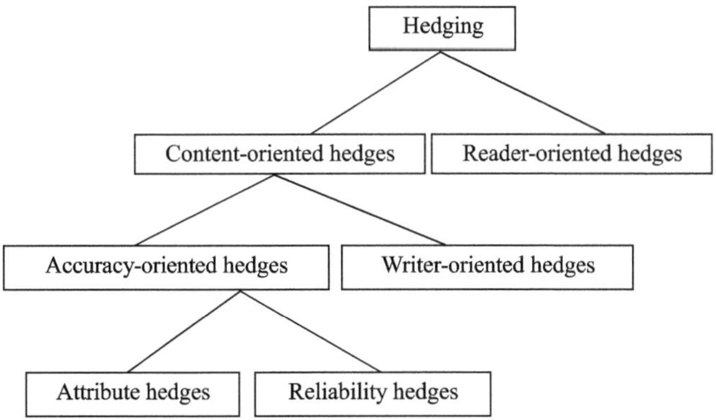

Figure 1 Hyland's Polypragmatic Model of Hedging (Hyland 1998a)

In the examples below (taken from Hyland 1996a: 437), (1) and (2) are examples of accuracy-oriented hedging. Hyland

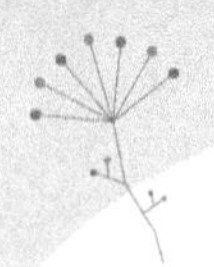

(1996a) in his study claims that example (1) reflects the use of a limited language to describe the variability of natural phenomena: 'staining was confined to the vascular issues'. The statement sounds too certain without the hedging adverbial *generally*, since in some circumstances it may not be true, while example (2) indicates the writer's confidence in the certainty of his/her knowledge:

(1) Staining was *generally* confined to the vascular issues (Hyland 1996a: 437).

(2) The photoreceptor involved is *somehow* related to the photosynthetic apparatus itself (Hyland 1996a: 437).

Somehow in example (2), is considered by Hyland (1996a) to be functioning as accuracy-oriented hedging in that an attempt is made to present the content as truthfully as possible, while acknowledging factual uncertainties. In example (2), the writer is trying to express that 'the photoreceptor involved' is 'related to the photosynthetic apparatus' to some extent or, in some cases, not always. In other words, the writer has discerned that in some cases 'the photoreceptor' is not 'related to the photosynthetic apparatus'. The writer admits that a precise understanding of the relationship that is thought to exist is not known.

While accuracy-oriented hedging is proposition-focused, writer-oriented hedging is writer-focused. Writer-oriented hedging aims to shield the writer from the consequences of opposition by limiting personal commitment. It indicates an unwillingness to make a commitment to conclusions and is therefore, often associated with higher level claims, or a greater generalisation of interpretation of findings than accuracy-oriented ones. Writer-oriented hedging, however, also belongs to the content-oriented category in that they function to hedge the writer's commitment to propositional content.

The most distinctive feature of writer-oriented HDs is diminished writer presence (see Section 3 for detail). Example (3) (taken from Hyland 1996a: 444) is an example of a writer-oriented hedge, which is realised by constructing an 'abstract rhetor' which minimises a personal projection. Hyland explains this as follows: 'By foregrounding "these data" (in bold), the writer presents a view where data, vested with agentivity, are attributed with primary responsibility by an interpretation; they become the source of the claim.'

(3) *These data indicate* that phyochrome A possesses the intrinsic ... (Hyland 1996a: 444)

The last main category of hedging devices distinguished by Hyland (1996a, 1998a) is reader-oriented HDs. Reader-oriented hedging devices function to express deference to potential readers, as a response to discourse norms (that is, the writer conforms to the social expectations of the scientific community). This practice acknowledges the reader's role in ratification of claims; because hedged statements mark claims as provisional, a potential reader is invited to participate in a dialogue or debate, which is a characteristic feature of scientific investigation (Hyland 1996b). According to Hyland, reader-oriented hedging often involves 'explicit personal alignment with findings, models and analyses' (Hyland 1998a: 182). Personal attribution, as in the example below can be regarded as indicating that there may exist alternative explanation concerning the state of affairs described by the writer and that what is said by the writer 'is a personal opinion', the information offered being 'left open to the reader's judgment' (Hyland 1998a: 182). The example below of a reader-oriented hedge is accomplished by specifying a personal source (taken from Hyland 1998a: 182):

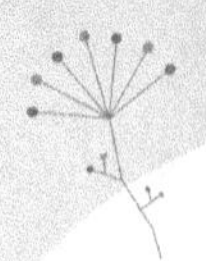

(4) *I believe* that the major organisational principle of thylakoids is that of continuous unstacking and restacking of sections of the membrane ... (Hyland 1998a: 182)

1.4.2.3 Distinction between the different categories of hedging functions

Having illustrated Hyland's approach to hedging in research articles, it is also necessary to point out that his treatment is not completely free of problems. To begin with, as Hyland (1998a: 161) himself suggests, 'analysing HDs according to the categorization presented is by no means a straightforward matter, there being variation in how different analysts interpret HDs'. Analysing a polypragmatic strategy such as hedging objectively and with absolute precision is undoubtedly an impossible task, and interpretations therefore always remain subjective and quite often ambiguous. In order to resolve some of these problems, the data dealt with by Hyland (1998a) was analyzed not only by himself but a group of expert readers to boost the validity of the findings, but, as Hyland admits, even then irresolvable cases remain.

The main problem that may be raised concerns the distinction between the different categories of hedging functions established by Hyland. Hyland's categorization takes into account that a hedge may have more than one of the functions postulated in the model, it is, in fact, at times difficult to determine what the primary function of a given hedge might be. Nonetheless, in establishing his categorization Hyland offers core examples representing each category. The core cases of the category of attribute HDs, for example, seem unproblematic in that identifying items with the primary function of adjusting terms to suit nonprototypical situations (e.g. *essentially*, *quite*, *more or less*, *approximately*, *generally*) is fairly straightforward

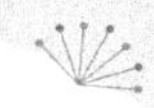

and there is no clear overlap with the remaining categories. However, when considering the other categories, the limits immediately seem less clear even in the case of some of the core examples cited by Hyland. For instance, the distinction between reliability HDs (accuracy-oriented HDs) and writer-oriented HDs does not appear obvious in examples such as:

(5) ... *it appears possible* that the mechanism causing the light activated fluorescence quenching may be triggered by either photosystem. (Hyland 1998a: 167)

(6) *It seems* that the stomata do not use the Calvin cycle ... (Hyland 1998a: 173)

According to Hyland, the example reproduced as (5) can be seen to involve hedging 'against complete accuracy, rather than a wish to seek protection against overstatement' (Hyland 1998a: 167), whereas in his opinion the latter example includes a writer-oriented hedge 'implying that the writer does not wish to be thought fully and personally committed to a belief in the proposed state of affairs' (Hyland 1998a: 173). When considered side by side, however, the difference in hedging between these examples seems less than clear, as the devices employed and contexts provided appear quite similar. Hyland (1998a: 170) implies that one way to differentiate between reliability HDs and writer-oriented HDs might be the possibility that HDs of the latter type are concerned with higher-level claims than the former, with writer-oriented hedging thus typically occurring when for example, research results are generalized. Unfortunately, the limited contexts provided in Hyland's examples do not reveal whether or not this is indeed the differentiating factor between the two cases above. Hyland might have considered long texts during his analysis, but he did not list them in his book.

Attempting to distinguish between higher and lower level claims is a problematic issue in the analysis with a short text of research articles. However, it is possible to draw a line between generalisations of results conceivably representing higher-level claims and lower-level claims with low degree of relevance to the topic dealt with in broader contexts. In this study, longer texts are considered in order to distinguish the higher-level and lower-level claims. The longer texts given in the current study are also related to move analysis of HDs.

Further problems appear to arise from Hyland's (1998a: 172) 'core examples' of hedging when concerning the distinction between the main categories of reader-oriented and content-oriented HDs. Hyland (1998a: 187) says that these two types of hedge can be distinguished on the basis of the contextual variable of agentivity, explicit author presence implying a reader-oriented function, whereas the absence of clear author agentivity suggests content-orientation. The first problem relates to one of Hyland's (1998a: 167) examples of content-oriented reliability (accuracy-oriented) HDs:

> (7) This insertion, which *we suspect* is the membrane anchor, *could* associate peripherally with the membrane or *might* span half the bilayer ... (Hyland 1998a: 167)

Although clearly marked by writer agentivity, Hyland and his informants regard this example as a core case of accuracy-oriented reliability hedging. However, provided that writer agentivity is central to reader-oriented HDs, one might question whether this example could equally be seen as a core case of reader-oriented hedging in the same way as example (8) exemplified below:

> (8) *I believe* that the major organisational principle of thylakoids is that of continuous unstacking and restacking of sections of the membrane ... (Hyland 1998a: 182)

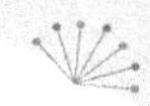

The differences between example (7) and example (8) is *we suspect in example* (7) is used to describe the subject 'The insertion' in the sentence; while *I believe* in example (8) is followed by the writer's claim. It seems that Hyland (1998a) implies that reader-oriented hedging and accuracy-oriented hedging can be differentiated in the same way as accuracy-oriented reliability HDs and writer-oriented HDs. Both reader-oriented HDs and writer-oriented HDs are concerned with higher-level claims than the accuracy-oriented reliability HDs. Reader-oriented hedging thus typically occurs for generalising results or putting forward arguments and claims.

Another issue is to do with the distinction between writer-oriented and reader-oriented HDs. As far as can be inferred from Hyland's examples, writer agentivity is understood to refer to explicit indications of authorial presence, as manifested by the use of pronouns like *I*, *we*, *my* and *our*. Thus, expressions with authorial presence such as *we propose*, *we infer*, *our analysis* and *our interpretation* may be taken as HDs signalling to the reader that what is said is a personal view, open to the judgment of the readers. In Hyland's study, examples involving authorial agentivity seem to be directly attributed to the choice of a personal subject. It is Hyland's (1998a: 181) contention that 'an overt acceptance of personal responsibility' can be seen as reader-oriented hedging. All in all, the primary feature distinguishing reader-oriented HDs from the other types is writer agentivity, and impersonality as realized by the use of abstract rhetors is a common strategy of writer-oriented HDs. For example,

(9) *These data indicate* that phytochrome A possesses the ... (Hyland 1998a: 172)

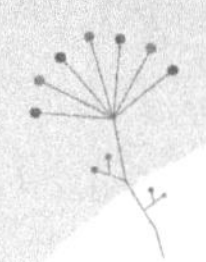

(10) *The model implies* that the function of grana is to (Hyland 1998a: 172)

(11) Thus *the evidence strongly favours* the conclusion that (Hyland 1998a: 175)

In all these three examples, we are dealing with sentences which include the hedging lexical verbs *indicate*, *implies* and *favours*, thus reducing the writer's commitment to what is being claimed. A central feature of these examples, Hyland (1998a) says, is the absence of writer agentivity, that is, sentences typically involve impersonal expressions. According to Hyland (1996b), impersonal expressions include: passive voice, abstract rhetors and empty subjects. As the examples illustrate, employing 'abstract rhetors', such as 'these data', 'the model' and 'the evidence', is a useful strategy in connection with writer-oriented HDs.

1.4.2.4 The approach adopted in the present study

Having illustrated ways in which the roles of HDs in academic papers have been approached in earlier studies, it remains to be determined how the present study will proceed in its analysis of hedging. The preceding discussion implies that earlier descriptions and taxonomies relating to hedging are not free of problems, particularly as regards the analysis of authentic academic writing data. Despite certain complexities involved in applying previous treatments of hedging to this author's analysis, some of the earlier studies provide useful principles which can be employed as starting points in the analysis. Thus, the present study shares Hyland's view that the best way to approach hedging in academic papers is to acknowledge that hedging has certain prototypical realisations, such as modal verbs, lexical verbs, adverbs, adjectives and nouns. The strategy of hedging is, thus, here understood to involve items that, due to their implicit

component of tentativeness, weaken the force of statements, express deference, signal uncertainty, and so on, it being taken for granted here that 'we can, generally, recognize a hedge' (Hyland 1998a: 160) by resorting to such a broad characterization. Hedging in academic papers, then, is here understood to refer to all linguistic phenomena that can be interpreted to signal less than full certainty regarding what is being expressed. For practical reasons, however, as mentioned in Section 2.3, certain potential ways (non-lexical hedging) of expressing hedging had to be left outside the analysis here due to the difficulties of determining which potential cases might or might not involve epistemic meaning.

Hyland's taxonomy of HDs combines earlier approaches to hedging with a particular focus on the communicative context of academic writing. By integrating aspects of the theories of prototypicality and fuzzy sets into treatment, Hyland manages to take into account the multiplicity of forms that hedging may take and the multifunctional nature of even a single hedging device. Varttala (2003) comments that Hyland's taxonomy succeeds in elucidating that in the context of academic writing, the role of HDs may not only be to contribute to accurate reporting of phenomena (attribute HDs) or to express a writer's assessment of the truth of a proposition (reliability HDs); they may also provide a means for the writer to express his/her viewpoint while allowing him/her to avoid taking responsibility for the propositional truth (writer-oriented HDs), or enable the writer to cultivate interpersonal harmony by allowing for the expert readers' attitudes and opinions, as expected by the academic community (reader-oriented HDs). Although Hyland finds his taxonomy difficult to uphold when applied to some of the core cases he describes (Varttala 2003), his taxonomy is valuable in summarizing the polypragmatic functions that HDs may have in the context of

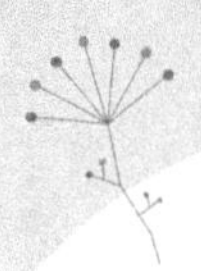

academic writing. Hyland's taxonomy has been discussed and successfully applied in research on hedging in academic writing in some published studies (e. g. Varttala 2003; Falahati 2004; Hyland 2005; Atai & Sadr 2008).

In the present research, Hyland's taxonomy of HDs is used for the initial analysis of the function of HDs. Attention is paid to the functions that HDs may have in different contexts. Hyland's taxonomy is regarded as open-ended, and the present analysis allows for an even wider interpretive framework, not excluding alternatives of interpretation extending beyond those offered by Hyland and other scholars.

Conclusion

The overall aim of this literature review is to examine the nature of academic writing and more, specifically, the role of hedging in academic writing. This review has shown that academic statements are both factual and interpretive, and that for the writer's interpretations to be accepted by readers, interpretive statements frequently need to be assessed and stated with an appropriate degree of certainty. It is furthermore indicated that this assessment can be communicated by hedging. In this regard, some studies show that, in general, second language English students have difficulty interpreting and expressing hedging. The review has also revealed that an appropriate theoretical framework for hedging analysis is one which emphasises the relationship among language, context and text. It could be pointed out that the politeness interpretation may explain the very basic motivations for hedging in academic writing. However, hedging in academic writing cannot be approached unproblematically in terms of politeness. The main problem in employing the politeness model has to do with the difficulty of analysing the use of HDs in a communally

constrained discourse such as academic writing. Hyland's (1998a) polypragmatic model with specific attention given to the social features is considered as the most suitable existing framework for analysing HDs in academic writing.

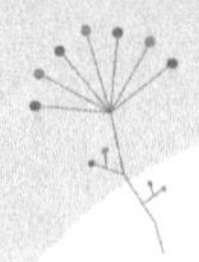

Chapter 2

The Corpus Linguistics Point of View

Introduction

This chapter reviews the research in the area where the current study is grounded. The use of large collections of text (corpora) and the field of corpus linguistics, in which computer programs are used to aid analysis of corpora, is discussed in Section 2.1. In this section, corpus linguistics is viewed as a lexical approach to the description of hedging devices (HDs) in undergraduate student writing, which focuses on the co-occurrence patterns of HDs in texts. The idiom principle (Sinclair 1991, 1996, 2004), pattern grammar approach (Hunston & Francis 2000), and the theory of lexical priming (Hoey 2005) are discussed as lexical approaches to the description of HDs in collocation and colligation patterns. Section 2.2 shows that the techniques developed by corpus linguists have been applied by genre analysts with varying degrees of success. For the purpose of the current study, genre analysis, especially move analysis, can demonstrate how students pattern their academic writings as a series of rhetorical actions, revealing variation in the writing of the NS and NNS students. Coupled with a close examination of recurring lexicogrammatical choices, move analysis can illustrate how students accomplish meso- and micro-rhetorical communication with the use of HDs. Conclusions are drawn from this which are then used in Chapter

3 to describe the methodology which can be employed to overcome some of the limitations inherent in the traditional approach to move analysis.

2.1 A lexical approach to the description of English

Over the past few decades, the work on corpus linguistics has stressed the interaction between lexis and grammar in language as well as the importance of collocational and colligational patterning in the construction of meaning (Sinclair 1991, 2004; Francis *et al.* 1996, 1997, 1998; Hunston & Francis 1998, 2000; Hunston 2002, 2007; Hoey 2005; Hyland 2008).

Collocates, a term first used by Firth (1957), is a word from Latin meaning 'place together'. The analysis of the collocations of a word would provide a great deal of information about its meaning. The central insight of collocation is that some words appear together more frequently than we would expect on the basis of traditional linguistic rules (syntax, semantics, register, etc.). Many attempts have been made to explain and illustrate the interrelationship between collocation and grammar, and the three most influential models, including Sinclair's idiom principle (1991, 1996, 2004), Hunston and Francis's Pattern Grammar (2000) and Hoey's lexical priming (2005). These three approaches have a number of things in common and they all contribute to our understanding of the interrelationship of lexis and grammatical patterning. The first observation common to the Idiom Principle, Pattern Grammar and Lexical Priming is that these studies of language are empirical and based on large amounts of naturally occurring text. The frequency of occurrence and co-occurrence of language items is crucial, and corpora and corpus tools are used to identify which items are common in which contexts and in which types of discourse. The core observations as to the interrelatedness of vocabulary and syntax and the conclusions the featured approaches arrive at, however, are largely similar which, according to Hunston (2008: 292) 'would tend to increase confidence' in all of them. They all find that form and meaning are inseparable and that the unit of meaning in language is not the word in isolation but a construction or phrasal unit (at a different level of complexity). The pervasiveness of co-selection features and collocations is emphasised in all strands. Finally, the most important shared observation which connects all described stances is that it is possible to divorce lexical items and grammatical constructions and those phraseological items should play a more central role in linguistic theory and description. It seems that a corpus-driven method of analysing can provide a starting-point for the identification of the lexis and grammatical patterns of HDs in academic writing. The difference amongst these three approaches is that lexical priming not only focuses on phraseology level, but also relates to the textual dimension of language. The focus on the textual level of lexical priming suggests a corpus approach to genre-level discourse analysis of the lexical pattern of HDs.

2.2 Corpus linguistics and discourse analysis

Schiffrin *et al.* (2001) note that discourse analysis can be grouped into three general categories: (1) the study of language use, (2) the study of linguistic structure 'beyond the sentence', and (3) the study of social practices that are associated with language and communication. According to Schiffrin *et al.* (2001), the study of language use focuses on surface linguistic features, such as phrase and clause structures. The study of linguistic structure beyond the sentence focuses on a larger object of study: how texts are constructed and organised. The study of social practices focuses on either the actions of participants in particular communication events or the

general characteristics of discourse communities in relation to issues such as power and gender.

Hoey's (2005) research on lexical priming covers the first two general perspectives of discourse analysis. One perspective focuses on the distribution and functions of surface linguistic features (collocations and colligation). These are typical corpus studies of language use in discourse. The other perspective focuses on the internal organisation of texts (text colligation), that is, the discourse studies of linguistic structure beyond the sentence in particular texts. Studies from this perspective have usually been qualitative and based on detailed analysis of a small number of texts from a single genre.

2.2.1 Move analysis

One specific research emphasis for discourse studies of structure 'beyond the sentence' has been the attempt to segment a text into higher-level structural units. The 'units of analysis' in corpus studies of discourse structure must be well-defined discourse units: the segments of discourse that provide the building blocks of the texts. As reviewed by Biber *et al.* (2007), there are many types of analysis that have been conducted from the perspective of discourse analysis as the study of linguistic structure 'beyond the sentence', with the focus on communicative/functional organisation. Move analysis (Swales 1981, 1990) is one of the most common examples of such a specific genre-level analysis. The notion of move (Swales 1990), defined as a functional unit in a text used for some identifiable purpose, is often used to identify the textual regularities in certain genres of writing and to 'describe the functions which particular portions of the text realize in the relationship to the overall task' (Connor *et al.* 1995: 463). Contributing to the fulfilment of the overall communicative purpose of the genre, moves can vary in length and size from several paragraphs

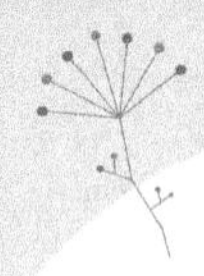

to one sentence, but normally contain at least one proposition (Connor & Mauranen 1999). Move analysis is a helpful tool in genre studies since moves are the semantic and functional units of texts, which can be identified because of the communicative purposes and linguistic boundaries (Nwogu 1997). The third aim of this study to understand more fully how HDs contribute to the rhetorical functions of different rhetoric move types in two corpora allows the combining of rhetorical move analysis with analysis of recurring lexical and grammatical choices of HDs with which students accomplish these moves in their academic papers. By doing move analysis of HDs in student academic writing, how the NS and NNS students in this study use HDs to make rhetorical moves in their writings can be generalised.

Move analysis in academic writing began with Swales's pioneering analysis (Swales 1981, 1990) of research genres in academic settings. His first well-known analysis of the structural organization of the genre was done in 1981 when he attempted to offer an alternative model to account for the rhetorical movement in research article introductions. The original aim of Swales's work on move analysis was to address the needs of advanced NNSs learning to read and write research articles, as well as to help NNS professionals who wanted to publish their articles in English. In his major work, *Genre Analysis: English in Academic and Research Settings*, Swales (1990) revises the previous model and identifies a pattern used in the introductory sections of English research articles that he calls 'the Create a Research Space model' (CARS). Three moves are identified: (1) Establishing a territory, (2) Establishing a niche, and (3) Occupying the niche (see Table 3 for steps in each move). The general aim of move analysis in academic writing is to identify the moves, a unit that relates both to the writer's purpose and to the

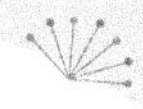

content that he/she wishes to communicate (Dudley-Evans & St. John 1998: 89). Move analysis has become a main approach in genre analysis. Its aim is to identify the moves, move sequences, and key linguistic features.

Table 3: CARS Model for Research Article Introductions (adapted from Swales 1990: 141)

Move 1: Establishing a territory
Step 1: Claiming centrality and/or
Step 2: Making topic generalization(s) and/or
Step 3: Reviewing items of previous research
Move 2: Establishing a niche
Step 1A: Counter-claiming or
Step 1B: Indicating a gap or
Step 1C: Question raising or
Step 1D: Continuing a tradition
Move 3: Occupying the niche
Step 1A: Outlining purposes or
Step 1B: Announcing present research
Step 2: Announcing principal findings
Step 3: Indicating RA structure

The CARS model has been referenced and evaluated by many other researchers, including Anthony (1999), Bisenbach-Lucas (1994), and Connor, Precht & Upton (2002). In his analysis of twelve articles on software written by engineers, Anthony (1999) applies the CARS model to the introductory sections of the articles and evaluates its usefulness for describing their structure. He investigates the kind of complexity and changes that occur within genres. Anthony finds that the introductions do not follow Swales's model. Although he agrees that the CARS model is useful in terms of identifying the main framework of the introductions, it does not address several important features such as extensive literature reviews, many definitions and examples, or evaluations of the results of the research. In conclusion, according to Anthony (1999), there are certain constraints in using

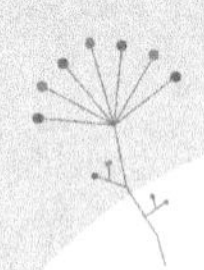

the CARS model, and it is necessary to understand these limitations in order to use the model effectively. The work done by Bisenbach-Lucas (1994) is another study conducted in order to prove the validity of the CARS model (Jogthong 2001). Bisenbach-Lucas (1994) makes a comparative genre analysis of research articles from *Scientific American Journal*, investigating the popularizations used in the articles. Bisenbach-Lucas (1994) studies across disciplines by selecting articles written in six different fields: medicine, zoology, geology, biology, astrophysics, and antiquity. She used the CARS model to analyse the introductory sections of selected articles and looked for textual features, rhetorical structures, and sequences of moves. The results of the study show that most of the articles followed the same pattern described by the CARS model. The second move is not found in the astrophysics article. However, all of the articles followed the same pattern, beginning with the first move and ending with the third. The moves that occurred most were: Reviewing Items of Previous Research (Step Three of the Third Move) and Announcing Present Research (Step One, Part B of the Third Move).

The work by Connor, Precht & Upton (2002) is an example of the application of the CARS model across several genres. These researchers applied Swales's CARS model to the study of a corpus of job application letters from the Indianapolis Business Learner Corpus (IBLC). By applying Swales's approach to the study, they find that different genres contain different rhetorical moves. While there are only three major moves in the introduction of research articles, seven types of moves are found in the job application letters. The study also compares the structure of the moves found in the letter with the moves in the introduction of research articles, finding that the structure in the letters is simpler. The study suggests that Swales's model is

applicable not only to research articles but also to other genres.

Swales (2004), in response to this subsequent research, modifies his model to better reflect the variability in how the three move types are realized in different sub-genres of research article introductions. His updated model, presented below in Table 4, has a broader description of the communicative purposes of Move 1 and Move 2; it also reflects—particularly in Move 3—the variation that occurs in the introductions in different research fields, and recognizes the possibility of cyclical patterns of occurrence of the move types (described further below) in the introduction section.

In the current study, concordance analysis and move analysis proceed from two different approaches. While the top-down approach, viewing genre moves as purposeful, relies on identification of communicative purposes, bottom-up processing concerns content and function (Biber *et al.* 2007).

Table 4: Create a Research Space (CARS) Model for Research Article Introductions (Swales 2004: 230)

Move 1: Establishing a territory (citations required) via Topic generalizations of increasing specificity

Move 2: Establishing a niche (citations possible) via:

- Step 1A: Indicating a gap, or
- Step 1B: Adding to what is known
- Step 2: Presenting positive justification (optional)

Move 3: Presenting the present work via:

- Step 1: Announcing present research descriptively and/or purposively (obligatory)
- Step 2: Presenting research questions or hypotheses (optional)
- Step 3: Definitional clarifications (optional)
- Step 4: Summarizing methods (optional)
- Step 5: Announcing principal outcomes (optional)
- Step 6: Stating the value of the present research (optional)
- Step 7: Outlining the structure of the paper (optional)

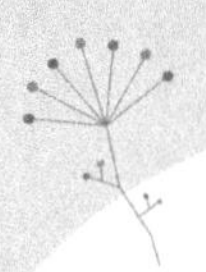

2.2.2 Using a corpus-based approach to move analysis

In discourse analysis, as Upton and Connor (2001) remark, most corpus studies have focused on the quantitative distribution of lexical and grammatical features, generally disregarding the language used in particular texts or higher-level discourse structures or other aspects of discourse organisation. Most qualitative discourse analysis has focused on analysis of discourse patterns in a few texts from a single genre, but they have not provided tools for empirical analysis that can be applied on a large scale across a number of texts or genres. Unlike some other branches of linguistics such as lexicology, morphology and semantics, corpus linguistics is not merely limited to analysis of a single aspect of language. On the contrary, it can be applied to the study of many linguistic areas. Corpus linguistics has been shown to be particularly compatible with contemporary usage-based linguistic frameworks, including move/genre analysis (Baker 2006).

The past few years have seen some studies attempting to combine the first two research perspectives of discourse analysis with corpus linguistics (Biber *et al.* 2007; Mahlberg & O'Donnell 2008; Mahlberg 2009; O'Donnell *et al.* 2012). These studies provide a useful starting point for the corpus approach to genre-level discourse analysis of lexical patterns. This study is further influenced by the work of a number of researchers in the field of corpus approaches to discourse analysis.

Mahlberg and O'Donnell's (2008) study focuses on newspaper texts and the study is part of a large project on the Textual Priming (Hoey 2005) of hard news stories. They divided a corpus of newspaper articles into two categories based on textual position: text-initial sentences and all other sentences. The analysis looks at the collocations and local patterns of a text-initial

key word, *fresh*, which has been found in the first sentence of hard news stories. The patterns are manually annotated as the basis for both quantitative summary and qualitative description of textual functions of the pattern in newspaper texts. It also presents a corpus approach to textual analysis of these patterns in view of their textual functions to begin news stories in newspaper texts. This study illustrates how the use of corpus annotation can reveal the extent and the variation of local patterns of a lexical word and how they are related to discourse functions. Mahlberg (2009) investigates the link between lexical and textual patterns in newspaper texts. The analysis starts with an overview of the distribution of the core *move follow* across different sections of the *Guardian* newspapers. Then, it presents the results of a concordance analysis which indicates the meanings that follow the *move* pattern. Lastly, it analyses the textual positions of the pattern in the newspaper articles. The preferred textual positions of the *move* pattern in the newspaper articles are linked to the news values that characterize a story. This analysis illustrates how corpus linguistics and text linguistics approaches can complement one another. Based on Mahlberg and O'Donnell's (2008) research on the example of *fresh* and the nucleus pattern, O'Donnell *et al.* (2012) describe a methodology for identifying textual colligations. The generation of key concgrams① is used as a new method to identify patterns that share the same items but vary in their ordering. Co-occurring text-initial items are then analysed in terms of their

① Cheng, Greaves and Warren (2006: 414) define a 'concgram' as 'it is all of the permutations of constituency variation and positional variation generated by the association of two or more words'. This means that the associated words comprising a particular concgram may be the source of a number of 'collocational patterns' (Sinclair 2004: xxvii).

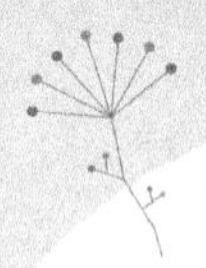

discourse functions in relation to theories of newspaper structure. This study illustrates how the new methodology presented can aid in the analysis of phenomena at the interface of corpus and text analysis.

Biber *et al.* (2007) also see the interface of these two perspectives in discourse analysis as one of the current challenges of corpus linguistics. The advantages of a corpus approach for the study of discourse, lexis, and grammatical variation include the emphasis on the representativeness of the text sample, and the computational tools for investigating distributional patterns across discourse contexts.

To achieve generalizable corpus-based descriptions of discourse structure with communicative or functional purposes of text as the starting point of analysis, Biber *et al.* (ibid) outline a top-down approach (the Biber, Connor & Upton Approach) to discourse analysis with seven major analytical steps to be followed, as shown in Table 5. In top-down approach to discourse analysis, the first step is to develop an analytical framework, determining a set of possible discourse unit types based on a priori determination of the major communicative functions that discourse units can serve in these texts. That framework is then applied to the analysis of all texts in the corpus. Thus, when texts are segmented into discourse units, it is done by identifying a stretch of discourse of a particular type which serves a particular communicative function. Once these discourse units are identified, they are then analysed and described for their lexical/grammatical features. Complete texts and then the full corpus are then analysed and described by organisational patterns.

Table 5: Seven Major Steps of Top-down Corpus-based Analysis of Discourse Organisation (Biber *et al.* 2007: 34)

1. Communicative/Functional: Categories determining the types of discourse units—the functional/communicative distinctions that discourse units can serve in these texts
2. Segmentation: Segmenting all texts in the corpus into well-defined discourse units
3. Classification: Identifying and labeling the type (or category) of each discourse unit in each text of the corpus
4. Linguistic analysis of each unit: analysing the linguistic characteristics of each discourse unit in each text of the corpus
5. Linguistic description of discourse categories: Describing the typically linguistic characteristics of each discourse unit type, by comparing all discourse units of a given type across the texts of the corpus
6. Text structure: Describing the discourse structures of particular texts as sequences of discourse units, in terms of the general type or category of each of those units
7. Discourse organisational tendencies: describing general patterns of discourse organisation that hold across all texts of the corpus

Apart from supplementing the inadequacy of bottom-up corpus analysis of HDs which limits the investigation to the level of truncated concordance lines, there are other advantages to using the corpus-based approach for move analysis of HDs.

In this study, corpus-based move analysis depends on both quantitative and qualitative techniques. The moves of the Introduction and Discussion sections in each text in the two corpora in this study have first been identified (and stored separately) by the author making qualitative judgments about the communicative purposes of the different segments of a text. In this research, corpus-based move analysis has been done on a relatively large representative collection of texts from the NS and NNS undergraduate student assignments. The NS and NNS corpora allow the author to clearly see and validate linguistic patterns of selected HDs in different move types. A traditional discourse analysis may only allow the author to analyse

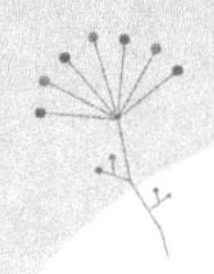

HDs on relatively few texts. A single text on its own is insignificant; however, with computers and the corpora, typical patterns and trends are more likely to show through when dozens of texts are looked at, rather than just one or two 'selected' texts. For example, if the results of bottom-up corpus analysis suggest that *should* frequently co-occurs with the first person pronouns in the move type 'making suggestions' from the NNS corpus, then this result provides a direction for further discourse analysis. The construction of 'the first person pronoun + *should*' is considered as a typical pattern in this Move Type. Therefore, move analysis has been carried out on how this construction of *should* fulfills the communicative purposes of the Move Type 'making suggestions'. Analysis of the typical linguistic features of HDs in specific move types provides information about how different communicative purposes are realized linguistically.

In this book, how bottom-up concordance analysis of lexico-grammatical features of HDs was complemented with top-down move analysis of the functions of HDs patterns in the different positions in texts. The previous studies reviewed above are considered as the guidelines for this research. Chapter 4 presents a more detailed consideration of methodologies adopted in the current study.

Conclusion

The analysis of patterns to be conducted in the current study has been undertaken in two forms: the first is a bottom-up concordance analysis and the second is a top-down corpus-based move analysis.

The first part of the present chapter has introduced and discussed the advantages of a corpus linguistic language description and the theoretical underpinnings of the major features that are analysed in the current study: lexico-grammatical patterns, collocations and colligations. It has been argued that lexico-grammatical patterns are

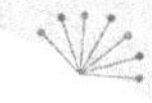

closely connected to textual meaning, that patterns, meanings and discourse are interrelated to one another, and that their interaction plays a major role in constructing the discursive identity in a disciplinary specific discourse. In other words, to identify patterns and their meanings is to identify features of a particular discourse. This is one of the main aims of the current study.

The second part of the current chapter has reviewed the top-down approach for the analysis of discourse structure: move analysis. The author presents a description of corpus-based move analysis, with steps that followed the guidelines proposed by Biber *et al.* (2007) for corpus-based top-down analysis of discourse structure. The chapter concludes with a discussion of advantages of a corpus-based approach to move analysis. These include the ease of identifying the linguistic characteristics of the moves, their frequencies and lengths, and the mapping of their use and location in the overall discourse structure of texts. Chapter 3 deals with the detailed methodological considerations within these two approaches.

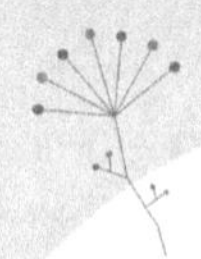

Chapter 3

Interpreting Corpus Data

Introduction

The present chapter describes in detail the research aim, corpora and data selection that are considered in the present study. Research questions for the current research study are presented in Section 3.1. Section 3.2 provides some brief information on the corpora compiled and used in the corpus study. Section 3.3 discusses issues of frequency count and the selection of hedging devices.

3.1 Aims of the book

In the current book, The author seeks to investigate the different aspects of descriptions of hedging devices by considering the following research aims:

(1) Generalize the most frequent HDs in the NS and NNS corpora. Compare the similarities and differences between the most used HDs in the NS corpus and the NNS corpus in terms of frequencies of occurrence.

We can see that corpus linguistics can provide the most straightforward approach to hedging devices in terms of the frequency of occurrence. Frequency information from the corpus studies provides the most general information on the use of HDs by the NS and NNS groups. In the present study, frequency is a selection criterion for

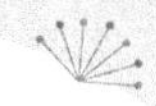

identifying the most used HDs in the NS and NNS corpora for an in-depth investigation.

(2) Analyze the collocations or co-occurrence patterns of the use of HDs in the NS and NNS corpora.

(2a) Figure out the differences between the NS group and the NNS group.

(2b) Find whether different co-occurrence patterns of each HD are related to a specific function of HDs in the NS and NNS corpora.

To better understand HDs, the second research question and sub-questions focus on repeated patterns of HDs. The sample concordance analysis reveals the co-occurrence patterns and collocations of selected HDs. Repeated co-occurrence patterns and collocations are indications of the relationship between a hedging device and its meaning.

(3) Study how HDs with different co-occurrence patterns or collocations interact with other rhetorical features in the move types of the Introduction and the Discussion sections to perform particular communicative purposes.

Hedges are seen as pragmalinguistic communicative features of academic language. It is essential to situate hedges in the rhetorical context to better understand the ways hedges interact with the rhetorical features of move types and contribute to the persuasiveness of academic writing.

In the present section, the methodology adopted (a two-fold approach) is explained in detail. The methodology used for the present book is a combined approach of methods from corpus linguistics and move analysis. These two approaches, which focus on different aspects in language, are closely related to each other.

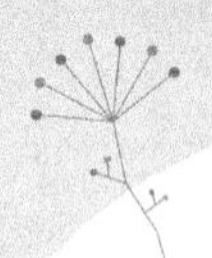

Corpus linguistics depends on real data while move analysis, evidently, focuses on the communicative purposes of each move type. Firstly, the concordance collocational analysis is performed on investigated hedging devices by means of AntConc 2. 2. 4 (Anthony 2011) in order to identify recurrent patterns. The second phase is based on move analysis in order to investigate how rhetorical functions of hedging devices contribute to the communicative purposes of move types. In Section 3. 2, the rationale for the use of the two methods described above, corpus and genre analysis has been described.

The following sections present a more detailed consideration of methodologies adopted in the current study. First details about the corpus are provided in order to describe the collected data.

3. 2 The corpora of the present study

The texts used for the current study are assignments written by university students. Details of each corpus, together with its characteristics and comparability, are described in the following sections to explain the criteria of data collection.

3. 2. 1 The non-native speaker corpus (NNS corpus)

Since there is no suitable existing learner corpus that can be used for the current study, the author compiled her own corpus. The data chosen to build the corpus was based on three main criteria. Since in China only students in English or Linguistics departments are required to write assignments and dissertations in English, the present investigation is restricted to one specific group of Chinese learners, who are undergraduate learners of English or Linguistics. These students are from four different universities with whom the author has maintained a good personal relationship. Since data from the same writer might be biased, students are only allowed to send in one

assignment so there would be a wider range of assignments from different contributors. Another criterion is that each assignment should have the traditional IMRD sections. Since this study is focusing on two rhetorical sections—Introductions and Discussions—it is important to have them among the rhetorical sections of assignments.

3.2.2 The native speaker corpus (NS corpus)

Native English students' assignments are available in an electronic format (text files), collected from the MICUSP (the Michigan Corpus of Upper-level Student Papers) (Arbor 2009) and the BAWE (British Academic Written English) corpus (see Alsop & Nesi 2009).

The MICUSP was developed by researchers at the University of Michigan English Language Institute. The corpus files are freely available for study, research and teaching. It contains around 830 A grade papers (roughly 2.6 million words) from a range of disciplines across four academic divisions of the University of Michigan. For the current study, only the category of argumentative essays or research papers (which contain Introduction and Discussion sections) written by NS students of English studies and linguistics related departments were selected in order to build up the Native-speaker Corpus. There are 55 undergraduate student assignments.

The BAWE corpus, released in 2008, contains approximately 3,000 pieces (approx. 6.5 million words) of proficient assessed student writing from British universities. The same criteria used to select data from the MICUSP are applied to choose from the BAWE corpus. There are 107 undergraduate student assignments.

With all the texts extracted from MICUSP and BAWE, two subcorpora have been compiled on the basis of student level. The NS

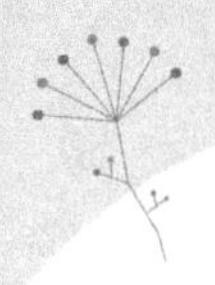

corpus consists of 162 assignments (486,000 words), 55 from MICUSP and 107 from the BAWE corpus. Since textbooks in both American and British English are adopted by the four universities where the author collected her data in English teaching, the author chose to include both American and British English student writing as a norm in her study.

All texts are collected and converted to Text file format and edited. Since the current book focuses on the main body parts of student assignments, the unnecessary parts: titles, abstracts, acknowledgements, tables, footnotes, reference lists and appendices were cut out in order to get neat texts and an exact total number of words of each corpus being analysed. Each section (IMRD) of student English academic writing has been stored in a separate text file.

There are approximately 480,000 words in the NS corpus and 825,000 words in the NNS corpus. The description of the NNS corpus and the NS corpus that the present investigation sets out to contrast is summarised in Table 6.

Table 6: Original Numbers of Words and Texts Collected

Corpus	Variety	Number of Words	Number of Texts
NS Data	UK Academic US Academic	486,000	162
NNS Data	Chinese Academic	825,000	150

Table 6 shows the total number of words and texts collected for the compilation of the NS corpus and the NNS corpus in this research. All texts were checked manually. Since HDs were examined in the moves of Introduction and Discussion sections, it is essential for all the texts in the corpora to follow the IMRD format. Texts which do not follow the IMRD format were deleted from the corpora. 110 and 160

texts meet this criterion in the NS and NNS data respectively. To make the comparison easier, an equal number of texts (110 texts) were selected to form both the NS and the NNS corpora (see Table 7 below).

Table 7: Computer Corpora Analysed in the Study

Corpus	Variety	Number of Words	Number of Texts
NS Corpus	UK Academic US Academic	282,392	110
NNS Corpus	Chinese Academic	729,445	110

3.3 Frequency

Having compiled the corpora, frequency count was carried out to provide quantitative information about HDs. Simple frequency count is a straightforward approach to quantifying linguistic data and it has often been used in corpus studies, because it provides a count of how many times within a corpus certain words appear. To select the hedging devices to be analysed in the current study, the frequency of occurrence of each hedging device was counted. Frequencies of occurrence were generated automatically by the computer.

3.3.1 Overview

In the present study, the frequencies of the 116 hedging items the author takes from Hyland (1998a) in the two corpora are dealt with at the preliminary stage of the analysis as they provide a good starting point for more detailed investigation into the lexical items in the corpora: it is the selection criterion for the hedging devices that will be investigated in a detailed concordance analysis. When the author counted the frequencies of the 116 hedging devices for the NS and NNS corpora, the software searched every hedging device in the

series in order to establish how many tokens there are for each hedging device. The software then ranked the hedging items according to their frequencies. Having established the list, the author turned her attention to what the list can tell.

The lists are useful because they highlight which HDs are most frequent in each corpus and may be worth investigating (Romer & Wulff 2010). This section gives an overview of the theoretical considerations of the information on frequency. The selection of the hedging devices seems to work with frequency of occurrence. The choice of the 10 most frequent hedging devices of the present study is based on comparing frequency information from the NS corpus and the NNS corpus (cf. Section 3.3.2).

3.3.2 The selection of hedging devices in the corpus study

It can be useful to compare the rank order of items in two or more corpora by looking at them side by side. However, raw frequency counts of linguistic features cannot be compared to each other because of the variable lengths of texts. Therefore, the counts have to be normalised to a common basis and hence rendered comparable (Biber *et al.* 1998). Biber *et al.* (1998) proposes a way to adjust raw frequency counts from differently sized data named 'normalisation'. To go into particulars, the raw frequency count should be divided by the number of words in the whole corpus, and then multiplied by a basis which is chosen for normalisation. For example, the hedging device *would* occurs 596 times in the NS corpus, and 767 times in the NNS corpus. However, because the two corpora are of such different sizes, these raw frequencies mean very little relative to each other. In order to normalise the figure for the NS corpus, the raw frequency of 596 is divided by 381,920 (the total word count of the NS corpus) and multiplied by 1,000, giving a

figure of 1.56 occurrence per thousand words. In order to compare this normalised frequency with that of *would* in the NNS corpus, the raw frequency of 767 was divided by 811,377 (the total word count in the NNS corpus) and then multiplied by 1,000, which results in a normalised count of 0.95 occurrences per thousand words. We can now see that *would* is more frequent in the NS corpus than in the NNS corpus. The results show that the overall frequency of HDs in the NS and NNS corpora is 18 and 14 per thousand words respectively and neither group of students uses all of the 116 HDs listed by Hyland (2004), but the native English speaking writers use a slightly wider range of HDs than the non-native English speaking writers (82 and 76 respectively).

As concordance analysis and move analysis is time-consuming, a small number of HDs seemed managcable in the concordance analysis and discourse analysis of the present study (10 in my study). Table 8 shows the top twenty hedging devices by rank order in the NS corpus and NNS corpus respectively.

Table 8: The Most Frequent HDs in the NS and NNS Corpora

Rank	NS Speakers		NNS Speakers	
	Device	Frequency per 1,000 Words	Device	Frequency per 1,000 Words
1	*would*	1.56 *	*should*	1.51 *
2	*may*	1.25	*most*	1.49 *
3	*seem*	1.23 *	*may*	1.14
4	*suggest*	1.21 *	*would*	0.95 *
5	*could*	1.07	*could*	0.86
6	*most*	1.05 *	*often*	0.84
7	*often*	0.82	*always*	0.61 *
8	*rather*	0.70 *	*seem*	0.43 *
9	*possible*	0.54	*usually*	0.42
10	*should*	0.52 *	*rather*	0.34 *

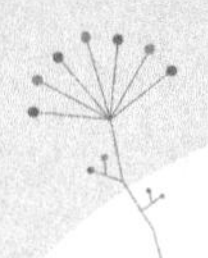

(continued)

Rank	NS Speakers		NNS Speakers	
	Device	Frequency per 1,000 Words	Device	Frequency per 1,000 Words
11	*perhaps*	0.52 *	*quite*	0.29 *
12	*might*	0.43 *	*mainly*	0.27 *
13	*imply*	0.41 *	*possible*	0.25
14	*argue*	0.40 *	*generally*	0.25 *
15	*always*	0.35 *	*suggest*	0.17 *
16	*almost*	0.30 *	*frequently*	0.16
17	*indicate*	0.28 *	*imply*	0.15 *
18	*likely*	0.26	*likely*	0.13
19	*frequently*	0.22	*tendency*	0.10 *
20	*assume*	0.21 *	*relatively*	0.09 *

Note: Z-score test for significant difference was carried out before normalization of the raw statistics. Significant differences of shared top twenty HDs are asterisked.

The top twenty HDs in the NS and NNS corpus of this study are listed respectively in Table 8. Both groups show similarities in their use of these HDs. The author did not examine all the HDs listed in Table 8 because of the purely practical reason of the time limit of the PhD. 10 items appeared to be a practical solution. As mentioned in Chapter 1, hedging can be realised through different forms of lexical expressions: modal verbs, lexical adverbs, adverbs, adjectives and nouns. It is reasonable to select at least one HD from each grammatical form for analysis in the current study. While frequencies and functions are related, this is not a one-to-one relationship and frequencies alone are not enough to explain differences between the uses of HDs in the two corpora. This is why, HDs whether with significant or non-significant differences in frequency were included in this study. If there are several HDs to choose for analysis from the top twenty lists of both corpora, for example hedging modal verbs, hedging lexical verbs and hedging adverbs categories, the author picked most frequent ones. For hedging modal verb, the top three from both lists *would*, *should* and *may* were selected. *Would* and

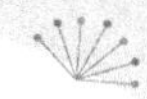

should are at the top of the list for the NS and NNS corpora respectively with significant difference of frequencies between the two groups. *May* is the second most frequent modal verb in both the NS and the NNS corpora with similar frequencies. For hedging lexical verbs, the top two hedging lexical verbs *seem* and *suggest* were selected to be analysed in the study. As for hedging adverbs, based on the same criteria, *most* and *often* were also selected. *Perhaps*, the 11th in the NS corpus, but not among the top twenty in the NNS corpus and *usually*, the 9th in the NNS corpus, but not among the top twenty in the NS corpus, are more noticeable due to the gaping ranking difference. *Possible* as the only hedging adjective was selected. In brief, the ten HDs selected for the current study were *would* *, *should* *, *may*, *suggest* *, *seem* *, *often*, *usually*, *perhaps* *, *possible* and *most* *.

Conclusion

This chapter has focused on the inquiry methods used in corpus linguistics and a genre analysis framework. The goal of this chapter is to outline an approach that is used to identify and analyse the HDs in the NS and NNS corpora, and to provide a specific and detailed description of how this type of analysis can be done. The NS and NNS corpora that form the basis of this analysis as well as the corpus tools used in retrieving data from them are presented and the comparability of these two corpora are evaluated based on selection criteria proposed by Bhatia (1993) in Section 4.2. The present chapter has shown that the frequency count can be considered as the starting point of the research. Frequency information has been viewed with regard to what can be counted. Ten HDs are selected according to the frequency counts for a concordance analysis and move analysis. The results of concordance analysis and move analysis of HDs are presented in the following chapters.

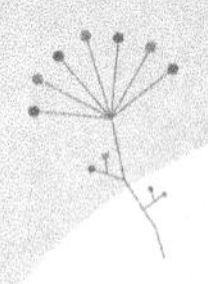

Chapter 4

Modal Verb Hedging

Introduction

Modal verbs are used to express a writer's stance, expressing either the degree of certainty of the proposition (epistemic modality), or meanings such as permission, obligation or necessity (deontic modality). They are one of the most common lexico-grammatical features used by the NS and NNS groups to express hedging.

The use of modal verbs as HDs in academic writing has been discussed by many researchers (Adams-Smith 1984; Hyland 1994, 1998a). Modal verbs do appear to be the most typical (54%) means of marking epistemic comments in medical RAs (Adams-Smith 1984) and constitute 27% of lexical HDs in Hyland's corpus of 26 molecular biology articles. Hyland (1998a) examines the epistemic functions of modal verbs and claims that modal verbs appear to be the typical devices used to express hedging in academic writing. He states that modal verbs are an important means of allowing a scientist to adjust the degree of certainty about his/her claims, and to build the writer-reader relationship that the writer wants to achieve. In this study, the statistical analysis reveals that in the overall frequency of modal verbs, the NNS writers employed them more than the NS writers, which constitutes 31.0% and 25.7% of the total HDs use respectively. This observation is in contrast with the findings of earlier

research (Ventola & Mauranen 1990). Ventola & Mauranen (1990), who studied only Finnish NNS writers' texts and the linguistic revision of their texts by the NS writers, found that the Finnish writers use fewer modal expressions.

When academic writers use such modal verbs as *would*, *may* and *should* in their academic papers, the epistemic modality expressed with these modal verbs can play an important role. When these modal verbs are used to express certainty or possibility toward findings and hypotheses, their roles seem to be more significant, and writers, therefore, need to carefully select an appropriate modal verb in order to convey his/her idea to potential readers precisely (Hyland 2004, 2005; Hyland & Tse 2007).

The present chapter starts with an overview of the meanings of the selected modal verbs *would*, *may* and *should*. Concordance analysis is presented in Section 4.1 to visualise the linguistic patterns and the relationships between the particular collocations or colligations of hedging modal verbs and their polypragmatic functions in the local textual context. Section 4.2 presents the move analysis by focusing on how selected hedging modal verbs achieve rhetorical functions in order to contribute to the persuasiveness of the students writing. The Discussion/Conclusion section summarises the main results with regard to modal verbs as a group of HDs. Similarities and differences between the NS and NNS groups in the use of hedging modal verbs *would*, *may* and *should* in various co-occurrence patterns and different move types are compared and presented in Sections 4.1 and 4.2.

4.1 Concordance analysis of *would, may* & *should*

In this section, concordance analysis is adopted in order to visualise linguistic patterns and polypragmatic functions of the three modal verbs *would*, *may* and *should*. Throughout, the emphasis of

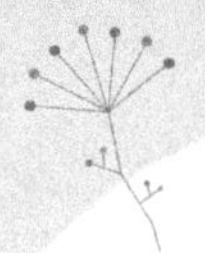

this chapter is to shed some light on how the NS and NNS English writers express hedging through the use of the three modal verbs in their dissertation/assignment writing. In particular, the analysis is intended to investigate how particular collocations and colligations are associated with polypragmatic functions of modal verb hedging. In Sections 4.1.1, 4.1.2 and 4.1.3, the author attempts to identify these three modal verbs used to hedge in the corpora, to explore their co-occurrence patterns and to determine the polypragmatic functions that these modal verbs may perform. Meanings and functions of *would*, *may* and *should* are introduced in Section 4.1.1. The co-occurrence patterns of these three hedging modal verbs are summarised in Section 4.2.2 with discussions on the similarities and differences between the NS and NNS corpora. In Section 4.2.3, polypragmatic functions that are associated with the different co-occurrence patterns of *would*, *may* and *should* are identified and compared between the NS and NNS corpora. These results are then discussed in relation to the previous studies and in terms of possible explanations of the findings.

4.1.1 Meanings of *would, may* & *should*

Modal verbs and their particular functions have been described by different sources such as Biber *et al.* (1999), Leech (2004) and Biber (2006). Leech (2005: 88) refers to 'a logical and a practical (or pragmatic) element' in the meanings of modals 'in terms of logical notions', such as possibility, ability, necessity, and obligation. Biber *et al.* (1999: 485) describe the meanings of modal verbs in written English as intrinsic and extrinsic. These authors similarly classify modals into three major categories according to their main meanings: a) permission/possibility/ability, b) obligation/necessity, and c) volition/prediction.

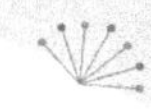

In epistemic use, Coates (1983: 208) has mentioned the use of *would*, namely as a past tense of *will* (marker of prediction). Hyland (1998a: 111) also states that a common use of epistemic *would* in scientific writing is as the hypothetical variant of *will*, which is used for showing past 'confident assertion or prediction' (*cf. It will be a failure.* Vs. *It would be a failure.*). Another important epistemic function reported for *would* is showing tentativeness or hypotheticality (*e. g. The findings would indicate.*) (Coates 1983; Huddleston & Pullum 2002).

According to Coates (1983), *may* is the primary modal used for epistemic possibility which can express a speaker's lack of confidence in the proposition expressed. It is often used to express uncertainty or possibility. The major distinction is normally made between epistemic and root possibility of *may*. The epistemic *may* shows that the occurrence of an event is not certain (e. g. *He may not come.*), whereas *may* shows possibility of an event in terms of natural facts (e. g. *He may not be at home.*). That is to say, *may* expresses either the occurrence of the event described, or its truth.

Should, alongside its other meanings, obligation is apparently the commonest one (e. g. *You shouldn't smoke so much.*) (Coates 1983; Bybee *et al.* 1994). *Should* is also occasionally used to convey an epistemic meaning (e. g. *He should be there by now.*). Since *should* is often used to express strong probability, this meaning can be described as a rather extreme likelihood, or a reasonable assumption or conclusion, which implicitly allows for the speaker to be mistaken (Palmer 1990, 2001).

4.1.2 Discussion on the similarities and differences of co-occurrence patterns of hedging modal verbs between the NS corpus and the NNS corpus

The two groups' preferences of individual use of modal verbs

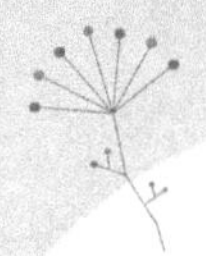

would, *may* and *should* bear some similarities as well as some differences. Table 8 in Section 3. 3. 2 shows that in the academic writing data the NS students employed *would* as an HD the most. This finding matches those of Coates (1983), Holmes (1988), Biber *et al.* (1999), Hyland (1998a), and Gabrielatos & McEnery (2005). However, the data shows that although the NNS writers also employed *would* with high frequency (ranking 4th), the use of *would* did indicate a significant difference based on Test significant of sample proportions (Z-test) in frequency of occurrence per 1,000 words when comparing the NS (1. 45) and the NNS (0. 85) data. *May*, which is considered to be the 'prototypical hedging device' (Hyland 1998a: 116), is also relatively highly frequent. This finding is consistent across the NS and the NNS corpora (1. 25 and 1. 14 per 1,000 words respectively). *Should* is the modal verb most frequently used by Chinese students to express hedging in their academic writing. The incidence of *should* in the NNS corpus (1. 36 per 1,000) is nearly triple compared to that of the NS corpus (0. 53 per 1,000). The finding that many NNS writers employ the modal verb *should* to express obligation and necessity at significantly higher rates than NS writers is not particularly new. According to the results of some studies (e. g. Hinkel 1995; Kwachka and Basham 1990), the uses of obligation/necessity modal *should* in the writing of Chinese writers can be particularly culture dependent. With regard to the linguistic manifestation of socio-cultural values in discourse, according to Scollon & Scollon (2001: 101), the Chinese social norm has largely remained 'post-Confucian'. That is, in language use, 'there is a strong carry-over from Confucianism' with its hierarchical view of social and kinship roles, responsibilities, and obligations. With the sense of duties and responsibilities, Chinese students employ the modal verb of obligation *should* significantly more

frequently than the NSs do (e. g. *Therefore we should raise our own real ability of bilingual transformation.* — NNS 083).

Based on the concordance analysis, in this study the meaning of the three modal verbs, *would*, *may* and *should*, mainly depends on details of the core pattern MOD v. For example, in combinations with infinitives of action verbs, such as *give*, the pattern MOD inf shows that the pragmatic force of the action verb has been weakened. From the concordance lines of each selected modal verb, we can see that modal verbs are followed by verbs in different forms which convey different meanings.

It is essential for the author of this study to go through the co-occurrence patterns of modal verbs identified in the previous studies in order to identify the modal verb phrase structures existing in the corpora. In the former research, Mindt (1995) reports five modal verb patterns including 1) modal + bare infinitive, 2) modal + passive infinitive, 3) modal + progressive infinitive, 4) modal + perfective infinitive, 5) modal + perfect passive infinitive. Kennedy (2002) on the other hand, adds four more patterns to Mindt's (1995) list including modal alone, modal + be + being + past participle (or adj.), modal + have + been + present participle, and modal + have + been + being + past participle.

This author does not simply look for the grammatical choices that co-occur with the three selected modal verbs, but searches based on pre-existing patterns, as Hoey *et al.* (2007) and Hunston & Francis (2000) suggest. They recommend studying colligation by making use of existing grammatical terminologies. The terminologies, according to Hoey *et al.* (2007: 35), are the product of 'pre-corpus investigations'.

These patterns, plus a code set which were used for this study with a sample example, can be seen below:

MOD inf

Otherwise they *would give* an overweening sense. (NNS corpus: 007)

MOD X inf

Two married parents *would significantly improve* the educational achievements of U. S. children. (NNS corpus: 023)

MOD be past pple

Linguists believe that a discourse analysis *should be based* on grammar. (NNS corpus: 001)

MOD be pres pple

They *may be suggesting* that they leave. (NNS corpus: 036)

MOD have pple

The translator *would have robbed* the reader ... (NNS corpus: 038)

MOD have been past pple

Charles Lamb *should have been* doomed to the drudgery of the desk for so long. (NNS corpus: 091)

For all these three modal verbs, the simple pattern MOD inf is, as expected, the most numerous in both the NS and the NNS corpora, since modal verbs are generally followed by the base form of the verb according to English grammar. According to the concordance analysis, we can see that *would*, *may* and *should* are principally used in the NNS corpus collocating with main verb. In both the NS and the NNS corpora they are followed by MOD be past pple, MOD adv inf and MOD have past pple (see Table 9 and Table 10).

Table 9: Frequencies of the Lexico-grammatical Pattern of *Would*, *May* and *Should* in the NS Corpus out of 100 Concordance Lines

	MOD inf	MOD be past pple	MOD adv inf	MOD have past pple
would	60	5	11	17
may	58	11	4	10
should	57	20	3	6

Table 10: Frequencies of the Lexico-grammatical Pattern of *Would*, *May* and *Should* in the NNS Corpus out of 100 Concordance Lines

	MOD inf	MOD be past pple	MOD adv inf	MOD have past pple
would	74	5	8	6
may	82	8	4	6
should	52	39	4	5

The modal verbs *would*, *may* or *should* occurring before lexical verbs can indicate a way to influence the action of lexical verbs, or give more information about the function of the main lexical verb that follows it. This can indicate if the writer thinks that something is true or not and can express prediction, possibility or obligation. The common feature shared by these examples is that *would*, *may* and *should* are incorporated into the main clause as part of the verb phrase, although it is understood semantically as providing hedging for the entire clause. It is notable here that the majority of examples of these three modal verbs are active, and used syntactically (*i. e.* subject to syntactic rules), in both the NS and the NNS corpora. The most frequent co-occurring main verb with *should* is *be*, followed by other action verbs, such as *avoid*, *act*, *give*, *forgive*, *try*, etc. The use of *should* to express obligation in academic writing displays a desire to control thoughts, inferences, and actions of potential readers, to lead them towards actions writers consider to be correct,

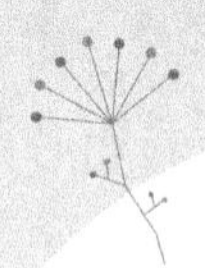

to impose the writers' opinion on the readers, and to demonstrate authority in their field. Frequently co-occurring main verbs in the *would/may* + (*adverb*) + *verb* pattern are mainly action verbs which relate to the modes of expressing lack of certainty, for example, *suggest*, *explain*, *guess*, *argue*, (*dis*) *agree*, *tell*, *fulfil*, *narrate*, *reproduce*, *reveal*, etc. in the concordance lines. Modal verbs in this lexico-grammatical pattern express tentative possibility of the basic aspect of meaning of the co-occurring verbs. In the case of both the NS corpus and the NNS corpus, the use of these hedged action verbs is evidence to indicate that there is some conjecture about the truth of a proposition.

An action verb is a transitive verb, a verb that takes an object, something you do to someone else. Typically, an action verb has both an emotional and physical component. The modal verbs *would* and *may* have the function of attenuating the pragmatic force of action verbs. For example,

> *I would argue that McCullough's assertion should be taken.* (NS corpus: 021)

In this example, the action verb *argue* is mitigated by the use of the modal verb *would*. It is believed that the mitigation through the use of the modal verb produces a semantic change in the utterance. Thus, when uttering: 'I argue that McCullough's assertion should be taken', although he/she is genuinely arguing, the meaning of the utterance is modified in some way. It is as if the writer was, in a certain way, forced (maybe based on evidence) to argue that McCullough's assertion should be taken.

The following two examples are from the NS and NNS corpora respectively with *would* combined with action verbs without hedging functions:

(1) Kristen and I theorized that people hear the elements in accents that they recognize as different which *would explain* why some English think I'm American and most Americans think I'm English or Australian, depending on the listener. (NS corpus: 0027)

(2) Aides say the foundation, similar to that of former US President Bill Clinton, *would focus* on sustainable development and dialogue between cultures, with a particular emphasis on Africa. It is to be launched later this year. (NNS corpus:026)

In these two examples, the verbs *explain* and *focus* are the actions that the subject 'which' and 'the foundation' in each sentence is going to take. *Would*, in these two examples, is used as the hypothetical variant of *will*, which makes a confident assertion and prediction about the action *explain* in example (1) and *focus* in example (2). In the case of both the NS and the NNS corpora, the use of these hedged action verbs is evidence to indicate there is some conjecture about the truth of a proposition.

In the following two examples, *may* was used to express the possibility of the action of *prove* and *matter*.

(3) As Norton states, 'The most popular literature in Britain during the late eighteenth... century was not the Romantic poetry, but "the latest trash of the day": the Gothic novel.' This *may prove* to some extent the theory that the Gothic was not as subversive as expected. (NS corpus: 3147e)

(4) However, the connotations of words used in English news headlines usually show the attitudes of the news. And these attitudes *may* matter as much as the surface information. (NNS corpus:006)

The statement in example (3) is based on research evidence

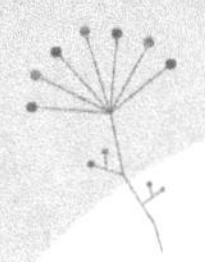

gleaned from a literature review of Norton's study. The use of *may* acknowledges the writer's uncertainty over his/her theory that '*the Gothic was not as subversive as expected*'. The modal *may* and the phrase *to some extent* are used as a hedge to convey the propositional content as reliably as possible. In example (4), the writer infers that it is possible that the attitudes shown by the connotations of words in English news headlines are as important as the surface information of the headlines. *May* offers an appropriate attitude and an expression of tentativeness and possibility for the writer's claim.

Moreover, in the examples from the NS corpus, some of the co-occurring action verbs are considered as HDs by Hyland (1998a) and can be found in his list of hedging devices (Hyland, 2005). These action verbs have tentativeness as part of their own meaning, and they are generally used to hedge either commitment or assertiveness. Their occurrence with *would* or *may* reinforces this aspect of meaning. For example,

> (5) The one example for this word came in a type 4 utterance, where a speaker asked a fellow conversant to reformulate his or her statement (yeah how would you say that? in a nifty little paraphrase like three words. five words. six maybe.). The speaker is obviously asking for a reduction of the original phrase, and one *would guess* that this would be how the word would be used in a type 1 utterance. (NS corpus: 0031)

In extract (5), an example was described by the writer to illustrate the word *paraphrase*. In the example, the speaker asked a fellow conversant to reformulate his or her statement by reducing the original phrase. The writer cannot determine how the listener interpreted the speaker's requirement of paraphrase. The use of the action verb *guess* here allows the writer to state his or her conjecture of

the listener's interpretation tentatively. The first modal verb *would* before *guess* in the extract further attenuates the proposition and conveys its hypothetical meaning. The hypothetical *would* does suggest a pragmatic interpretation. It expresses a tentative expression rather than merely making a prediction. It also softens the assertion in the extract and avoids forcing the potential reader to accept the writer's claim 'this would be how the word would be used in a type 1 utterance'. *Would guess* is given particular polypragmatic hedging function by collocating with the subject *one*. This will be further discussed in Section 4.1.3.

The collocation of *may* + hedging lexical verb also forms a compound-hedged expression, such as *may imply* and *may indicate*. Similar to the analysis of *would* + hedging lexical verbs, these hedging lexical verbs have tentativeness as part of their own meaning and their occurrence with modal verb *may* reinforces this aspect of meaning.

> (6) This is perhaps worth remarking on because it *may indicate* that writers at different levels in their education may hedge with a different level of strength and frequency. (NS corpus: 0030)
>
> (7) In contrast, the word 'adversary' *may imply* 'aggression', 'enemy' and 'rival'. (NNS corpus: 006)

In example (6) and example (7), lexical verbs *appear* and *imply* already contain expressions of uncertainty. The writers choose to heavily hedge their claims with a combination of *may* and a hedging lexical verb to indicate their uncertainty and protect themselves against the dangers of overstatement.

This combination of modal verb and hedging lexical verb in one proposition provides more protection to this proposition as well as to the author's face, since in this case the degree/strength of hedging is

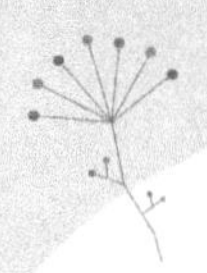

intensified. The combination is considered as a compound hedge (Salager-Meyer 1995). The presence of compound hedges in the NS corpus represents another significant finding. The role of these hedges has been highlighted in Salager-Meyer's (1994) taxonomy of hedges. Accordingly, compound hedges can be realised as a double or treble hedge and normally collocate between two different categories of hedge. Modal verb *would* tends to collocate with hedging action verbs. Note the following examples (8) (9) and (10) of such collocations in the data below:

(8) This *would imply*, in the post-Lacan sense that the continual search for meaning, which many groups of people have projected into the idolisation of a form of deity, is merely a sense of something missing that can be rediscovered. (NS Corpus: 3007b)

(9) It *would seem* that men are responsible for controlling and defining her role. Like Gruoch, the way her name is said metamorphoses. (NS Corpus: 3008g)

(10) Graphologically it *would appear* that the extracts share a similar form, as both are examples of dialogic prose that use the presence of a narrating voice to engage with the reader. (NS Corpus: 3008a)

There are seven compound hedges *would* + hedging action verb in the 100 examples from the NS corpus, but none are found in this 100 examples from the NNS corpus. For *may*, five compound hedges *may* + hedging action verb appeared in the 100 examples from the NS corpus, two were found in the 100 examples from the NNS corpus. From the results we can see that most Chinese students in this study tended to employ a simple style of writing using modal verb hedging. In contrast, the hedging that occurred in a sentence written by the NS

students consisted of double hedges (modal verb *would/may* + hedging action verb). Therefore, it can be said that Chinese students are likely to employ HDs in a less complex way or to employ fewer compound hedges than the NS students.

The initial analysis suggests that similarities and differences exist in the use of *would*, *may* and *should* in various co-occurrence patterns between the NS and the NNS corpora. However, hedging modal verbs *would*, *may* and *should* are further linked to different polypragmatic functions in various local context surroundings or co-occurrence collocations. This is elaborated and exemplified in Section 4.1.3.

4.1.3 Polypragmatic functions of hedging following modal verb patterns

To identify the polypragmatic functions that are associated with the lexico-grammatical patterns of *would*, *may* and *should*, this author took both the preceding and the following textual context into account. Functions that follow the modal verb lexico-grammartical patterns can be categorised into three groups as outlined in Chapter 2: accuracy-oriented hedging, writer-oriented hedging and reader-oriented hedging.

The overall distributions of *would*, *should* and *may* used by the NS and NNS groups of students to express writer-oriented, accuracy-oriented and reader-oriented hedging are presented in Appendix B. The co-occurrence patterns by which these functions are often expressed through *would*, *may* and *should* in the data of students writing have been identified and these are also listed in Appendix B.

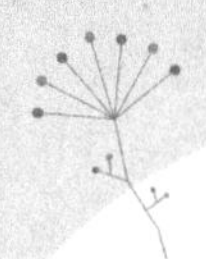

4.1.3.1 Principal devices in realisation of reader-oriented hedging

In the reader-oriented hedging category, the NS students used as many HDs as the NNS students, but with a wider range of linguistic choice. From Table 11, we can see that making suggestions by using *should* in grammatical patterns *should be + past pple/ should be* and personal attribution expression of *would* and *may* were adopted by both the NS and the NNS groups to convey reader-oriented hedging. In addition to this, NS student writers also expressed reader-oriented hedging by addressing readers indirectly and using the hypothetical conditional *would*.

Table 11: Reader-oriented Hedging and the Co-occurrence Patterns of Modal Verbs Often Used to Express Them from 100 Concordance Lines

Reader-oriented Hedging				
Function: Hedges Assertiveness				
NS Corpus			NNS Corpus	
	F	Patterns	F	patterns
would	11	hypothetical: *would* (3) personal attribution (7) addressing reader directly: *one would* (1)	5	personal attribution: *I would* (5)
may	6	personal attribution (3) addressing reader directly: *one may* (2)	6	personal attribution: *we may* (6)
should	37	make suggestion: *should be + past pple/ should be* (26)	58	personal attribution: *we should* (10) make suggestion: *should be + past pple/ should be* (44)

4.1.3.1.1 First person pronoun *we/I + would/may/should* functions as reader-oriented hedging

A number of studies have identified a range of functions that

personal pronouns *I* and *we* can play in academic writing (Bernhardt 1985; Vassileva 1998; Kuo 1999; Tang & John 1999; Hyland 2001, 2002; Harwood 2003, 2005). For example, *I would* like to make a comparison and discussion on the eastern and the western senses of color and its symbolic meaning as follow. (NNS corpus: 104). The personal attribution *I would* refers to the writer's acknowledging personal views, conclusions, or research limitations. 'By specifying a personal source ... the writer shifts the interpretive frame, drawing attention to the relation of the work of the investigator, and signaling that the claim is left open to the reader's judgment.' (Hyland 1998a: 121) Adams-Smith (1984) also notes that personal attribution, or what he refers to as the subjective element in writing, is accomplished by use of the first person in preference to the impersonal passive. That is to say, personal pronouns have been acknowledged as one of the main means used by writers in order to express their stance, to communicate with their readers and to establish their relations with the academic community of which they are, or aspire to be, part (Kuo 1999). Thus while some uses of *I* and *we* are said to be low-risk, discrete instances of textual authorial intervention, other uses, such as when a writer makes a claim, carry much greater threat to face, and are potentially points at which the writer exposes themselves to attack by the audience. Hence those who have constructed functional pronoun taxonomies (Ivanic 1998; Tang & John 1999; Hyland 2002) link pronoun functions with authorial presence.

Most taxonomies proposed for the pragmatic functions of personal reference revolve around the core issue of authorial presence and the relationship of the author with her/his readers and the academic community (Tang & John 1999; Hyland 2002; Harwood 2005). For example, Hyland (2002) identified the following categories: stating a purpose; explaining a procedure; stating results/claims; expressing

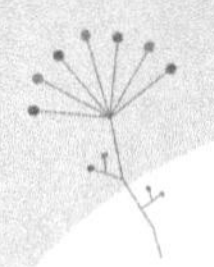

self-benefits; elaborating an argument, which he then used for the categorisation of pronouns and the quantitative analysis of his results. Harwood (2005) elaborates on the functions previously proposed in the literature by adding functions which capture the subtle effects that an author can create, such as describing or critiquing disciplinary practices. The first person pronoun *I* is stated as being used when writers make claims, or want to reduce the gap between writer and reader and to claim authority (Harwood 2005) and to exhibit some form of ownership of the content (Hyland 2002).

The recurring personal pronouns in reader-oriented hedging examples in both the NS and the NNS data revealed that self-attribution is favoured among the writers of both groups to express reader-oriented hedging. In the corpora, personal attribution was conveyed by the personal pronouns, *I* and *we*. From Table 11, we can see that both groups use modal verbs *would*, *may* and *should* to express reader-oriented hedging largely by specifying a personal source. In the NNS corpus, all these three modal verbs in the reader-oriented hedging category were found to collocate with personal pronouns, but only *would* and *may* were used together with personal pronouns to express reader-oriented hedging by the NS writers. It seems that there is an overuse of *should* in personal expression in the NNS corpus. Examples of *would*, *may* and *should* being used as reader-oriented hedging with personal attribution will be presented and discussed in the following text.

As presented in Table 11, within the 100 concordance lines, there are 11 and 5 examples of *would* functioning as reader-oriented hedging in the NS corpus and the NNS corpus respectively. And among them, there are seven cases in the NS corpus and five cases in the NNS corpus in which the writers used this rhetorical option to present their knowledge claims, in a way that displays personal

attribution but is mitigated by the co-occurrence of modal *would*, which shows respect for the reader's opinion.

Example (11) and example (12) show the use of a first person pronoun plus *would* in the NS corpus and the NNS corpus respectively. Example (11) is from the concluding paragraph of an assignment with the title 'Which words collocate with the words Islamic and Muslims?'.

> (11) The main problem faced with such an investigation is that analysis and annotation of data necessarily involves native speaker intuition. The decisions made regarding these matters are likely to vary greatly across individuals. Often in long and complex text, particularly from broadsheet newspapers, it was not clear when a lexical item was behaving in one way, and when it functioned as something else entirely. In a further study *I would* like to extend the searches and look at each emotive word and find the frequency in which it appears in that text. I believe this would highlight the tendency of tabloid newspapers to refer to Muslims with connotations of terrorism. (NS corpus: 6061b)

In example (11), the discussion section of this assignment starts by stating the main problems and limitations encountered within the investigation. The writer then seeks solutions for the problems of the NS speaker's intuition. The term *further study* is used to indicate a following statement of suggestion. In example (11), the writer then explicitly brings up the recommendations that he/she suggests for this research. According to the analysis of the problems and limitations, the writer proposes the suggestion by telling the reader what he/she is going to do in a further study by using the construction *I would like to + action verb*. The first person pronoun *I* here indicates the author's

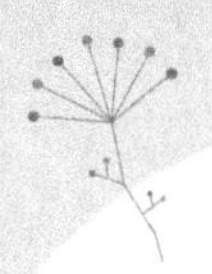

personal involvement with the suggestions for further research. By specifying a personal source however, the writer shifts the interpretive frame, drawing attention to the relation of the further work to the writer him/herself. The pattern *I would* also signals that the claim is left open to the reader's judgment. That is to say, the suggestion 'to extend the searches and look at each emotive word and find the frequency in which it appears in that text' is the writer's contribution to solve the problems existing in the study from his/her perspective. Potential readers of this study are free to agree with this suggestion or have their own response to the problems in the study and have their own suggestions for further study.

Example (12) illustrates an occurrence of *I would* in the NNS corpus, announcing to the reader that the definition of *idiomatic*, which is the topic of the assignment, is to come:

> (12) First of all, let's come to the basic differences: different definitions and structures of English and Chinese idiomatic expressions. The idiomatic expressions have different definitions in Chinese and English usages. According to the Oxford Dictionary, an idiom is a phrase or sentence whose meaning is not clear from the meaning of its individual words and which must be learnt as a whole. At the same time, in Chinese there are many four-character allusions, sayings, proverbs, and tow-part allegorical sayings, which are different from the English usages in many aspects, so the difference also exists in the structure of English and Chinese idiomatic expressions. The structure of an English idiomatic expression may be a phrase, a clause or a sentence, while Chinese idiomatic expressions are abundant in four-character phrases and two-part allegorical sayings, which are greatly different from English ones. But at the

same time, both the Chinese and English idiomatic expressions are phrases commonly used with semantic unity and structural stability; however, for the comparison's sake, *I would* like to define idiomatic expressions in general to cover all-type expressions: proverbs, sayings, colloquial phrases, allusions, idioms, slangs and so on. (NNS corpus: 056)

In this example, the extract is to introduce the term *idiomatic*. The writer commented on how to interpret the concept of 'idiomatic' which is central to the assignment. The writer first compared the basic different meanings of the word *idiomatic* in English and Chinese usage. Then, the writer chose a way to define the term *idiomatic* taking into account both definitions in Chinese and English. Similarly to example (11), the pattern *I would* in example (12) was used to show the writer's awareness of the tentativeness of their statements in defining 'idiomatic'. Naturally, the writer could have skipped the personal hedging element marked in italics above, and contented him/herself with saying '*In general to cover all-type expressions, the definition of idiomatic expressions is* ... '. The occurrence of *I would* shows that the writer is careful not to present him/herself as an expert in this field. Through the personal expression that anticipates the reader's response, an interaction was built up between the writer and potential readers of this paper. That is to say, the expression with authorial presence *I would* in the sentence defining the term *idiomatic* can be taken as a hedge signalling to the reader that the definition of *idiomatic* is a personal view, open to the acceptance and judgment of the readers.

Table 11 shows that in the NNS corpus another common type of co-occurrence pattern contains examples with the combination of first person pronoun *we* + *may*. For example,

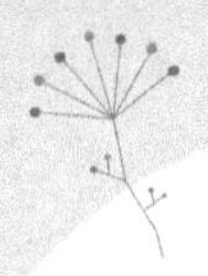

(13) If we open a magazine or newspaper, *we may* easily find advertisements like the following: (NNS corpus: 045)

The use of the first person pronoun *we* in example (13) alone would not be hedging, but in this case, *we* occurs with epistemic modal verb *may* which is considered as hedging. The writer and the potential readers of example (13) are binding together through the use of inclusive *we*, which straightforwardly expresses the writer's responsibilities to his/her uncertain or arguable proposition of 'easily find advertisements like the following'.

As shown in Table 11, *should*, used to make suggestions for further research or pedagogy by the NNS writers, is frequently found collocated with the first person pronoun *we*, which acts as the subject of the sentence. However, it is seldom used by the NS writers. The example below contains typical sentences with the use of the first person plural pronoun with the modal verb *should* in the NNS corpus.

(14) Through the introduction of multiple points of view of different scholars, we put a few of beneficial opinions towards number concord, which let our learners know the current development of this area. However, *we should* know that this is not the satisfactory answer. Language changes constantly, and any linguistic rules and theories are instructive just for a certain period of time. Therefore, the most important thing *we should* do is paying attention to the development of the language and making scientific summary. The emergence of any logistical linguistic phenomenon or any new selection of words have certain preconditions, background and the process for the public to accept, therefore, *we should* bear in mind each of them whenever and wherever we see it without making up story. Our suggestion

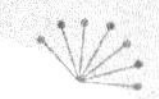

is that *we should* focus on the basic grammatical rules which are fundamental and instructive. In the meanwhile, those important and unconventional but reasonable phenomena need to be handled with flexibly in order for practical use. (NNS corpus: 012)

The examples of *should* in the sample discussion section of the NNS corpus are shown in example (14) above. We can see the four examples of *should* in the sample text all co-occur with *we*. In this text, *we should* is used to both indicate the limitations of the study and to recommend or identify useful areas of further research. *We should* in line 4 negotiates a position with the potential reader by stating the claim *this is not the satisfactory answer* as an opinion of the research limitations and leaving it open to judgment. Having pointed out the limitations of the study, the writer makes four main recommendations for further study. The first three suggestions were put forward by the writer through the expression of obligations. The collocation *we should* in these three sentences are considered in the light of expressing obligations in order to make suggestions for further research. They are: *paying attention to the development of the language and making scientific summary*, *bear in mind each of them* and *focus on the basic grammatical rules*. In this case, the writer states his/her suggestions for further research, but the readers are allowed to judge for themselves. The personal strategy seeks to hedge assertiveness by representing the tension between a personal conviction and the need to relate the claims to the existing knowledge currently recognised by the potential readers.

The results suggest that the NNS students are less neutral than the NS students in stating limitations and making suggestions for further research in their use of the modal verb *should*. The overuse of

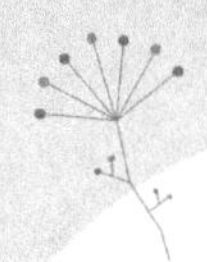

the HD *should* may have something to do with first language transfer and mode of thinking. In Chinese students' dissertations, there is a tendency to promote and impose what they take for granted as a brilliant idea. Especially, in the Discussion section, Chinese students are accustomed to initiate expectations to encourage the readers to join their action. The collocation *we should* is often used for emphasis or expressing determination. The results indicate that Chinese students' suggestions for future research are more fully elaborated, but may be more subjective and ignore the objective evidence. We can say that in giving out suggestions, Chinese students over hedged in the use of the hedging device *should* compared to the NS students in their English academic writing.

The personal attributions in the above examples are critical and clearly acknowledge the desire of the writer to defer to the audience in presenting the new claims and statements he/she hopes to gain acceptance for proposing. The choice of personal subjects signifies a reader-oriented hedge. Thus the reader-oriented hedge *I would* represents the tension between a personal conviction and the need to relate the claims to the existing knowledge currently sanctioned by the potential readers. It might be tentatively suggested that the writers' employment of personal hedging to make suggestions may result from a perceived need to respond to the potential readers' concerns with effective support for their statements. An acceptance of personal responsibility mitigates the expression of a proposition and signifies a reader-oriented hedge. By marking the proposition as a personal belief with the first personal pronoun *we/I*, the writer recognises the possible interpersonal effects of their claim and simply labels it as an alternative position without weakening its probability in any way.

4.1.3.1.2 Address to reader

A relationship with potential readers may also be invoked by

addressing the readers indirectly (For example, *one would* find mainly differences, and not similarities. —NS Corpus: 0229b). Here, the claim is hedged by explicitly drawing the reader into the process of academic enquiry. This expression was only found in the NS corpus towards a reader-oriented hedge. Regarding the use of *one*, Luukka & Markkanen (1997) find that this is characteristic of English first language academic discourse. In their corpus, the NS English writer does not use one single explicit reference to him/herself, whereas in contrast, the NNS English writer refers explicitly to him/herself by using the first person pronoun.

In the NS corpus, the impersonal pronoun, *one* was used to involve both the writer and the potential readers in the reasoning process. For example,

> (15) As evidence for this transformation, *one may* examine the treatment of new prisoners by the established veterans. (NS corpus: 0014)

In example (15), the writer leaves open the possibility for *anyone* to examine *the treatment of new prisoners*. In this case, the writer used an awkward expression skilfully as a way of engaging the reader, or acknowledging the reader's active role in evaluating information. The construction involving *one* in the above example is a strategy of anticipating the reader's reaction. In the example, *one* serves to introduce arguments, whether accepted or rejected by the writer. The writer used *one* + modal verb to soften the taking of positions in argumentation, and directly cued the potential readers to evaluate the information, encouraging them to take an active role.

In the example, the reason for the NNS student writers' not addressing the readers directly and employing a conditional may be because they find the construction difficult or they have not been

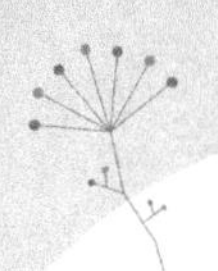

taught how to use *one* in academic writing, or there is not enough exposure to it in textbooks.

4.1.3.1.3 Hypothetical *would*: suggesting alternative interpretations or possibilities

Reader-oriented hedging is also accomplished by suggesting alternative interpretations or possibilities. Hyland (1998a: 182 – 183) states that in comparison with explicit personal alignment with findings, models and analyses, a more subtle way of deferring to the reader is to offer a claim as one possibility among many. In the following examples, writers used hypothetical conditionals, which were expressed as if-clauses in combination with *would*, to suggest alternative interpretations. The following extract is an example of *would* being used as a hypothetical marker where the conditions for the realisation of the hypothesis are stated.

> (16) *If* we take the former function, "leader" *would* be read as the pre-modified noun object of the phrase—a "Helpless.../leader". (NS corpus: 3006f)

In this example, the writers provided alternative results of their research under the hypothetical conditions of *we take the former function* in example (16).

The reason for the NNS students' not employing conditionals may be two-fold. Perhaps they find the construction difficult, or they do not have sufficient background for considering conditional relationships that could obtain between aspects relating to the research topic.

To sum up, reader acceptance is an important factor in academic communication, and hedging here results from the fact that claims may often present a challenge to the values of the potential readers. In the reader-oriented hedging category, the NS students used not only more hedges in expressing reader-oriented hedging than the NNS students, but also employed a wider range of linguistic expressions and collocation patterns than the NNS students. This observation runs in line with the findings of Ventola & Mauranen's (1990) research. In their study, the NNS writers employed little variety in their application of choice of modal verbs. The major differences pertaining to the extent of use were in respect to addressing the reader and using the hypothetical conditional to suggest alternative interpretations or possibilities. The lower incidence of these two patterns in the NNS student writing could, perhaps, be attributed to the NNS students not fully comprehending how modals can function as reader-oriented hedges. The difference between the NS and the NNS students' use of modal verbs in the reader-oriented hedging category may mostly be explained in terms of the writer's cultural background (Markkanen & Schroder, 1989), educational background, and also the multifunctionality of *would*, *may* and *should*.

4.1.3.1.4 Make suggestions and recommendations

As mentioned above, the collocation patterns *should be + past pple/ should + be* were used by both the NS and the NNS students to express obligation in order to give advice and make suggestions (Coates 1983; Bybee *et al.* 1994). For example, 'The translator *should* be aware of the cultural differences and pay sufficient attention to the possible barriers arising from the different cultural functions of various languages.' —NNS corpus: 004. The use of *should* to express obligation as in 'the translator *should*' in the example aims to control the thoughts, inferences, and actions of the reader, to lead the reader towards actions the writer considers to be correct, to impose the writer's opinion on the reader (Bybee *et al.* 1994). Through conveying thoughts to the potential readers by expressing obligation, writers also involve potential readers in a joint quest for

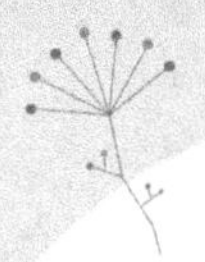

knowledge. Extracts (17) and (18) are examples of how patterns *should be* + *past pple* and *should* + *be* (main verb) were used to make recommendations by the NS and NNS writers. In examples (17) and (18), the writer made recommendations and suggestions in relation to his/her research, as a response to insights he/she may have gained from his/her research. This indicates a reader-oriented hedge using *should* for making recommendations and suggestions.

> (17) In my opinion, advanced English writing *should be* removed for its old content and is repetitive with the writing class of the first and second year. (NNS corpus: 086)
>
> (18) Therefore, college level writing courses *should be* mandatory. (NS corpus: 0002)

The above two examples from the NS and the NNS writing illustrate a strong sense of necessity and obligation entailed in the duties of the institutions of higher education in example (18), and the department of Curriculum development's choice to remove advanced English writing from National English Curriculum constrained by their obligations and responsibilities in example (17).

In example (17), the NNS writer argues that the curriculum developers have a responsibility to consider the removal of advanced English writing from the curriculum. The modal verb *should be* is useful when advising on the best course of action to take. The hint of obligation is milder than *must*, allowing the reader the freedom to choose. In example (18), the NS also approaches a similar situation of curriculum development in terms of duties and obligations. The NS writer in example (18) explains his/her view on the best way to set up college level writing courses. The occurrence of *should be* is employed in the context to mildly express the writer's advice that it is the curriculum developers' obligation to involve college level writing as

compulsory courses.

4.1.3.2 Principal devices in the realisation of writer-oriented hedging: Empty subject + *would/may* and writer-oriented hedging

As shown in Table 12, there are no significant differences in the overall density and principal patterns of modal verbs in the realisation of writer-oriented hedging between the two groups, the NS and the NNS.

Table 12: Writer-oriented Hedging and the Co-occurrence Patterns of Modal Verbs Often Used to Express Them out of 100 Concordance Lines

Writer-oriented Hedging				
Function: Hedges Writer Commitment				
	NS Corpus		NNS Corpus	
	F	Patterns	F	Patterns
would	11	empty subjects: *it*, *this*, *there* (9)	18	empty subject: *it*, *this*, *there* (13)
may	30	empty subjects: *it*, *this*, *there* (15)	28	empty subject: *it*, *this*, *there* (17)
should	0	N/A	0	N/A

From the concordance lines of writer-oriented hedging, a common type of collocation, containing examples with the combination of *empty subject* (*it/there/this*) + *would*, can be distinguished in both the NS and the NNS corpora. The impersonal pattern of the modal verb indicates a strategy which is intended to 'shield the writer from the possible consequences of negotiability by limiting personal commitment' (Hyland 1998a: 172). In fact, Hyland (1998a) states that a central feature of writer-oriented hedging is the absence of writer agentivity that involves impersonal constructions. *Would* and *may* co-occurring with an empty subject are normally used as a writer-

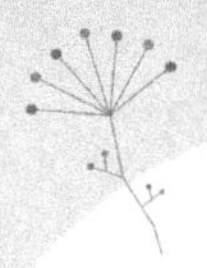

oriented HD which avoids commitment to the proposition and also provides some protection against reader rejection. In the following examples, we are dealing with hedged sentences including modal verbs *would* and *may* in impersonal constructions which reduce the writer's commitment to what is being said. For example,

> (19) The data set is perhaps a bit too small to allow for any definite conclusions, but this preliminary analysis places the rate of triple hedging at around 30% of all double-hedged expressions. *It would* be interesting to examine as well the occurrence of even larger congregations of hedging expressions (i. e. quadruple hedging) to see where this relatively strong occurrence rate drops off. (NS corpus: 0030)
>
> (20) One limitation of the present paper is its scope of research. *It would* be more persuasive if an English-Chinese case was included. (NNS corpus: 085)
>
> (21) Yet it *may* also be argued that without a standardised International language the need to follow Inner circle norms is stronger than ever in order to gain from the international opportunities which English can offer. (NS corpus: 6020d)
>
> (22) It *may* be useful to think of a semicolon as an addition sign joins related ideas. (NNS corpus: 055)

In examples (19) and (20), the writers put forward their propositions for further research based on the described results and the proposed limitations in an impersonal construction 'empty subject + *would*'. The pattern *it would* implies that the writer is not prepared to personally guarantee the proposition. The tentativeness is realised through using *would* relating principally to the commitment the writer wishes to bestow on the statement, rather than a strict concern with the truth of its propositional relationships. As the examples illustrate,

employing *would* as an impersonal construction is a strategy found in writer-oriented hedging.

Similarity to *it/this would*, the purpose of using *may* in the contexts of examples (21) and (22) above were also considered as writer-oriented hedging in the light of stating an argument of the study from the research's part. In example (21), the writer tried to propose his/her own argument on the norm for international English language based on his/her exploration and research. In example (22), the argument was proposed followed by an extensive literature review. The writer aimed at announcing an idea for his/her research. In these two examples, the use of *may* and an empty subject, which indicates lack of writer agentivity, or writer presence, constitutes a writer-oriented hedge. The writers carefully expressed their claims by using modal *may* and distanced him/herself from the proposition by constructing the sentences in an impersonal way, for the purposes of not provoking opposition and to have his/her ideas accepted.

To summarise this section, it is clear that writer-oriented hedging is a significant communicative resource for both the NS and the NNS students. On one hand, it enables the students to present statements with appropriate accuracy; on the other, it makes the strongest claim possible, while limiting the damage of being wrong, to protect the writers. Both groups of students rely on the impersonal strategy 'empty subject + *would/may*' to accomplish writer-oriented hedging.

4.1.3.3 Principal devices in the realisation of accuracy-oriented hedging

In Chapter 1, it is stated that the principle motivation of accuracy-oriented hedging is the writers' desire to clarify the state of knowledge, and to acknowledge factual uncertainties. Accuracy-oriented hedges, as Hyland (1998a) states, serve to present the content as accurately as possible.

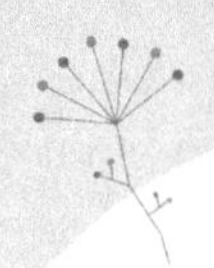

In both the NS and the NNS corpora, in general, the three modal verbs *would*, *should* and *may* investigated in this book were most frequently employed for conveying accuracy-oriented hedging (see Table 13). In the expression of accuracy-oriented hedging, what these three modal verbs have in common is that the majority of examples are active, and frequently co-occur with action verbs or adverbs. Despite differences in the frequency of occurrence, the NS and NNS groups use *would*, *should* and *may* to express accuracy-oriented hedging in a similar way. This indicates that both the NS and NNS writers are well aware of the use of *would*, *may* and *should* to qualify the intensity or the validity of the state of affairs expressed in the propositions, in order to seek precision in their expressions.

Table 13: Accuracy-oriented Hedging and the Co-occurrence Patterns of Modal Verbs Often Used to Express Them out of 100 Concordance Lines

Accuracy-oriented Hedging				
Function: Hedges Propositional Content				
NS Corpus			NNS Corpus	
	F	Patterns	F	Patterns
would	78	would + action verb/adverb (71)	80	*would* + action verb/adverb (72)
may	64	may + action verb/adverb (63)	66	*may* + action verb/adverb (66)
should	63	should + action verb/adverb (35)	42	*should* + action verb/adverb (31)

As stated in Section 4.1.1, *would* can be used to express the writer's desire to clarify the state of knowledge, and acknowledge factual uncertainties. In other words, writers can use *would* to pronounce their degree of certainty in the expected outcomes of their research. *Should* links the writer's attitude to the propositions in order to indicate what he/she believes is probable. Also, since the meanings of *may* are permission and possibility, it can also express the writer's lack of confidence in the truth of the proposition

expressed.

This is clear in the following examples, where modal verbs *would*, *may*, and *should* are used to specify the attributes of the phenomena described more precisely.

(23) The embellished diction in Beowulf serves as a cue to the reader about the nature of the characters. Without it, the reader *would* certainly still interpret good characters as good and bad characters as evil. (NS corpus: 0017)

(24) So, for example, films that depict aggressiveness as an inalienable part of human nature *would* not be classified as social drama. (NNS corpus: 094)

(25) I chose these two expressions because, unlike some of their counterparts, they are almost always used as hedges and thus *should* give a good starting ground to the present research. (NS corpus: 0030)

(26) An excellent translation of film title *should* maximize the charm and popularity of the film, and it's really challenging for the translator to do a good English film title translation. (NNS corpus: 033)

(27) The words of the same meaning in different languages *may* have different semantic domain. (NNS corpus: 073)

(28) This attempts maybe in relation to a specific history that the author may be trying to revive or in other cases, the author *may* simply try to bring to light the fact that histories may be lost in general. (NS corpus: 0049)

In the context of examples (23) and (24) the function of *would* is considered to be a means for the writers to make their statements as reliable as possible. In example (23), the writer's judgement on the reader's interpretation of *good characters* and *bad characters* is

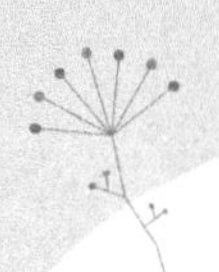

expressed accurately. In example (24), the writer's opinion is that *film is not social drama*. The use of *would* in these two examples allows the room for the writers to convey their opinions and assertions, as reliably as possible, by basing the hypothesis on their prior theoretical or experimental premises.

Hypothetical *should* in examples (25) and (26) is used to hedge the predictions *give a good starting ground to the present research* in (25) and *maximize the charm and popularity of the film* in (26). In these two examples, the writers use *should* to make tentative predictions and to precisely convey their hypothesis.

The other modal verb with a high frequency of use for accuracy-oriented hedging is *may*. The function of *may* in contexts as in both examples (27) and (28) is considered as expressing possibility on the writer's part. In example (28), which is taken from the Introduction section of the NS corpus, the writer uses *may* to speculate about the possibility that the *author may simply try to bring to light the fact that histories may be lost in general*. In example (27), *may* is used to indicate that it is possible for *the words of the same meaning in different languages* to *have different semantic domains*.

Overall, from Table 13 we can determine that the modal verbs *would*, *should* and *may* are used frequently to express accuracy-oriented hedging in both the NS and NNS students writing, and these three modal verbs show a common collocation pattern 'modal verb + action verb/adverb' in conveying this hedging function. These modal verbs express possibility, prediction or hypothesis to the action of the lexical action verbs or the description of adverbs in order to accurately and tentatively express the writer's factual interpretation to the propositional information in the text.

4.2 Move analysis of modal verbs

In this section the major communicative uses of hedges are analysed in greater detail by studying extracts of each move type in Introduction and Discussion sections. As mentioned in Chapters 2 and 3, situating hedges in their appropriate linguistic and rhetorical context gives a better picture of the ways hedges interact with other rhetorical features and contribute to the persuasiveness of the students writing. In addition, it can be seen more clearly how writers seek to vary their discussion of possibilities and manipulate their attitudes to the truth of statements through the combination and concentration of HDs. Hyland (1998a) argues that the analysis of longer stretches of discourse can thus more explicitly reveal how distribution and use of hedges reflects different rhetorical purposes of academic papers stages. In the current book, how the use of hedges reflects the different rhetorical purposes of assignments stages can be examined by looking at longer stretches of discourse as Hyland (1998a) suggested. Table 14 shows information on a number of Introduction and Discussion sections analysed in both the NS and the NNS corpora and summarises the results of occurrences of each modal verb in different moves.

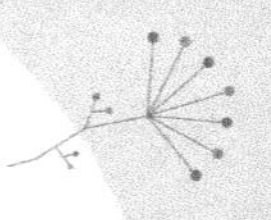

Table 14: Summary of Raw Occurrences and Normalised Frequencies of Modal Verbs *Would*, *May* and *Should* in Different Moves in Introduction and Discussion Sections (110 Sample Assignments in Each Corpus)

	NS—Introduction (110)			NS—Discussion (110)			NNS—Introduction (110)			NNS—Discussion (110)		
moves (occurrence of each move in 110 samples)	establish a territory (110)	establish a niche (22)	occupying a niche (56)	consolidate important points (110)	state limitations (39)	make suggestions (54)	establish a territory (110)	establish a niche (15)	occupying a niche (44)	consolidate important points (110)	state limitations (19)	make suggestions (50)
would	32/1.16	0/0	10/2.06	89/1.62	8/6.03	16/5.29	51/0.76	2/2.02	5/0.57	29/0.62	7/11.50	12/5.58
may	31/1.13	8/3.60	3/0.62	82/1.50	9/6.79	3/1.00	53/0.79	6/6.06	4/0.45	47/0.10	3/4.93	9/4.19
should	11/0.40	0/0	3/0.62	19/0.35	2/1.51	15/4.96	52/0.78	31/31.30	4/0.45	79/0.17	4/6.58	63/29.30

* *Numbers in the row of 'moves' present how many assignments have each move list in the table*

* *The figures in the rows of 'would', 'may' and 'should' indicate the raw number/number per 1,000 words*

4.2.1 Modal verb hedging realisations in the Introduction sections

As mentioned in Chapter 1, Swales (1990) points out that the structure of academic writing Introductions can be analysed with reference to the writers' need to 'create a research space', a task involving three major moves, namely 'establishing a territory', 'establishing a niche' and 'occupying the niche'. In general terms, then, the Introduction section involves presenting the topic to be dealt with by placing it in perspective with regard to the existing research paradigms and previous work, demonstrating that there is a need for work in the area due to gaps, lack of evidence or shortcomings in previous studies. One of the aims of the Introduction is thus to explain how this need will be addressed by the research at hand.

It appears that hedging is particularly linked with Introduction sections, as the strategy allows writers to introduce their research projects to the scientific community without being too bold as to the importance and definiteness of their work. However, as we have seen above, HDs may be found in a variety of contexts in the academic writing, not only in preliminary discussion of the writers' own work in occupying a niche, but more frequently in connection with establishing a territory, for instance when giving an overview of previous work, as well as in establishing a niche, by pointing toward a gap, shortcoming or lack of evidence in previous work. In each case, the use of HDs may be seen as a cautionary strategy, allowing the writers to 'diplomatically' indicate less than full commitment to what is being said (Swales 1990:175).

As can be seen from Table 14, the NS group's use of the three modal verbs *would*, *may* and *should* to realise the three moves of the Introduction sections of their writing bear some similarities as well as some differences with those of the NNS group. The analysis of

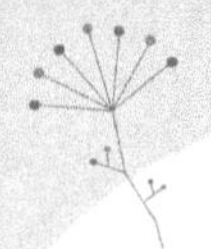

Swales's CARS model of moves and steps in the NS students' writing reveals that all texts in both the NS corpus and the NNS corpus have a Move 1 (establishing a territory) in the Introduction section and the majority of them also have a Move 3 (occupying the niche) but a relatively small number of them have a Move 2 (establishing a niche). As reviewed in Chapter 3, 'establishing a niche' (indicating a gap in the previous research or extending previous knowledge in some way) in the CARS model when writing the introduction of an academic paper, which is often thought to be obligatory in major academic papers (Swales 2004). However, although all the papers in the corpora are research papers, majority of student writing in both the NS and the NNS corpora did not have this essential move. This indicates that students in both groups did not sufficiently elaborate criticisms or denials of previous knowledge claims to create a gap in their research papers. In all the three moves examined, the occurrences of *would* and *should* in the NS corpus mostly occurred in the moves 'establishing a territory' and 'occupying a niche', while in the NNS corpus, *would*, *may* and *should* were frequently found distributed in all the three moves. Although a large number of *would*, *may* and *should* were found to be used by the NNS group to establish a niche, no examples of *would* and *should* were found to be used to accomplish this rhetorical function in the NS corpus. To occupy the niche, *would* and *may* were more frequently used by the NS group than the NNS group through announcing present research.

4.2.1.1 Establishing a territory (Move 1)

The first move, 'establishing a territory', occurs in all Introductions in both the NS and the NNS texts. The communicative function of this first move type is to introduce the topic of the study. As Swales (2004) notes, this move usually begins with topic

generalization and ends with topic specific information. As outlined in Chapter 1, according to Swales's (1990) CARS model for article introduction sections, academic writers realise the first move of the Introduction sections of their research articles 'establishing a territory' by 'claiming centrality' and/or 'making topic generalisations' and/or 'reviewing items of previous research'. A widely realised sub-move by both the NS and the NNS groups is 'reviewing items of previous research'. Modal verbs can be said to be characteristic of the third step of reviewing items of previous research. The third step is generally used to report other researchers' findings or arguments. More precisely, according to Swales (1990), writers need to provide a 'specification' of previous findings, an 'attribution to the research workers who published the results', and 'a stance towards the findings themselves' in order to establish a research territory in an Introduction section (Swales 1990: 148).

Both the NS and the NNS writers tend to use modal verbs *would*, *may* or *should* as shown in the following six examples in their discussion or interpretation of previous studies:

(29) Move type: establishing a territory (NS corpus: 6120b)

McCarthy (1998) is one of very few researchers who has actually looked into the specific area of indefinite pronouns and from his work gives the impression of a completely different view point to that which Lakoff <accuracy-oriented_M1> would </accuracy-oriented_M1> <accuracy-oriented_M1> likely </accuracy-oriented_M1> have. He feels that the uses of such indefinite pronouns as 'something' or 'anything' are simply a form of vague language. He feels that in certain situations when people are interacting with each other, there are often instances

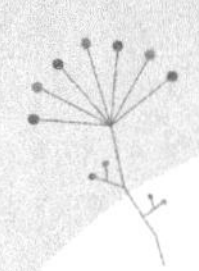

where it would not be appropriate to be precise as it can sound overly authoritative, patronising and assertive, especially in informal contexts.

(30) Move type: establishing a territory (NNS corpus: 008)

According to some critics, the most outstanding achievement of this novel is the discovery of the inadequacy of Western models, which always appear in the myth and Bible, for those who have been tied up with bitter experience and repelled by the dominating white culture. Aristotle once wrote that the tragic plot might indeed play upon our humane feelings, but it <accuracy-oriented_M1> would </accuracy-oriented_M1> not arouse either pity or fear; for our pity is awakened by undeserved misfortune, and our fear by that of someone just like ourselves, 'pity for the undeserving sufferer and fear for the man like ourselves' so that the situation in question <accuracy-oriented_M1> would </accuracy-oriented_M1> have nothing in it either pitiful or fearful.

Example (29) is from an Introduction section of the NS corpus. Both *would*, and the adverb *likely* after it, are expressions of uncertainty. The compound-hedged expression shows the greater tentativeness of the writer's statement. The writer uses *would likely* to modify the main verb *have* in the sentence in order to accurately express the writer's tentative attitude to Lakoff's point of view to *indefinite pronouns* when comparing it with McCarthy's standpoint. Then he/she tries to explicitly review McCarthy's opinion on *indefinite pronouns* with the writer's tentative expression. Similarly, in example (30), the NNS writer also uses *would* to show his/her awareness in referencing Aristotle's research on the *tragic plot*.

(31) Move type: establishing a territory (NS corpus: 0030)

As with any identifiable aspect of academic writing, much of the research on hedging attempts to define it, theoretically and functionally. Because of the negative treatment hedging has received in the past, many studies (Skelton 1988a, 1988b; Myers 1996; Channell 1990; Banks 1998; Hyland 1994, 1998a) aim to validate the presence and legitimacy of hedges in academic writing. Other research (Hyland 1994, 1998a) has offered advice on how best to teach hedging in an EAP context. Research has been undertaken on the pragmatics of hedging and its link to politeness, its social implications, and how it affects the negotiation of meaning between writer and reader (Lakoff 1972; Myers 1996; Salager-Meyer 1994). Several contrastive rhetoric studies have looked at hedging in different cultures (Martin & Burgess 2004) and the possible linguistic transfer that <accuracy-oriented_M1> may </accuracy-oriented_M1> result from attempts to hedge in the L2 (Clyne 1991; Hinkel 1997).

(32) Move type: establishing a territory (NNS corpus: 002)

The definition of conflict varies in with different cultures. The Chinese <accuracy-oriented_M1> may </accuracy-oriented_M1> see conflict as intense fighting and contradictory struggle, while the Americans <accuracy-oriented_M1> may </accuracy-oriented_M1> imply broader meaning, such as perceived incompatible goals or perceived interference of the other in achieving the desired outcomes (Lulofs & Cahn 2000).

Example (31) addresses the literature of previous research on

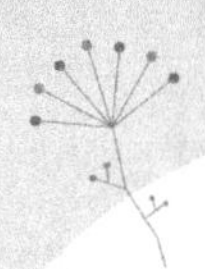

hedging. The statement of the relationship between different cultures and hedging in the L2 is based on research evidence gained from previous literature reviews from Clyne's research and Hinkel's research. *May*, in the last sentence, expresses the possibility of the action of the lexical verb *result* and acknowledges the writer's tentativeness towards the statement on *linguistic transfer* and *attempts to hedge in the L2*. In example (32), the writer reviews Lulofs and Cahn's research on *how the definition of conflict varies in with different cultures*. The modal verb *may* modifies the action of lexical verb *see* and reinforces the tentative meaning of the hedging lexical verb *imply* in the example. The writer tries to infer the possibilities of the claim that *Chinese see conflict as intense fighting and contradictory struggle*, *while the Americans imply broader meaning*. References or citations are scattered throughout Move 1 (establishing a territory) in the NS example (31) and the NNS example (32), even from the very beginning of the move. These references seem to be used to provide readers with background information or knowledge, as in the definitions of key terminologies, narration of a research topic history, in order to establish a territory for the hedging study in example (31) and the conflict study in example (32).

By using *would* and *may* in these examples, the writers display their tentative stance in reviewing previous studies, which aims to provide information on the territory within which the topic of the study is situated. In all the examples, writers address the literature in order to assert those matters that are taken to be true for the purpose of the paper. Because the background is assumed to be shared knowledge, the information is cited categorically in order to build a foundation of substantiated facts upon which the argument to follow can be constructed. Both the NS and the NNS writers achieved this purpose by the use of accuracy-oriented HD realised through modifying the

action of the lexical verb by the modal verbs *would* and *may*.

Compared with the NNS group, a lower number of tokens of *should* was used by the NS students in the Introduction sections, most of which were used to establish a territory. The co-occurrence pattern *should be + past pple* was largely used by the NS students in expressing the writer's obligation to review the related knowledge or accurately indicating the previous researcher's attitude to their statements in order to establish a territory.

(33) Move type: establishing a territory (NS corpus: 0040)

The playwright Eugene O'Neill brought many innovations to American drama. His voluminous works reflect a harmonious integration of elements from anachronistic and seemingly disparate traditions such as classicism, modernism, impressionism, and naturalism. Further, much of what make such a heterogeneous texture of dramatic writing so rich are its implications for what it means to be human. Specifically, if literature is supposed to offer examples of how it is people can, should, or actually do live, it makes sense that human life <accuracy-oriented_M1> should </accuracy-oriented_M1> be represented multi-dimensionally with different people, in different settings, struggling against different obstacles. In this sense, O'Neill brings to audiences and readers plays that portray tragedy within the self and outside of it, arising from the mind as well as acting upon it.

(34) Move type: establishing a territory (NS corpus: 0032)

There are several terms relevant to the discussion of Nicaraguan Sign Language data that <reader-oriented_M1>

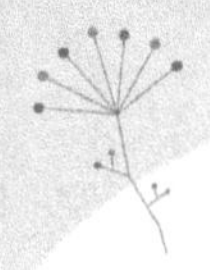

should </reader-oriented_M1 >be clarified. Idioma de Seas de Nicaragua (ISN) refers to the full Creole nativized by the second generation of children, and continuously restructured by subsequent generations. ISN is the only one of the three manifestations of Nicaraguan Sign Language that can be considered a structurally complete Creole. Lenguaje de Seas de Nicaragua (LSN) refers to the signed Pidgin created spontaneously by the first generation of children in the community. Pidgin de Seas de Nicaragua (PSN) is the term used to refer to the more traditional Pidgin used for communication purposes between deaf and hearing individuals. PSN uses a mixture of spoken Spanish lip movements, signs borrowed from ISN or LSN, and common Nicaraguan gestures.

Example (33) is from the NS corpus. It illustrates the use of *should* as an accuracy-oriented hedge in the Introduction section for expressing the writer's desire to review the previous research explicitly.

In example (33), the writer reviews O'Neill's work to American drama. The phrase *should be represented* accurately expresses O'Neill's opinion on *human life* and *heterogeneous texture of dramatic writing*. Since the literature review is assumed to be shared knowledge, the reason O'Neill's contributions to American drama are reviewed categorically is in order to build a reliable foundation upon which the argument to follow can be constructed. By reviewing his research, the writer aims at realising the first move type 'establishing a territory' of the Introduction section.

Example (34) is also from the NS corpus, which demonstrates the use of *should* as a reader-oriented hedging device in an Introduction section for declaring the writer's obligation to review the

background information of research relevant terms. In example (34), the writer suggests the necessity to clarify 'terms relevant to the discussion of Nicaraguan Sign Language data' through the use of the reader-oriented HD *should be + past pple*. The hint of obligation is milder than *must*, allowing freedom to potential readers to judge the necessity of the clarifications. The use of *should be* expresses an obligation. The reader-oriented HD *should be* aims to control the thoughts and inferences of the potential reader, to lead the reader towards the following actions of reviewing *terms relevant to the discussion of Nicaraguan Sign Language data*, to gain reader acceptance.

Similar to the NS students, the NNS students applied the co-occurrence pattern *should be + past pple* in reviewing items of previous research to 'establishing a territory'. In addition, the NNS students also used the co-occurrence pattern *we should* in claiming the importance and centrality of the topic to be studied. These are exemplified as follows:

(35) Move type: establishing a territory (NNS corpus: 0067)

The study on the connotation has been the focus of linguists for a long time. Many linguists contribute to the study of connotation. One of the most important scholars, Geoffrey Leech, says connotations are unstable. He further illustrates that connotations vary from individual to individual and from society to society. Another important figure, Bloomfield, considers connotations as the supplementary values of words. He places connotations from social standing in the most important position. What he declares clearly is that connotations vary according to the social standards. Compared with the above two linguists, F.

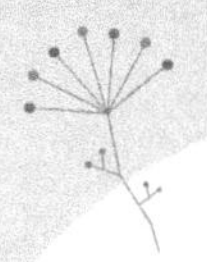

R. Palmer does not give a positive view on connotations. He says connotations are not useful. But Palmer points out that connotations are closely related to society. Then Greimas studies on connotation from the perspective of sociology. He concludes that connotations <accuracy-oriented_M1 >should </accuracy-oriented_M1 > be postulated in individual and social fields. Greimas further concludes that connotation can gain more territory as it enters into other fields. Roland Barthes says connotation relates the meaning to another text. He points out connotation implies additional meaning to the communication so that communication is not a pure activity.

In example (35), the writer uses *should be* to conclude the findings of Greimas' research. *Should be* expresses Greimas' attitude to the claim of *connotations*. In other words, the writer of example (35) would like to claim that Greimas' point of view is that it is necessary to postulate connotations in individual and social fields. This obligation is milder than *must*, but stronger than *could*. The wrong choice of modal verb may misinterpret the intention of the original researcher. The modal verb contributes to the precision with which a claim is made. The major function of *should be* here is to provide a specification of the state of knowledge rather than hedge the writer's commitment to the claim.

The move 'establishing a territory' can also be realised by claiming centrality through the use of *should* in a reader-oriented expression.

(36) Move type: establishing a territory (NNS corpus: 0032)

Colorful pigments to palette are what idiomatic expressions to language. Without those colors, even though you, as the greatest master, move heaven and earth, the jig is up. Without

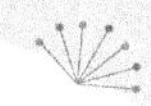

those idiomatic expressions, even though you, the smashing chatterbox, bend over backwards to talk away, you can not hold water. So in order to complete a wonderful painting, we must know pigments like the palm of our hands, and accordingly, we <reader-oriented_M1> should </reader-oriented_M1> be familiar with the idiomatic expressions to get the hang of language study. For us Chinese students who learn English as the second language, it is extremely important to understand the differences between Chinese and English idiomatic expressions if we want to get to the bottom of language study.

As shown in example (36), the writer claims that his/her research of *idiomatic expressions* is important at the very beginning. By so claiming, the writer called attention to potential readers to consider the concept of *idiomatic* by using the pattern *we should* to indicate the necessity to *be familiar with the idiomatic expressions*. The expression *we should* negotiates a position with the reader by stating the proposal as an opinion and leaving it open to ratification. The sentence with the opening phrase *we should* also plays a role of a connecting link between what comes before and what goes after. Understanding the importance of *idiomatic*, the readers know that the writer is going to give out the relevant concepts. By emphasising the importance of studying *idiomatic* and claiming the necessity of understanding the concept of it, the writer tried and partly established a territory for his/her study.

4.2.1.2 Establishing a niche (Move 2)

Move 2 'establishing a niche' mainly involves pointing out the weaknesses of previous relevant work, denying earlier claims made by earlier investigators and making claims that may dispute other's work; this is the common way writers establish a niche or create a space for

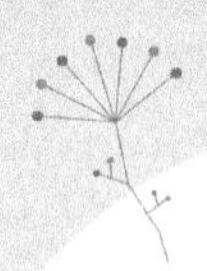

research (Swales 1990). In other words, in this move, writers seek to find a gap in the existing literature in the field under review in order to justify their own current research. It implies distancing oneself from other researchers who have already investigated the field. In so doing, writers may be led to express disagreement or even criticism in such a way as to show respect for fellow researchers. As shown in Table 14, only a small number (22 and 15 out of 110 texts in the NS and NNS corpora respectively) of the NS and NNS writings have a segment which can be classified as a Move 2. The NS writers rarely used the modal verbs *would* and *should*, preferring *may* to realise the second move 'establishing a niche', while the NNS writers used all these three modal verbs quite often in the second move, especially in the use of the modal verb *should*. In the NNS corpus, the frequency of *should* is several times higher than *may* and *would* in 'establishing a niche'. The niche establishment segment, realised through modal verbs, is mainly expressed using the rhetorical work of stating that research on a particular area is important or in need of being carried out or reported. As elaborated in Section 4.1.1, *may* is the primary modal verb used to express uncertainty or possibility and *should* is commonly used to convey obligation. The different preferences of using *may* and *should* in the NS and NNS corpora may indicate that the two groups of students followed different strategies in establishing a niche. The following two typical examples reveal how the NS and NNS students use *may* and *should* respectively to establish a niche in their assignments.

(37) Move type: Establishing a niche (NS corpus: 6206b)

What this lack of focused attention leaves unclear is just how often multiple hedging occurs, whether or not it is considered

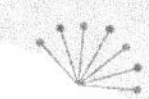

acceptable (and if so how many hedges must be used before multiple hedging becomes overhedging), and what, if any, factors, such as level of education, native vs. non-native speaker status, etc, <accuracy-oriented_M1 >may </accuracy-oriented_M1 > affect the strength or amount of a given writer's use of hedges.

(38) Move type: Establishing a niche (NNS corpus: 032)

For the foreign audience, the translation of a film plays a significant role in cultural communication between two countries. It is through translation that foreign audiences get the chance to understand and appreciate other countries' art, culture, people and way of life. So the importance and effect of film translation < reader-oriented _ M1 > should </reader-oriented_M1 > not be ignored. And it is necessary to study on the translation method of film title translation.

In the above two examples, both the NS and the NNS writers address Move 2 by concluding that research on a particular aspect has been neglected by other researchers. Therefore, their research project could be very important or significant. These conclusions or claims about the unavailability or non-existence of studies on a particular aspect of research in example (37) and example (38) are proposed with the writers' hedging. The modal verb *may* is concerned with precision in example (37) and indicates accuracy-oriented hedging and the obligation expression *should not be ignored* marks the hedge in example (38) as a reader-oriented strategy. In example (37), the tentativeness, which is expressed through the modal verb *may*, relates principally to the writer's concern with the truth of its proposition *affect the strength or amount of a given writer's use of hedges*. According to the analysis of Section 4.1.3, the co-occurrence pattern

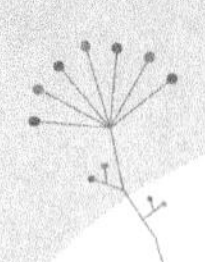

should be + past pple is used to express obligation in order to give advice and make suggestions. In example (38), the writer attempts to advise that attention be paid to *the importance and effect of film translation*. Through conveying the writer's entreaty to potential readers by expressing obligation, writers also involve potential readers of this study in a joint quest for knowledge on *film translation*. It could be argued that different strategies were adopted by the NS and NNS students in 'establishing a niche' in their assignments. The results show that the NNS students tended to indicate a gap of previous research through making suggestions by using *should* as a reader-oriented HD. However, the strategy used by the NS students was to evaluate the gap of previous research tentatively.

4.2.1.3 Occupying a niche (Move 3)

The role of Move 3 in the CARS model is 'to turn the niche established in Move 2 into a research space that justifies the present research' (Swales 1990: 159). In Move 3, academic writers offer to substantiate the particular counter-claim that has been made, fill the created gap, answer the specific questions or continue the rhetorically-established tradition. Swales (1990) suggests that the obligatory step in Move 3 is 'to indicate the main purpose of research'.

Compared to Move 1, the rhetorical work in Move 3 is more straightforward and simpler syntactically and semantically; this part of a piece of academic writing, therefore, often requires shorter textual realisation or statements than Move 1 does (Ahmad 1997). The main communicative purpose of this move is to announce or indicate the research purposes, research specific features, principle findings or academic writing structure. Unlike Move 1 which is more persuasive, Move 3 seems to be more informative rather than argumentative.

The final move of the two groups realised in the Introduction

sections of their writings was 'occupying the niche'. This was achieved through the use of *would*, *may* and *should* to varying percentages (see Table 14). *Would* is predominantly used in Move 3 'occupying the niche' by the NS students, while fewer examples of *may* and *should* were found to be used in occupying the niche through the analysis of the NS data. In the NNS corpus, there is no difference in the frequency of occurrences among the three modal verbs *would*, *may* and *should* in Move 3. All these three modal verbs were used by the NNS students, but in a low frequency, to 'occupy a niche'.

Both the NS and the NNS students used *would* to realise the final move 'occupying the niche' by describing the purpose of their research with a preference in use of personal attribution.

The purpose of using *would* in example (39) from the NS corpus and example (40) from the NNS corpus is to tentatively propose the aim of the research:

> (39) Move type: Occupying a niche (NS corpus: 6120d)
>
> For the purposes of this assignment, I decided that I <reader-oriented_M3 >would </reader-oriented_M3 >look at a specific aspect of language and compare its use in both tabloid and broadsheet newspapers. In order to make the most accurate comparisons, equivalent stories from the newspapers had to be collected and so I decided to look at the recent events surrounding the former Liberal Democrat leader, Charles Kennedy. It then had to be decided which aspect of language to investigate. Eventually it was therefore decided that my final research question < reader-oriented _ M3 > would </reader-oriented_M3 > be: How does the use of superlative adjectives differ between the broadsheet newspaper *The Guardian* and the tabloid newspaper *The Mirror*?

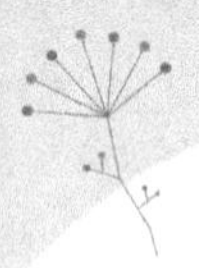

(40) Move type: Occupying a niche (NNS corpus: 0084)

This article attempts to analyse and probe into the cultural influence on color words from the angle of the cultural contrast of Chinese and Western. I <reader-oriented _ M3> would </reader-oriented _ M3> like to make a comparison and discussion on the eastern and western senses of color and its symbolic meaning as follow.

The personal attributions in all the examples are critical and clearly acknowledge the desire of the writer to defer to the audience in presenting the new claims and statements he/she hopes to gain acceptance for. Thus the personal expression *I would* represents the tension between a personal conviction and the need to relate the claims to the existing knowledge currently sanctioned by the potential readers. It might be tentatively suggested that the writers' employment of personal hedging to outline purpose may result from a perceived need to respond to the potential readers' concerns with effective support for their statements.

A reasonable interpretation is that an acceptance of personal responsibility mitigates the expression of a proposition and signifies a reader-oriented hedge. By marking the propositions as personal beliefs with the personal pronoun *I*, the writer recognises the possible interpersonal effects of his/her claim and simply labels it as an alternative position without weakening its probability in any way.

4.2.2 Modal verb hedging in Discussion sections

According to the frequency counts, discussion sections in the NS and NNS corpora are also heavily hedged. The reason why hedges occur frequently in this rhetorical section is obviously linked to the

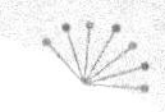

kind of information it encompasses. Hyland (1998a: 154) summarises the motivation for hedging in the Discussion section by saying that

> It is in Discussions that authors make their claims, consider the relevance of results and speculate about what they might mean, going beyond their data to offer the more general interpretations by which they gain their academic credibility. The level of generality, and therefore the density of hedges, is much higher here, as writers explore the ramifications of their results.

Contrary to the Introduction section, the Discussion section moves incrementally outward. Considering the fact that the findings are foregrounded and the work of others are cited to confirm, compare, and contrast with the present findings, the Discussion sections are expected to be general and tentative rather than particular and precise. According to Hopkins and Dudley-Evans (1988), research article writers realise a number of sub-moves to realise three moves 'consolidating important points', 'stating limitations' and 'making suggestions'. These sub-moves range from providing background information to stating their results, from expressing their (un) expected outcomes to referring to previous research, and from explaining and exemplifying to making deductions in order to be able to consolidate important points. In addition to these strategies, they also state their limitations and make recommendations. The analysis of moves and steps in NS students writing reveals that all texts in the NS corpus have a Move 4 (consolidating important points) in the Discussion section and the majority of them also have a Move 6 (making suggestions), but only one third of them have a Move 5 (stating limitations). The analysis of moves and steps in the NNS

students' writing also shows that all texts in the NNS corpus have a Move 4 'consolidating important points' in the Discussion section followed by Move 5 'stating limitations'. However, very few of them have a Move 6 'making suggestions'. The reason that far fewer NNS writers in the data have a Move 5 in their Discussion section could be due to the fact that many NNS writers make suggestions for further research without evaluating the limitations of his/her current research, or because most of the suggestions the NNS writers made in their Discussion sections are pragmatic suggestions.

In their attempts to realise these moves of the Discussion section, which is general and tentative, both the NS and the NNS groups conveyed their imprecision by employing the three modal verbs to varying degree as shown in Table 14.

As was the case in the Introduction section, the NS group used *would* the most in the Discussion section as well, whereas, the NNS group employed *should* the most, followed by *would* and *may*. Moreover, these three modal verbs were not evenly distributed in Moves 4, 5 and 6. In both the NS and NNS corpora, Move 5 'stating limitations' and Move 6 'making suggestions' had a higher incidence of the three modal verb HDs together than Move 4 'consolidating important points'. The NS students employed *would* and *may* more frequently than *should* to 'consolidate important points' and 'state limitations', while they preferred to use *would* and *should* rather than *may* to 'make suggestions'. In the NNS corpus, *would*, *may* and *should* were used with high frequency to 'state limitations' and 'make suggestions'. The most commonly used modal verbs by the NNS group in Move 5 'stating limitations' and Move 6 'making suggestions' are *would* and *should* receptively.

4.2.2.1 Consolidating important points (Move 4)

As underlined in Chapter 1, according to Hopkins and Dudley-

Evans's (1988) model for the Conclusion section, academic writers realise the first move of the Conclusion sections of their academic writing 'consolidating important points' by 'giving background information' and/or 'stating their results', and/or 'stating their (un)expected outcomes', and/or 'referring to previous research', and/or 'making explanations', and/or 'making exemplifications'.

As presented in Table 14, both groups made use of *would* and *may* more often than *should* in this move. The use of impersonal expressions is a common feature shared by the examples of *would* and *may* in Move 4 of both the NS and the NNS writing. The use of an 'abstract rhetor' as a subject of a sentence indicates the absence of writer agentivity which is a distinctive characteristic of writer-oriented hedges as generalised by Hyland (1998a). Modal verbs which were used as writer oriented HDs in the following examples imply that the writers aimed to shield themselves from the possible negative consequences in stating results and making explanations about these results.

(41) Move type: Consolidating important points (NS corpus: 6206b)

L was also found to use SVO structures most frequently, (refer to LARSP charts within appendix) with the majority of her utterances falling into the stage 3 category. Similarly, this is the category occupied most by Sophie at 2;4 and 3;0, with a gradual progression towards more stage 4 clauses being shown at 3;0. Stage 3 is estimated to be the equivalent of age 2;0 -2;6 and therefore it's dominance in L's and Sophie at 2;4's language is to be expected. It is apparent though that as Sophie is showing signs of more stage 4 clauses at 3;0 (2;6 - 3;0), L is also beginning to do so at 2;6. This <writer-oriented_M4 >may

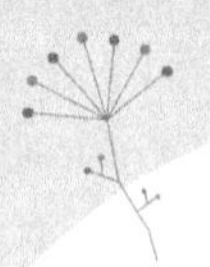

</writer-oriented_M4 > < writer-oriented_M4 > suggest </writer-oriented_M4 > that L's syntactic development is in fact ahead of Sophie's, however as previously emphasised this is only a suggestion and further investigation would be necessary to form any significant conclusions.

(42) Move type: Consolidating important points (NS corpus: 6020c)

From this analysis it <writer-oriented_M4 >would </writer-oriented_M4 > < writer-oriented_M4 > appear </writer-oriented_M4 > that the distribution and primary function of some discourse markers, in particular 'well' can be maintained across different speech events ('well' occurring in initial position and as an introductory, framing device).

(43) Move type: Consolidating important points (NNS corpus: 0002)

Based on the argument that Chinese people value group harmony and avoid conflict to preserve relationships, the author predicted that in Chinese families people would show a preference for avoiding and obliging styles. The results of the survey partially supported the hypothesis. In the sample, Chinese showed a strong preference for avoiding and compromising styles over dominating and obliging resolution styles in conflict situations. It is beyond the author's expectation that integrating outweighed obliging style in the survey. This finding <writer-oriented_M4 >may </writer-oriented_M4 > <writer-oriented_M4 > indicate </writer-oriented_M4 > that Chinese people have become more practical and more solution-oriented, and would like to make both parties satisfied in addition to family harmony. Furthermore, the finding < writer-oriented_M4 > may </writer-oriented_M4 > also < writer-oriented_M4 >

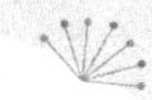

reflect </writer-oriented _ M4 > the influence of Western cultures on Chinese people after China opened its door to welcome other cultures.

(44) Move type: Consolidating important points (NNS corpus: 0028)

To sum up, it < writer-oriented_M4 > would </writer-oriented_M4 > be rather difficult for a translator to achieve the ideal effect of ' form resemblance ' in literary translation due to the special characteristic of literary works. Generally it should be a harmonious unity of a translator's thorough understanding of the original text and his good skill of expression as well.

The above examples deal with hedged sentences including modal verbs to reduce the writer's commitment to what is being said. A central feature of these HDs is the absence of writer agentivity, that is, sentences with writer-oriented HDs typically involve impersonal constructions. As the examples illustrate, employing an ' abstract rhetors' (Hyland 1998a) is a useful avoidance strategy in connection with writer-oriented hedging. Accordingly, in examples (41), (42), (43) and (44), modal verbs *would* and *may*, in connection with an impersonal subject as well as lexical verbs *suggest*, *appear*, *indicate*, *reflect* and *be*, may be interpreted as linguistic choices implying that the writer is not prepared to personally guarantee the proposition. Lexical verbs *suggest*, *appear* and *indicate* in examples (41), (42) and (43) are also considered as HDs. The writers choose to heavily hedge their arguments with a compound HD (a hedging modal verb and a hedging lexical verb) to indicate their uncertainty and protect themselves against the dangers of overstatement.

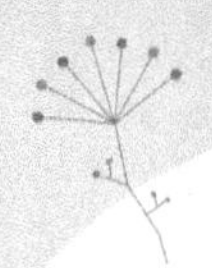

4. 2. 2. 2 Stating limitations and making suggestions (Move 5 & Move 6)

Move 6 'making suggestions' of the Discussion section is often immediately after Move 5 'stating limitation' in the NS and NNS data. The differences between the NS and NNS writers in the realisation of Move 5 and Move 6 by using modal verbs *would*, *may* and *should* are displayed in Table 14. The most noteworthy is *should* is extensively used by the NNS writers to make suggestions. As discussed in Section 4. 1. 1, the uses of obligation/necessity of modal *should* in making suggestions for further research by Chinese writers can be particularly culture dependent.

The results of the concordance analysis shows that the NS writers applied *would* more with personal expressions than the NNS writers in stating limitations and making suggestions. While there are many more personal expression co-occurrences with *should* in the NNS data than in the NS data in realising Move 5 and Move 6. In this section, modal verb *would* and *should* for the purpose of 'stating limitations' and 'making suggestions' in the Discussion section will be exemplified below.

Example (45) is extracted from a Discussion section of the NS corpus. It contains two move types, namely 'stating limitations' and 'making suggestions'. Five occurrences of *would* are used in making suggestions for further research by the NS writer.

> (45) Discussion section (NS corpus: 6061b)
>
> Move types: 'indicating the limitation of study' (lines 1 – 7) and 'recommending or identifying useful areas of further research' (lines 8 – 35)

The main problem faced with such an investigation is that analysis and annotation of data necessarily involves native speaker intuition. The decisions made regarding these matters are likely to vary greatly across individuals. Often in long and complex text, particularly from broadsheet newspapers, it was not clear when a lexical item was behaving in one way, and when it functioned as something else entirely.

In a further study I <reader-oriented_M6> would </reader-oriented_M6> like to extend the searches and look at each emotive word and find the frequency in which it appears in that text. I believe this <reader-oriented_M6> would </reader-oriented_M6> highlight the tendency of tabloid newspapers to refer to Muslims with connotations of terrorism. When reading the articles it is clear that tabloids treat Muslims with a certain bias. Broadsheets on the other hand, although often use the same words to refer to Muslims, also feature articles where Muslims are considered in contexts other than terrorism. The BNC results are predominantly nouns, often inanimate, illustrating that Muslim/Islamic is mainly found as an adjective. This differs from tabloids which tend to involve what Muslims do and which attributes they have. There are many advantages of using a larger Corpus. Primarily it enables the comparison of different types of text. In this case it <writer-oriented_M6> would </writer-oriented_M6> have been useful to compare articles of a different time period. Searching for Muslim/Islamic in the last year necessarily included coverage of July 7th bombings and the earthquake of Pakistan so it was inevitable that this study <accuracy-oriented_M6> would

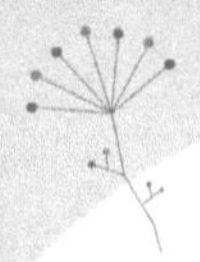

</accuracy-oriented_M6> uncover perhaps an unrepresentative amount of words with a certain type of meaning. Another useful continuation of this theme <accuracy-oriented_M6> would </accuracy-oriented_M6> look at a diachronic as opposed to a synchronic corpus, enabling a comparison of language across time.

In example (45), the writer starts with a discussion of the major problem/limitations faced in his/her study. Then the move 'stating limitations' is followed by 'making suggestions' for future research. In this example, the move 'making suggestions' was realised through different polypragmatic functions of the HD *would*. The personal attributions in line 8 and line 11 are critical and clearly acknowledge the desire of the writer to defer to the audience in presenting the new and radical claims he/she hopes to gain acceptance for proposing. Thus the reader-oriented HD *I would* represents the tension between a personal conviction and the need to relate the claims to the existing knowledge currently accepted by the potential readers or even the discourse community. It might be tentatively suggested that the NS writers' employment of reader-oriented *would* to make suggestions may result from a need to respond to potential readers' concerns with effective feedback of their research finding (Myers 1990; Hyland 1998a). The repeated use of hedging *would* (lines 29 – 33) is interesting in this regard. *Would* in lines 29 and 33 are considered as accuracy-oriented HDs, mitigating the reliability of the conclusions by making them dependent on the premises. *Would* in line 18 is considered as a writer-oriented hedge. It therefore contributes to the persuasive character of the argument by deferring to the reader in suggesting hypothetical consequences of unreal conditions to make suggestions for future research. In lines 12, 29 and 33, *would*

collocated with the verbs *highlight*, *uncover* and *look*. The meanings of these three verbs are weakened by the co-occurrence with *would*. It could be argued that the use of *would* is carefully selected by the writer to make suggestions in a manner which reduces the risk of challenging readers and provoking the possibility of immediate negation of the suggestions.

Example (46) is extracted from a Discussion section of the NNS corpus. It also contains two move types, those are 'stating limitations' and 'making suggestions'. Five occurrences of *would* were found in 'stating limitations' and 'making suggestions' for further research by the NNS writers, mostly in an impersonal way, which is different from the examples from the NS corpus.

(46) Discussion section (NNS corpus: 085)

Move type: 'indicating the limitation of study' (lines 1 –8) and 'recommending or identifying useful areas of further research' (lines 9 –17)

One limitation of the present paper is its scope of research. It <writer-oriented_M5> would </writer-oriented_M5> be more persuasive if an English-Chinese case was included. Although great efforts has been made for the case study of Chinese-English subtitle translation, it won't well describe the wild usage of skospos for all languages. Anther limitation is the author of the paper receives most information from Internet not the original version, which can't let us know the real original thinking of the translator. Practice makes truth, research should be absolutely true and accurate.

In view the limitations of above, further study is encouraged to investigate English-Chinese cases and compare the result

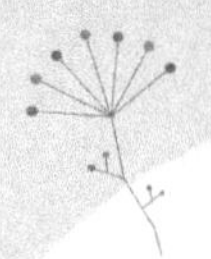

with that of Chinese-English cases. A bolder attempt <accuracy-oriented_M6> would </accuracy-oriented_M6> be to include different language versions of a same movie distributed in different foreign markets to see what insights the functionalist approach can provide. The ideology issue, which is not the focus of the present paper, <accuracy-oriented_M6>would </accuracy-oriented_M6> be worth discussing once the translator is available. The author believes that a comparison between the original and the edited versions <accuracy-oriented_M6> would </accuracy-oriented_M6> also be fruitful if they are available. Here the author <accuracy-oriented_M6>would </accuracy-oriented_M6> like to call for more cooperation and also it will be better for the research if could consult the director of the movie *Crouching Tiger*, *Hidden Dragon* and the screenwriter.

In example (46), the NNS writer begins by drawing attention to the limitations of the study mentioned from the researcher's point of view. Then the move of 'stating limitations' is followed by 'making suggestions' for future study. In the argument of the suggestion for further study, the writer builds on the acceptance of his premise with the modal verb *would* five times. The suggestion is hedged with a concern for propositional precision, indicating less assurance by the writers on the direction that future research should take.

The impersonal construction of *it would* in line 2 indicates a writer-oriented HD which implies that the writer does not wish to personally commit to the proposed suggestion. The repeated use of *would* (lines 15 – 26) are examples of accuracy-oriented HDs. They mitigate the reliability of the suggestions by making them dependent

on the validity of the premises. In line 23, the subject 'the author' is the writer himself/herself. Thus personal alignment with suggestions conveys a reader-oriented HD. By specifying a personal source, the writer draws attention to the relation of the work to the investigator, and signals that the suggestion is left open to the reader's judgment.

Sample text (47) below gives examples of *should* functioning in two move types 'stating limitations' and 'making suggestions' found in Discussion sections.

(47) Discussion Section (NS corpus: 6206b)

Move types: 'indicating the limitation of study' (lines 1 –5) and 'recommending or identifying useful areas of further research' (lines 5 –38)

This investigation did not use a control of the same age. Although the data on Sophie was thought to be satisfactory for the purpose of this case study, in hindsight an age matched control <reader-oriented_M5> should </reader-oriented_M5> have been used. Future research <reader-oriented_M6> should </reader-oriented_M6> consider using matched pairs of premature and full term infants in relation to SES, age and family history of language delay. L's utterances were often difficult to decipher, resulting in many utterances being marked as unintelligible. This may not necessarily have been the case. Noises within the natural home environment may have contributed to these difficulties, as well as L's use of varying pitch often causing utterances to become distorted. These factors add to the naturalistic environment which the investigation chose to adopt, however it may have been beneficial to use more

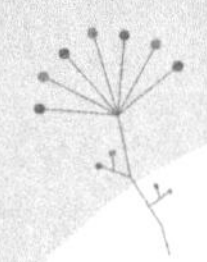

sophisticated recording equipment which would not influence the subject or cause observer's paradox. Coding system used within SALT is often problematic to use, with Brown (1973 as in Bennett- Kastor, 1988: 78) stating that he was "never confident that he knew what the full coding should be". The use of the Sophie data proved difficult to compare to that of L at times. This was mainly due to L's data being based on a series of mean scores, so features such as TTR, VTTR and bound morphemes which had to be assessed in each individual transcript, could not be compared adequately as examples could not be given. There is no way of telling if the data is representative of L's full language production abilities due to it being a sample, and there is no way of assessing comprehension directly through SALT (Bennett-Kastor, 1988: 36). Comprehension assessments may be a useful tool for future research in order to assess whether receptive language is affected in a healthy, premature sample. The form of a case study does not allow any conclusions to be drawn from the investigation. In order to establish whether the finding presented are true of the majority of healthy, premature infants a larger sample of premature infants is required.

The opening statement of example (47) indicates the limitations of his/her research. The hypothetical meaning of the first HD *should* in line 4, therefore, contributes to the persuasive character of the statement by deferring to the readers in expressing the research action that needs to be taken. Thus the HD *should* acknowledges the desire of the writer to gain acceptance for the claims him/her proposed from the potential readers. The extract then goes on to make suggestions for

future research. In line 6, the second modal verb HD *should* co-occurs with *further research* and links what the writer suggests is probable. The writer uses *should* here to express obligation in order to make suggestions for further research. The use of an obligation expression aims to lead the reader to *consider using matched pairs of premature and full term infants in relation to SES, age and family history of language delay* in future research and to impose this opinion on the readers.

The examples of *should* in Move 5 and Move 6 in the NNS corpus are shown in sample text (48) below. We can see that four occurrences of *should* in the sample text co-occurred with *we*. The pattern *we should* appeared frequently in Move 5 and Move 6 of Discussion sections in the NNS corpus. In total, 159 instances of *should* appeared in all the Discussion sections of the NNS corpus. Fifty-eight instances of *should* were used in the NNS corpus together with first person plural subjects compared with 2 out of 48 in the Discussion sections of the NS corpus.

In example (48), *we should* are used in both 'indicating the limitations of study' and 'recommending or identifying useful areas of further research' move types. The acceptance of personal responsibility mitigates the expression of a proposition and signifies a reader-oriented hedge.

(48) Discussion section (NNS corpus)

Move types: 'indicating the limitation of the study' (lines 1 –8) and 'recommending or identifying useful areas of further research' (lines 8 –18)

Through the introduction of multiple points of view of different scholars, we put a few of beneficial opinions towards number concord, which let our learners know the current

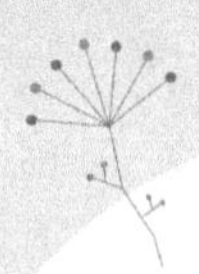

development of this area. However, we <reader-oriented_M6 >should </reader-oriented_M6 > know that this is not the satisfactory answer. Language changes constantly, and any linguistic rules and theories are instructive just for a certain period of time. Therefore, the most important thing we <reader-oriented_M6 >should </reader-oriented_M6 > do is paying attention to the development of the language and making scientific summary. The emergence of any logistical linguistic phenomenon or any new selection of words have certain preconditions, background and the process for the public to accept, therefore, we <reader-oriented_M6 > should </reader-oriented_M6 > bear in mind each of them whenever and wherever we see it without making up story. Our suggestion is that we <reader-oriented_M6 > should </reader-oriented_M6 > focus on the basic grammatical rules which are fundamental and instructive. In the meanwhile, those important and unconventional but reasonable phenomena need to be handled with flexibly in order for practical use.

We can see that the four tokens of *should* in the sample text all co-occur with *we*. In this sample text, *we should* is used in both indicating limitations of study and recommending or identifying useful areas of further research. *We should*, in lines 4 and 5, negotiates a position with the potential reader by stating the claim *this is not the satisfactory answer* as an opinion of research limitation and leaving it open to judgment. While pointing out the limitations of the study, the writer makes four main recommendations for further study. The first three suggestions are put forward by the writer through the expression of obligations. The collocation *we should* in these three sentences are

considered in the light of expressing obligations in order to make suggestions for further research. Theses suggestions are *paying attention to the development of the language and making scientific summary*, *bear in mind each of them* and *focus on the basic grammatical rules*. In this case, the writer states his/her suggestions for further research, but the readers are allowed to judge for themselves. The personal strategy seeks to hedge assertiveness by representing the tension between a personal conviction and the need to relate the claims to the existing knowledge currently recognised by the potential readers.

Conclusion

These findings of concordance analysis show the use of modal verbs *would*, *should* and *may* in expressing hedging. The most frequent co-occurrence pattern of these selected modal verbs is MOD *inf* in both the NS and the NNS corpora. The lexico-grammatical patterns of modal verbs served as three different categories of polypragmatic functions of hedging in different expressions. The findings are discussed in relation to the major specific functions of hedges proposed by Hyland (1998a), namely accuracy-oriented, writer-oriented and reader-oriented type hedges.

The NS and NNS writers have almost the same patterns in the accuracy-oriented and the writer-oriented categories. In the reader-oriented hedging category, the NS writers consistently use a wider range of patterns than the NNS writers, that is, (1) hypothetical conditional *would*, (2) addressing the reader directly, (3) personal attribution and (4) make suggestion (*should be*). The NNS writers' methods to express reader-oriented hedging are limited to the latter two patterns (cf. Section 4.1.3.1). The major difference occurred with respect to modal verbs in making recommendations or

suggestions, referring to shared assumptions, and using hypothetical conditionals to suggest alternative interpretations or possibilities.

The analysis of a long extract demonstrates the cumulative effect of hedging through a paper and how writers use different types of hedging to achieve different purposes. By the use of different hedging functions the writers are able to achieve a balance of scientific accuracy, self-protection and deference to their audience. This chapter has shown that the two groups have displayed, through the employment of the modal verbs to express hedging, that they are aware of the fact that 'academic discourse is not just a mere collection of facts' (Wishnoff 2000: 128). In the same vein, both the NS and the NNS writers demonstrated that they know the importance of modifying their assertions, toning down uncertain or risky claims, and conveying opinions to the potential readers of their research. However, the NNS writers showed differences in overall distribution of modal verb use across the sections and moves in their writing. They displayed different tendencies in the choice of modal verb patterns in the Introduction and Discussion sections and moves within these two sections. Broadly speaking, the NNS writers behaved more subjectively than the NS writers in stating limitations and making suggestions for further research in their use of the modal verb pattern *we should*. While the personal attribution, *I would*, shows the desire of the NS writers to defer to the audience in presenting the new claims and statements he/she hopes to gain acceptance for proposing to establish a niche.

This book reveals problems of the NNS writers' use of modal verbs in academic writing such as an underuse of *I would* and hypothetical conditional *would*, but an overuse of *we should* to make recommendations or suggestions, to present new claims or statements, and to suggest alternative interpretations or possibilities in comparison

with the NS writers. The results of this study could give the NNS students a notion of their inappropriate use of reader-oriented hedging expressions and how the NS writers use reader-oriented HDs in academic writing. As discussed in Section 4. 1. 3. 1, the inappropriate use of *would* and *should* could be due to not having enough exposure to the different usages of these modal verbs, first language transfer and mode of thinking. It is important that Chinese undergraduate students majoring in linguistics or English studies, especially those for whom academic writing is a qualification requirement, be informed about using modal verbs to express reader-oriented hedging, and be shown what kinds of linguistic expressions could be used in order to accomplish particular reader-oriented hedging functions. Chinese undergraduate students are suggested that they analyse some model texts in their field of study to see how the NS writers express reader-oriented functions.

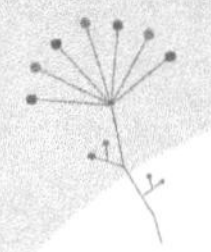

Chapter 5

Lexical Verb Hedging with *Suggest* and *Seem*

Introduction

On the basis of Hyland's analysis of the formal aspects of hedging, lexical verbs (e. g. *suggest*, *seem*, *indicate*, *appear*) with epistemic meanings are considered as HDs in this book. It could be argued that lexical verbs are central to the linguistic construal and communication of meaning in academic discourse, not only because many verbs have domain-specific meanings, but also in view of the fact that verbs establish the relations between concepts denoted by nouns (Halliday & Martin 1993).

The focus of this chapter is on the contribution of the two selected hedging lexical verbs *suggest* and *seem* to the communication features of academic knowledge. Many of these hedging lexical verbs are of interest as an object of research in academic texts because of their discursive and hedging function in the communication of the academic research. Their occurrence in specific colligational patterns is indicative of their function. For example, *that* clauses following lexical verbs can be shown to be frequently employed in the reporting of research results, whereas *to*-infinitive clauses tend to present the writer's ideas or statements of known facts (Bartsch 2009).

Lexical verbs with an epistemic meaning encompass verbs expressing what Hyland (1998a: 20) refers to as 'epistemic judgement'. These are, verbs of speculation (e. g. *suggest*, *believe*) and deduction (e. g. *conclude*, *infer*), as well as verbs expressing evidentiary justification (Hyland 1998a: 124 – 126), that is, verbs of quotation, which are used to report the findings of other researchers, and at the same time express the degree of the writer's commitment to these findings (e. g. X *shows*, Y *claims*), verbs of perception (e. g. *seem*, *appear*) and narrators (e. g. *seek*, *attempt*), verbs which relate the goal of the book with the results achieved; they contribute to the construction of an identity and a narrative, which relates to evidence by hinting at the fallibility of knowing (Hyland 1998a:125).

5.1 Frequency of hedging lexical verbs

Lexical verbs constitute 25.6% of the major grammatical classes expressing hedging in the NS corpus. Proportionally, they are used much less frequently in the NNS texts, which constitute 9% of all the HDs in the NNS corpus. A z-score test has furthermore confirmed the statistical significance of the difference between the mean values between the two sets of corpora.

When comparing the lexical verbs which are used as HDs in the two corpora, it has been observed that the verbs *suggest* and *seem* occurred quite frequently in the NS corpus, whereas they were used much less frequently in the NNS corpus. Table 8 in Chapter 3 shows the difference of the incidence of occurrence of *suggest* (1.21 in the NS corpus and 0.17 in the NNS corpus) and *seem* (1.23 in the NS corpus and 0.43 in the NNS corpus). The marked differences in the frequency of the use of *suggest* and *seem* between the NS and the NNS assignments made these selected hedging lexical verbs worthy of

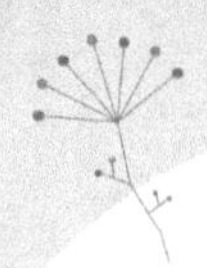

investigation.

Various meanings of *suggest* and *seem* are connected to different patterns, which help to disambiguate them. When the hedging lexical verbs were searched for across the NS and the NNS corpora, their lemma verb form, which includes simple present base form, simple present -s form, past form, past participle and -ing participle, are considered as the search term. In this book the term 'lemma' refers to the base form of each lexical verb, disregarding inflectional morphemes. For example, *suggest*, *suggests*, *suggested* and *suggesting* are realisations of a single lemma *suggest*.

A body of example sentences of these two verbs and their lemma was obtained for the analysis of co-occurrence patterns. Both significant and non-significant patterns were considered, provided that they contributed to the hedging meaning of the lexical verb being studied. The lemmas contain information about both meaning and syntax. When a lemma is activated, its syntax becomes available and the semantic roles must be mapped onto the syntactic roles (Levelt 1989). The advantages and disadvantages of taking word forms or lemmas as units of analysis are discussed below.

Any corpus-driven investigation of lexical verbs needs to consider the advantages and disadvantages of using verb lemmas or verb forms as units of analysis. If lemmas are used, the different inflectional forms, e. g. *suggest*, *suggests*, *suggested*, *suggesting*, are merged. This is a useful option if the aim of the analysis is to give a general overview of learners' lexical repertoire and/or to detect patterns of use that cut across verb forms (e. g. the use of a *that*- clause with the lemma SUGGEST). However, as rightly pointed out by Sinclair (1991), lemmas are an abstraction and only using lemmas amounts to losing important information as each word form has its own individual patterning. Sinclair (1991: 41) sees a future for a new

branch of study that focuses on the interrelationships of a lemma and its forms as 'it is not yet understood how meanings are distributed among forms of a lemma'. He even goes as far as to suggest that lexicographers change the traditional practice of using the 'base' or uninflected form as headword and use 'the most frequently encountered form' instead (Sinclair 1991: 42), a pioneering view that has so far gone unheeded. In Granger and Paquot's (2005) study, they carried out an automatic comparison of a one million-word corpus of academic writing and a similar-sized fiction corpus. One of the interesting results of the study is that verbs regularly function as keywords in only one or two inflectional forms.

Sections 5. 2 and 5. 3 present the study of the two selected lexical verbs *suggest* and *seem* used in the NNS corpus and compare the results with those used in the NS corpus. This study first focuses on verb lemmas for the insights they provide into learners' lexical stock of these verbs and then on verb forms to uncover new perspectives on learners' preferred and dispreferred patterns.

Table 15: Lexical Verb Lemmas and Forms in the NS and NNS Corpora

Lemma	Word Forms	Frequency of Occurrence (NS Corpus)	Frequency of Occurrence (NNS Corpus)
SUGGEST	suggest	**121**	32
	suggests	**186**	**51**
	suggested	81	**42**
	suggesting	63	5
SEEM	seem	**132**	**85**
	seems	**265**	**171**
	seemed	47	55
	seeming	26	9

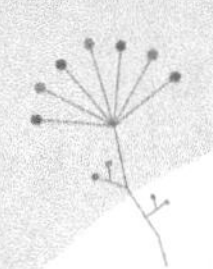

Table 15 lists these two verbs in each verb form. It shows that the verb lemma SUGGEST, just like SEEM, appears as a distinctive item in student academic writing in different forms. From Table 15, we can see that frequencies have been counted for different forms of *suggest* and *seem*. Since different forms of *suggest* and *seem* tend to occur in different patterns and with manageable frequencies of occurrence, all concordance lines of each form of these two lexical verbs were looked at in the concordance analysis. As shown in Table 15, most of the occurrences of SUGGEST and SEEM in the NS and NNS corpora appear in two word forms. Table 15 shows that the verb lemma SUGGEST in the NS corpus mainly appears in two forms: the base form and the -s form, while in the NNS corpus it appears mainly in -s form and -ed form. For SEEM, it is the base form and -s form that are distinctive. As pointed out by Hyland and Tse (2007: 243), we need to 'be cautious about claiming generality for families whose meanings and collocational environments may differ across each inflected and derived word form' (cf. also Oakey 2005). This word of caution has been at the forefront of the analysis of lexical verbs in the NS and NNS writing, the results of which are presented in Sections 5.2 and 5.3.

5.2 Judgment verb—*suggest*

The epistemic lexical verb *suggest* under consideration in this chapter is termed a 'judgment verb' by Hyland (1998a: 120 – 124). This verb is further subsumed into 'speculative judgment verbs' (Hyland 1998a: 126). A speculative verb marks a writer's tentative evaluation; the truth value of the proposition evaluated by the writer is uncertain. In example (1), the writer has a tentative stance in stating and claiming on his/her findings by using *suggest* with an epistemic possibility meaning:

(1) Recent evidence *suggests* that Hofstede's dimensions are applicable not on... (NNS corpus: 002)

The distinct meanings of *suggest* found in the two corpora match the three meanings in the *Collins COBUILD Advanced Dictionary* (online) as follows:

❶ to offer an idea or a plan to someone to consider or make a proposal or declare a plan for something (e. g. 'I would *suggest* a more in-depth study of articles and sentence structure for Max, as well as more time spent in Germany.' —NS corpus: 0029)

❷ to tell someone about something that may be useful or suitable for a particular purpose (e. g. 'I would *suggest* a more in-depth study of articles and sentence structure for Max, as well as more time spent in Germany.' —NS corpus: 0029)

❸ to say or to make you think that something is likely to exist or to be true (e. g. 'These findings *suggest* that the development of social roles although beginning before the age of five is not complete representations by this age.' —NS corpus: 6020b)

❹ to remind you of something or bring something to mind through an association of ideas (e. g. 'while candle suggests warmth and life'. —NS corpus: 3006b)

These meanings are connected to different grammatical patterns, which help to disambiguate them. While meaning ❶ is followed by a noun phrase or a finite clause, usually a *that* clause or gerund, meaning ❷ and ❸ usually occurs with *that* clause and meaning ❹ is followed by a noun phrase. Meaning ❸ appears more frequently in both the NS and the NNS corpora.

100 concordance lines of the HD *suggest* from the NS and NNS

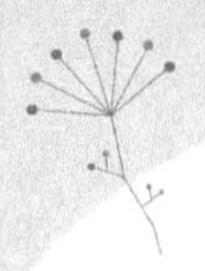

corpus have been investigated respectively. The concordance lines were sorted with the first word to the left of the node word (1L) as the main sort, the second word to the left of the node word (2L) as the second sort, and the first word to the right of the node word (1R) as the third sort. Words like *findings*, *evidence*, *seems to*, *possible to*, *may* and *would* are found repeatedly combined with *suggest*. Still, some patterns are not obvious from the concordance lines. Based on a closer look at *suggest* in the concordance lines, another collocation has been found, e. g. 'Coates *suggests*' and 'Mikhail Bakhtin *suggests*'. These co-occurrence patterns and collocations are then defined into different meaning groups. Some of the meaning groups have been mentioned and discussed in Hyland's study (1998a). Co-occurrence patterns and collocations are discussed in the following Sections 5.2.1, 5.2.2 and 5.2.3.

5.2.1 Personalised and depersonalised constructions of *suggest*

There are different ways in which the NS and NNS groups use *suggest* to express hedging. The HD *suggest* found in the NS and NNS data carries a hedging meaning. It occurs both in personalised and depersonalised constructions. Since s*uggest* can be used to introduce an opinion with a certain degree of emotional implication, it appears in the two corpora with first person subjects to convey the writer's strong attachment to a proposition, but with lower frequency of occurrence. For example,

> (2) *I would suggest* a more in-depth study of articles and sentence structure for Max, as well as more time spent in Germany. (NS corpus: 0029)

It can be inferred from Hyland's examples that writer agentivity is

understood to refer to explicit indications of authorial presence, as manifested by the use of pronouns like *I*, *we*, *my*, and *our*. Thus, expressions with authorial presence, like *I suggest*, may be taken as HDs signalling to potential readers that what is said is a personal view open to the judgment of the readers. Since personal attribution is frequently used to express the reader-oriented hedging when introducing claims, it seems relatively easy to identify the reader-oriented *suggest*. *Suggest* in example (2) is categorised as the reader-oriented HD. In the example, the writer's intention was to give some acceptable suggestions to the potential readers. The personal expression *I would suggest* represents the tension between a personal conviction and the need to relate the claims to the existing knowledge currently sanctioned by the discourse community. This leaves adequate leeway for readers to evaluate the suggestion proposed by the writer.

The HD *suggest* is more predominantly used in both the NS and the NNS corpora in depersonalized constructions. The NS and the NNS writers in this research often use *suggest* to attribute their arguments to other sources. Among the examined concordance lines, most instances of *suggest* in the NS and the NNS corpora, for example, follow the third-person subject + *suggests* + *that* pattern. These constructions are what Holmes (1988) terms 'depersonalised expression'. These expressions shift responsibility for statements away from the writer by attributing them to another. The NS and the NNS writers show a remarkable tendency to distance themselves from their propositions through the manufacture of 'abstract rhetors' and an 'empty subject' (*it*, *this* or *there*). For example,

(3) This would *suggest* that the narrator is [...], they do share some intimacy. (NS: 3009b)

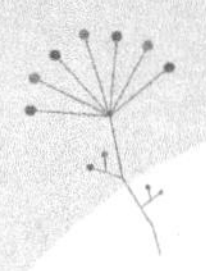

Abstract rhetors' that accompany the lexical verb *suggest* in the NS and NNS corpora follow the meanings of 'surveys', 'evidence', 'findings', 'research/paper' or 'fact' predominantly functioning as a subject (see Concordances 9 and 10).

Concordance 9 Examples of collocation '*abstract rhetors*' +*suggest* in the NS corpus

tactic signifiers as well. These findings suggest that the development of social roles

sions (Libben 1996: 434). These findings suggest that the whole brain contributes

in her subservience to man. This further suggests that if a woman has pronounced sexual

women's actions in divorce. This passage suggests that he sees women as holding equal st

's painful experiences. These revelations suggest that there has never been a time when

God. The women's fear and initial silence suggest that they are not the ceaselessly

understanding the text on this level might suggest that it si one which concerns and

re is no evidence or proof. The statement suggests collective denial, even though at the

be concluded that some evidence seems to suggest that at least certain villagers might

yncrasies of a generation, it can also suggest impressions of individual issues and e

d responses of the women in Mark, and it suggests that the Gospel of Mark is still quest

rm infants. </heading> These findings suggest that premature children can perfo

to a 'rose'. These expressions, which suggest life, precede images of death. The

entant or not. An argument against would suggest that, especially compared with Tess,

Concordance 10 Examples of collocation '*abstract rhetors*' + *suggest* in the NNS corpus

lose scrutiny of recent advertisements suggests that the soft-sell technique is now popu

e use of these types of sentences does suggest something about who is listening or read

word. The meaning of the name exactly suggests she will always stand the tests of the

nd the news agencies. This paper also suggests that the teaching and learning of E

cern is appropriate. Such declarations suggest that women are injudicious and shortsigh

ed value orientations. Recent evidence suggests that Hofstede's dimensions are applicable

e examination of recent advertisements suggests that the soft-sell technique is now popula

true nor false, but it does typically suggest that the hearer might know something that

before these phases. The effect is to suggest that we already have these desires, that

word. The meaning of the name exactly suggests she will always stand the tests of the f

es, trade figures of the two sides both suggested an average annual bilateral trade growth

S exports. Both countries' statistics suggest that between 1990 and 1996, US exports t
of both of those paths. This novel has suggested, for the most part, that the professor's
ims of a lesson. Research on teaching suggests that the opening or 'entry' of a lesson
s can not be gotten rid of, findings suggest that negative transfer does reduce wi

This collocation pattern is strategic. It contributes to 'the impersonalisation of the discourse by appearing to make the text or the data the source of epistemic judgments' (Hyland 1998a: 123). The entire construction 'abstract rhetors + *suggest* + *that*' hedges the strength of a statement by suppressing human agency and volition in the evaluation of the statement. These indicate that the writer is not prepared to personally guarantee the proposition, which aims to shield the writer from the possible negative consequences.

Example (4) is from a Discussion section of the NS corpus. The purpose of using *suggest* in context as example (4) is considered in the light of generalising and stating the findings from the researcher's part:

> (4) These findings *suggest* that the development of social roles although beginning before the age of five is not complete representations by this age. Instead development continues from the initial prosodic differences which mark social status (Clark 2003), and progresses to incorporate lexical and syntactic differences in determining social roles (Grunwell 1986). This shows the way in which children's knowledge and schemas are being created and extended all the time, as Clark (2003) points out 'as children do the voices for puppets they reveal what they have observed so far (...) children have a long way to go. They will discover more and more roles and learn how to mark those too.' (NS Corpus: 3006g)

These findings in example (4) support the following

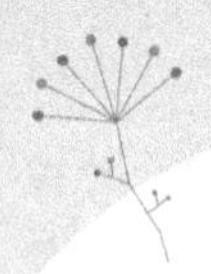

interpretation after the *that*-clause. In example (4), the writer has a tentative stance in stating and making claim about his/her findings by using *suggest* with an epistemic possibility meaning. The construction *these findings suggest that* in the example suppresses writer agency in the evaluation of the claim.

In Hyland's (1998a) study, he summarises that the common strategies of writer-oriented hedging are the construction of 'abstract rhetors' and an 'empty subject' which, by nominalising a personal projection, suggests that the situation described is independent of human agency. Therefore, the hedging device *suggest* collocates with 'abstract rhetors' or 'empty subject' and usually marks the hedge as a writer-based strategy.

5.2.2 'Authors' +*suggest*

The presence of 'authors' +*suggest* in the two corpora represented another meaning of *suggest* (see Concordances 11 and 12). *Suggest* mitigates by referring to some outside, often authoritative, sources as supporting evidence. The left collocations, such as 'authors', co-occur frequently with *suggest*, downplaying the commitment of the writer to the truth value of the propositional information.

When reviewing other scientists or researchers' work, both the NS and the NNS students preferred to use *suggest* to express the writer's desire to explicitly state the commitment to knowledge. In this case, *suggest* often co-occurs with 'authors' (e.g. Tolstoy *suggests*) as mentioned above. This co-occurrence in collocation can usually be considered as a sign of accuracy-oriented hedging in discourse.

Concordance 11 Examples of ' authors ' + *suggest* in the NS corpus

t a few lines of each other, Tolstoy suggests that Nicholas may have traded his life for
l mentioned. John Skelton (1988a), who suggests that hedges should be broken down into two
depose (Stanza 4, Lines 13 – 16). Marvell suggests that Fate has a vested interest in preventi
probability and necessity as Aristotle suggested is ideal, she shapes one that resists clea
thout the sex-object? David M. Halperin suggest that Greek and Roman men.. generally understo
h Adam. In celebrating Bacchus, Storni suggests that the male participates in unrestrained
en, Charrington or Squealor. Winston suggests that the power lies in the proles, but is

Concordance 12 Examples of ' authors ' + *suggest* in the NNS corpus

ale and female athletes. So Mr. Cheng suggested it be translated into "For better(athletic
he name of Celie's husband, Mr.___, suggests ambiguity and uncertainty. Such a naming
aty ports of China" (35). George suggests that "were Chinese Pidgin English not widel
the law" (101). Third, Williams suggests that the absence of westerners proficient i
orm the social institution. Reynold suggests in his The Scarlet Letter and Revolution Ab

Example (5) is from the NS corpus and illustrates the use of *suggest* as an accuracy-oriented hedging device in an Introduction section. The following paragraph starts by addressing the literature in order to assert those matters that are taken to be true for the purpose of the paper. This background is assumed to be shared knowledge.

> (5) Gender is a hugely nebulous concept, representing it often proves as difficult as defining it; Butler goes so far as to argue that, 'There is no proper gender' believing all gender to be performance. If so, Dickinson appears to *suggest* that speech is a formative part of this 'performance', but the polarity established in her opinion is highly problematic as it utterly divides both men and women, and speech and silence. The central weakness of her statement lies in its generality, as no one author or character is capable of representing the manifold aspects

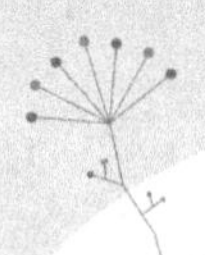

of an entire sex. As a result, I am not trying to ascertain how valid Dickinson's opinion is, nor do I wish to debate the extent to which the texts disprove or support her argument. Instead I am examining what people see as stereotypically gendered writing and characteristic of male and female in relation to speech. I will however investigate what the binaries of speech and silence may be implying about gender. I intend to concentrate on how each author uses language to create the voice or its absence, depict speech and generate eloquence. (NS Corpus: 3008f)

In example (5), the writer used *suggest* to summarise the findings of Dickinson's research on speech and performance of gender. By using *suggest* in this excerpt, the writer displayed his/her tentative stance in reviewing previous research, which aims to express the writer's desire to explicitly state the commitment to the knowledge. S*uggest*, which aims to achieve precision as presented in example (5), can be categorised as accuracy-oriented hedges.

5.2.3 Compound hedges

The hedging device *suggest* is also found collocating with other HDs together as compound hedges. The role of these hedges had been highlighted in Salager-Meyer's (1994) study of hedges which has been discussed in Chapter 4. Accordingly, compound hedges can be realised as double or treble hedges and normally collocate between two different categories of hedges. Salager-Meyer (1995) describes and indicates the patterns of compound HDs which include:

a) Modal with hedging verb (It would appear that ...).

b) Hedging verb with hedging adverb/adjective (It seems reasonable that ...).

c) Double hedges (It may suggest that; This probably

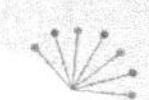

indicates that ...).

d) Treble hedges (It seems reasonable to assume that ...).

e) Quadruple hedges (It would seem somewhat unlikely that John will tell anyone).

The overall number of compound hedges found in the NS and NNS corpora are 36 (6.9 per 100) and 3 (1.6 per 100) times respectively. In Chapter 4, we found that compound hedges consist of certain modal verb collocates with various hedging action verbs (see Section 4.1.2). In the study of the judgment verb *suggest*, most concordance lines from the NS corpus contain compound hedging through the use of different epistemic modal verbs and the use of the epistemic lexical verb *suggest*. For example, *would suggest*, *might suggest* and *may suggest* are repeated in Concordance 13. Other examples from Concordance 13 below contain compound hedging created by the use of double hedges (for example, *seems to suggest*; *it is possible to suggest*).

In line with the findings of the Chapter 6, compound hedges are more often used by the NS writers. Most Chinese students in the study tended to employ single HD in one sentence. In contrast, the hedging that occurred in a sentence written by native students consisted of up to three devices (treble hedges).

The linguistic devices of hedging can be characterised as stronger or less strong HDs, depending on the strategy they implement/belong to. Therefore the combination of two or more HDs in one proposition provides more protection to this proposition as well as to the writer's face, since in this case the degree/strength of hedging is intensified.

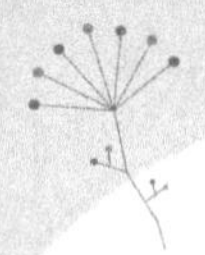

Concordance 13 Examples of compound hedges (*suggest*) in the NS corpus

be concluded that some evidence seems to suggest that at least certain villagers might not

Twelfth Night, Shakespeare also seems to suggest that courtship somehow cheapens or bastardi

character of Viola, Shakespeare seems to suggest that true love does not need to rely on

ualized. Thus, Marvell not only seems to suggest that there is an impossibility associated

ct of the play, his language seems to suggest that he is, in a sense, returned to his

ety of determiners in use which seems to suggest that L's vocabulary is relatively good.

n ambivalent ending, the notes seem to suggest that Offred does succeed in escaping,

ints throughout the transcripts seem to suggest that her vocabulary is developing at a

hear and process information, seeming to suggest that the temporal lobes role in hearing

th Tager-Flusberg (1999: 328) seeming to suggest that language deficits lead to the social

planations..." </quote> It is possible to suggest that in fact T. S. Eliot does not invi

It is possible to suggest that the most clearly obvious way int

sense of alienation. It is possible to suggest that this opening passage of Heart of

sponse to his tale." It is possible to suggest that Marlow is evidence of Conrad cre

Jelinek p. 50 </fnote> It is possible to suggest that the narrative of Mrs Dalloway in

of the past tense in the title might also suggest a metaphorical journey through time; the

upon. Although the act of kneeling might suggest an element of religious worship the cushio

ll collection into account, then, might suggest desires motivated by some other factor

is called after their function which might suggest that "they are types rather than strongly

self invisible; unseen; unknown". One might suggest that Clarissa's conflict is one of identit

, and bear children." Indeed, this might suggest that Esther's 'madness' lies in the way

erstanding the text on this level might suggest that it is one which concerns and quest

when and where the text was written might suggest that this opposition is a comment of disse

of mood is quite different. It might be suggested that "mood" in Mrs Dalloway is generate

y I resembled at heart." It might be suggested that Esther is in fact searching in

a total life situation." It might be suggested then that whilst Esther struggles to

o account the binary structure might suggest that Othello is still protesting with

. In the context of the play, this might suggest that Othello regards the murder of his

trained their eyes to see him. This would suggest that the narrator is closer to Estha than

g the reader to do the same. This would suggest that the typical role of women as the

a second whistle is blown. I would also suggest that Atwood is exploring again the ways

switching during our interview. I would suggest a more in-depth study of articles and

pon male power are indeed valid, I would suggest that in Atwood's novel, the men involved

ifying Buda and St Augustine, Eliot may suggest an amalgamation of Western and Eastern

also beginning to do so at 2;6. This may suggest that L's syntactic development is in fa

rformance. If so, Dickinson appears to suggest that speech is a formative part of thi

Concordance 14 Examples of compound hedges (*suggest*) in the NS corpus

there are several aspects that could be suggested as the directions for the relevant s
small town America, though cynics might suggest a new setting for The Truman Show, or
he alleged thieves. To use "be" here would suggest that they were only intermittently

5.3 Evidential verb—*seem*

Seem is categorised as an 'evidential verb'. This refers to perception or apprehension based on reports of others or evidence of the writer's senses, or feasibility of matching evidence to goals (Hyland 1998a). That is to say those evidential verbs can be used by authors to imply that they do not wish to be thought fully and personally committed to a belief. As Chafe (1986) argues, evidential tells us a writer's stance toward the knowledge he/she relates. Thus evidential verbs suggest that the writer's belief is based on reports of others or on the senses of the writer.

The frequencies of occurrence of *seem* in the NS and NNS corpora show us that the NS writers applied significantly more tokens of *seem* to express hedging than the NNS (Chinese) writers. However, it does not provide us with information about how the verb is actually used in the two corpora.

The two main meanings of the verb *seem* defined in *COBUILD Advanced British English Learners' Dictionary* (2009) that were used in the two corpora are shown as follows:

❶ Use *seem* to say that someone or something gives the impression of having a particular quality, or of happening in the way you describe. In this sense, *seem* is used to give the impression or sensation of being something or having a particular quality. It is used to suggest in a cautions, guarded or polite way

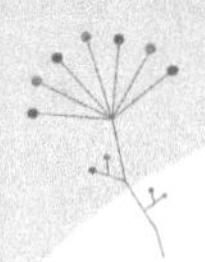

that something is true or a fact.

❷ Use *seem* when describing your own feelings or thoughts, or describing something that has happened to you, in order to make your statement less forceful. In this sense, *seem* is used to make a statement or description of one's thoughts, feelings or actions less assertive or forceful.

Meaning ❶ allows the writer to state their impression rather than to mitigate an opinion (meaning ❷) (see Concordances 15 and 16). It would be reasonable to argue that the former meaning is commonly used in descriptive text in order to accomplish accuracy-oriented hedging and the latter meaning usually occurs in discursive text which is more related to writer- or reader-oriented hedging (see Concordances 17 and 18). The accuracy-oriented group contains the largest number of examples in both the NS and the NNS corpora. The writer-oriented group illustrates an important aspect of the verb *seem* in mitigating a statement or description of one's thoughts, feelings or actions.

Concordance 15 Examples of accuracy-oriented *seem* in the NS corpus

interesting that the narrator of this novel	seems	so convinced that he and his family are
embodiment of Christian ideals. His wife	seems	more conniving that pious. London is the
s haven't changed so much as the timeline	seems	to have changed? areciprocity can happen
r negative connotation, in that they still	seem	to be seen to have the power to subvert
eality is a desirable place to return to	seems	to vary, but the fantastic can, at the
narrator, his cold-blooded murder of Pluto	seems	to result in Pluto's reincarnation as a
on that the entire production of the pageant	seems	a bit futile; in the context of the impen
arlier work in which her philosophy always	seemed	to be resolutely on the side of women's
male figures. Queen Wealhtheow initially	seems	to be a powerless woman dominated by the
that Wealhtheow is serving the men makes it	seem	as though she is subservient to them;
heow's presentation of gifts to Beowulf may	seem	to signal his dominance, the gifts are
God's commandments. In Hosea, the covenant	seems	less specific and more human; God desire
ant with this new covenant about love. He	seems	to want to unite the previous notion o
th the idea of strengthening a covenant that	seems	again and again to be too weak is Hosea's

oor. A God who can provide for them may not	seem as necessary; it may be easy for this
m. However, the covenant in Hosea does not	seem to be so concrete. The book presents the
fe, God will also take back his people. They	seem to know that it is he who has torn, and
ter metaphors about God's love covenant that	seem almost too big to be contained by the
ield empty of the cattle which had	seemed so beautiful(63). He laments over the
e. How, then, can one judge the kapos? Levi	seems to place the kapos perilously at the
hrough the eyes of an existentialist. It	seemed unreal. I faced them knowing that a
. When confronted with spring, autumn often	seems pale in comparison. Anne acknowledges
ouisa's energy. Her own autumnal situation	seems not the view of the last smiles of the
me opens wide, / To which the Hell I suffer	seems a Heav'n (IV, 73 – 78). He expresses
ore perfect with the addition of Eve: what	seemed fair in all the world seemed now / Mea
on of Eve: what seemed fair in all the world	seemed now / Mean (VIII, 472 – 3). This
miles / Wanted, nr youthful dalliance as be	seems / Fair couple linked in happy nuptial
e is Regarded, / such delight till then as	seemed / In fruit she never tasted whether t
is on the Pardoner's deliberate attempts to	seem admirable. Whereas Chaucer simply prese
es other religious figures in his work who	seem more reasonable and, in the case of the
is profession as a whole, but the critique	seems limited in scope. Chaucer builds on
oup, each one fails. The Prioress and Monk	seem to excel at the type of posturing for w
the end of the plays, Jessica's marriage	seems doomed and Hermia's appears successful.
us undertone. Later in the scene the lovers	seem to be disconnected and lacking
d in an all encompassing sense. He does not	seem to notice that this grave accusation of

Concordance 16 Examples of accuracy-oriented *seem* in the NNS corpus

." By the meaning of the product this truism	seems equally obvious as regards to More Cigarett
bet, I say. They do, he say, surprise. Harpo	seem to love me. Sofia and the children, I think
ce Celie begins to make pants at home, she	seems unable to stop. She changes the cloth. S
____ has been hiding Nettie's letters, she	seems to show disappointment in God. Celie de
he seeming last letter Celie writes to God	seems to convey Celie's misunderstanding and
transformation. Naming of characters, which	seems a subtle device, helps to portray Walker's
she would never see her again, Mr. Bennet	seemed to be serious but very humorous to give
her father. The Collins who should be miff	seems like he is ignorant of the fact, because
ot help from resisting: "Being a Mrs. Darcy	seems a pretty good chance." Finally, naturally
Colossus, the publication of Ariel in 1965	seems to stun, astound, shock and excite th
with two children. The hardness of het life	seemed to increase her feeling of self-missing,
ind: they merit severe reproof: they would	seem inexcusable" (Brontë 417). However, Jane
erson's approbation. But in fact, Jane Eyre	seemed to have found out the fun that could not
permanent fame of it. Film title translation	seems quite simple but actually it's a very compl
tan outcast and the Puritan world, Hawthorne	seems to convince us readers that a bright future

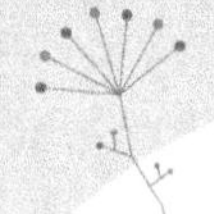

r writing skills, while the writing classes seem unnecessary to help enhance the ability to
s several confusing sounds, but the teacher seems too busy to pay much attention to me. All
ed. However, in China, that debate does not seem to go as what the news has reported. The
d hardness that can bear the heavy snow. It seems common sense. While easterners think that
ill express their modesty for some time and seem not to accept the praise, this will make
the last few years. The position of the dog seems to change to some extent. But the derogator
ng, they... ", the appearance of translation seems to adhere to the original work, but readers
t also all human beings, which make the male seem to be the representative of all human bein
essage. By the 1980s, Chinese scholars seemed to have reached a consensus which favors
mblance" and "Theory of Spiritual Resonance" seem to be unfathomable while "reaching the acme
resent economic and political situation, it seems like oriental and occidental cultures are
means that we, finding that something that seems especially desirable is unattainable, may

Concordance 17 Examples of writer-oriented *seem* in the NS corpus

r's mind in a forceful way, yet overall it seems that books have lost most of their negative
e are confusion and holes in the text, it seems that Hosea does present the idea of the c
dy and something else. That is to say, it seems that what is meant by the heart is not the
than develop good programs. In general, it seems that while at the federal level the Supreme
e in certain circumstances (p. 117). It seems that these articles, especially Hyland (19
s difficult to determine. In fact, it seems that not even experienced linguists and
of hedging in the claim); and finally, it seems that a Wordsmith search turns up a few rep
of course, a more complex language, and it seems that even though the LSN model was incomple
Creole language to form. 5. Discussion It seems that our language acquisition abilitie
ion. However, as the play progresses, it seems that Orsino is more concerned with merely
id, but also, Do as I say, not as I do. It seems that we would prefer to predicate who we
characters (or vice versa) either. It seems that in both plays under consideration,
mpanionship (if not friendship), and it seems that nothing is really at stake. Michael
ough it certainly isn t finished, and it seems that for Beckett, nothing ever truly is.
x. Though he is virile and handsome, it seems that most of his dealings with women end
presentatives of their age. However, it seems that in both societies though they were
egins with the use of Kirpal Singh, and it seems that instantly the author is discussi
efore he receives official news of it, it seems that it must be God speaking when it was
ral times "DOWN WITH BIG BROTHER." (20) It seems that revelation and consciousness are the
create our own moral codes and beliefs. It seems that Oswald may not have just inherited
quote > <fnote> Atwood p. 104 </fnote> Thus, it seems that in order to aid patriarchal power in
quote > <fnote> Atwood p. 26 </fnote> Hence, it seems that it is not only the Handmaids who suffer
e importance Blake placed on symbolism. It seems that Frye (1947, 230) would have a more
03), Volume I, Chapter I, p. 11 </fnote> It seems that this 'sensible' character is acting

at this scene portrays sexual violence. It seems that Stoker is explicitly exhibiting his
fication of conventional gender roles. " It seems that the vicious battle between good and
examining the research in these areas it seems that five marks a functional shift, for
] insisted upon [the name] Olivia (39). This seems to have a negative connotation, as the
e > Some view Othello a poetic drama, but this seems unlikely as it exhibits the characteri
ng it availible to the masses. Although this seems liberatory and positive, to the critic
this poem's irritating habits. In turn, this seems to stress the special nature of the re
ie Home Companion' without explanation. This seems to make the poem feel more intimate. T
sh as perhaps a new variety of English? This seems a little far off and to explain why pe
ly, I decided to look at adjectives but this seemed too broad an area and so it was narro
ch gender being socialised differently. This seems to be supported through the evidence t
be challenged and possibly interrupted; this seems to support the notion that men try to
until after eighteen months gestation. This seems to be supported anatomically due to th

Concordance 18 Examples of writer-oriented *seem* in the NNS corpus

, and the general state of the world, it seems that there is no end to the number of things
Nes reflect positive attitudes. Though it seems that the attitude of each news is individual
And negative meaning. In other words, it seems that the journalists of these four news ag
creation in developing technology, so it seems that America is always energetic with more
randa asks her to do in busy time. It seems that she is reborn to fit this job, and
B's answer is neither of the two. It seems that B's utterane is about his private
To be mocked, Teased and avoided. Once it seemed that Pecola made friends with Maureen Peal
ppearing femininity and masculinity. It seems that, in Hemingway's view, a liberated woman
and it was thought queer, at the time. It seems that houses had become insupportable to hi
ey confront problems in their marriage. It seems that the relationship between the professor
are many factors influencing it, but it seems that social factor plays a more important
up on something. 3.4 Blue. It seems that blue is a favorable word to Chinese.
i the fork in the right hand and this seems acceptable and normal to people who hav

The concordance analysis of the data from the NS and NNS corpora appeared to show some patterns in the way in which the verb *seem* is used in the corpora. In both the NS and the NNS corpora, the examples were found occurring in certain kind of pattern forms: *seem* JP (adjective phrase), *seem* IP (infinitive phrase) and *it seems that* ' abstract rhetors' *seem that*.

Looking at the concordance lines in which the verb *seem*

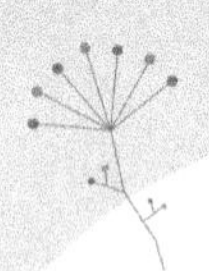

occurs, we find emphatic and strong adjectives [such as *important* in example (6)] as complements to stress the writer's views. The expression of *seem* can semantically be interpreted as evidentials or as an expression of sensory evidence. Thus, when the complement is an adjective, hedged reading is more plausible, if the characteristic described by the adjective cannot be perceived directly but depends on reasoning. In the written opinions, the writer's perception as well as the reader's, are focused on the written evidence. The reasoning is then based on the evidence perceived in the text and it represents the writer's attitude towards that evidence through reasoning.

(6) Hosea's metaphor certainly reestablishes the idea of the covenant as one of love, but it is unclear why this new covenant is expressed here or why it is important. It does *seem* <u>important</u> to Hosea to weave together the old ideas of the covenant with this new covenant about love. (NS corpus)

In example (6), the argument that *it is important to Hosea to weave together the old ideas...* is not based on evidence or data obtained, but depends on the writer's perception. *Seem*, in the example, hedges the degree of importance of *to weave together the old ideas with the new covenant about love* to *Hosea*. This makes the writer representing his/her attitude dependant on reasoning.

Evidential verbs, similarly to judgmental verbs, produce writer-oriented hedges when they are found in impersonal constructions with 'empty subjects': *it seems that*. It is evidential verbs of the sensory type that are almost always found in such constructions. By using such constructions the writers present their interpretations and observations as objective, based on evidence from their data, and again attribute their evaluation to the findings:

(7) And finally, *it seems that* a Wordsmith search turns up a few repeated examples, which I tried to be aware of and exclude. (NS corpus)

(8) Overall *it seems that* books have lost most of their negative connotation and are viewed as healthy, moral objects. (NS corpus)

(9) *It seems that* the relationship between the professor and his wife will never be good again. (NNS corpus)

(10) *It seems that* blue is a favorable word to Chinese. (NNS corpus)

Accuracy-oriented hedges and writer-oriented hedges, therefore, hedge either the accuracy of propositional content or the writers' relationship to propositional content. Accuracy-oriented hedges are motivated by epistemological reasons and academic uncertainty, while writer-oriented hedges are motivated by social reasons to provide protection from personal criticism.

With the total numbers of forms of *suggest* and *seem* in the NS and NNS groups, it has been observed that active forms of *suggest* and *seem* exceeded passive form in both the NS and the NNS corpora. From Table 16, we can observe that the frequencies of the base form and the simple present tense of *suggest* and *seem* are greater, and that of the past tense is less. Tenses, with very few exceptions, follow the standard pattern reported in the literature (Wingard 1981; Hanania & Akhtar 1985; Malcolm 1987).

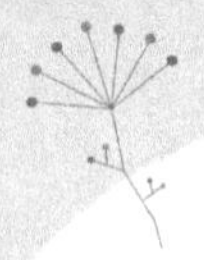

Table 16: Verb Forms and Co-occurrence Patterns: Patterns with Frequencies in the NS and NNS Corpora from All Concordance Lines

HD	NS	NNS	HD	NS	NNS
suggest	personal pronoun 6 author 8 abstract rhetor 41 compound 46	author 4 abstract rhetor 14 third person subject 14	*seem*	infinitive 67 adj 54 compound 10	infinitive 52 adj 24
suggests	third person subject 20 author 42 abstract rhetor 27	third person subject 5 author 19 abstract rhetor 23	*seems*	that 31 infinitive 118 adj 110 it 80	it 47 adj 46 that 20 infinitive 71
suggested	passive construction 43 author 11 abstract rhetor 16	passive construction 10 abstract rhetor 13 third person subject 6	*seemed*	infinitive 24 adj 12 it 10	it 17 that 4 infinitive 20 adj 17
suggesting	abstract rhetor 42 author 6 by suggesting 6	abstract rhetor 5	*seeming*	adj 8 infinitive 19	adj 5 infinitive 4

From the above analysis, we can summarise that active forms of *suggest* can be subdivided into those with a human subject (author; personal pronoun) and those taking an inanimate subject (abstract rhetor; third person subject), or into those taking a nominal clause. Choices of these forms revealed two main functions of *suggest*: to cite previous research either by other researchers or by the same author; and to frame statements about the current research. The use of passive

suggest with inanimate subjects toned down the writer's assertion. Such use, not only for one's own previous research but also for that of others, indicates that criticism does not invalidate the findings as such, but queries their significance and theoretical implications. The simple present tense of *suggest* with inanimate subjects mostly refers directly to the current research through 'abstract rhetors' (e.g. *this finding*, *this evidence*). This pattern consists of 'abstract rhetors' (*findings*, *evidence*, *results* and *observations*) and the present tense. The other pattern, with specific nouns (*analysis*, *assessment*, etc.) and in the past tense, introduces results: e.g. 'thus emphasizes the sense of time *suggested* earlier in line two' (The NS corpus: 3006f). The most noticeable feature of *seem* in Table 16 is that the majority of the verb appears to be used in the simple present tense and is relatively active. The simple present tense of *seem* displays no significant difference in patterns between the NS and the NNS corpora. It displays a large amount of the use of the simple present tense accompanied with the adjectives/adverbs and *that* clause. The use of the verb of sensory evidence (*seem* in this study) expresses the writer's opinion and attitude towards the meaning of the proposition. Rather than *seem* itself, the company of the adjective and adverbs they keep denote the writer's opinion. Writers seem to choose the tense of *seem* depending on the purpose of a sentence. *Seem* is used in the present tense when presenting findings and their interpretation in discourse. The main aspect of the *that* clause refers to the writer's attitude towards the proposition in the *that* clause and is typically realised by the controlling predicate (through the use of hedging lexical verb *seem*) in the projecting clause.

As noted in previous research (Salager-Meyer 1992; West 1980; Halmari & Virtanen 2005), the density of these lemmas and these constructions differed significantly between rhetorical sections of the

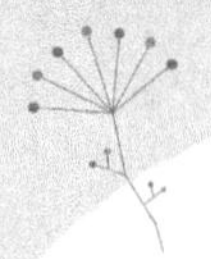

text. The following section demonstrates that hedging lexical verbs *suggest and seem* in academic writing vary according to the specific purpose of the written material.

5.4 Move analysis of hedging lexical verbs *suggest* and *seem*

Lexical verbs are important in academic discourse, as 'they allow the writer to clearly convey the kind of activity reported and to precisely distinguish an attitude to that information, signalling whether the claims are to be taken as accepted or not' (Hyland 1998b: 351). Lexical verbs perform an essential rhetorical function in academic writing: they are used to quote and report what other scholars have written (Aarts & Granger 1998). In the studies of author comment (Adams Smith 1984) and hedging (Salager-Meyer 1994) in medical discourse, the authors point out the importance of the scale of intensity, or the degree of author commitment, as reflected by the choice of verb. There are a variety of verbs that can be used to hedge the certainty or generalisability of a claim. They enable writers to modulate their ideas and position their work in relation to other members of the discipline. Hyland (2002), for example, points out that, words like *suggest* and *seem*, which appear to be the most frequently used hedging devices in the NS corpus of this study, can mitigate the writer's responsibility toward this certainty. With the feature of tentativeness, hedging lexical verbs contribute significantly to academic writing rhetorical functions such as expressing personal stance, reviewing the literature, quoting, expressing cause and effect, summarising and contrasting (Granger & Paquot 2009).

In Section 5.1, the concordance analysis of the two selected hedging lexical verbs *suggest* and *seem* focuses on the relations

between meanings, co-occurrence patterns, and their polypragmatic functions. The purpose of this section is to give attention to the contextual aspect of these two hedging lexical verbs. The following analysis focuses on verbs as instruments of rhetorical activation in academic writing. Genre/Move descriptions of student academic writings in the data have varied in their focus, from whole selected sections, such as the Introduction and the Discussion sections, to different move types (see Swales and Dudley-Evan's modal of moves) in each section. The genre analysis of *suggest* and *seem* in the following section focuses either on the rhetorical structure of the assignments in the two corpora or on a particular feature, such as verb form, tense and co-occurrence patterns of selected verbs.

In this section of the study, the overall distribution of *suggest* and *seem* used by the NS and NNS groups across their writing are dealt with, as different sections and moves of the academic writing seem to govern the choice of hedging lexical verbs.

Frequency analysis shows there are significant differences between the NS and the NNS writers in the use of these two selected hedging devices *suggest* and *seem*. They were the most frequent lexical verbs in hedging use in the NS data. *Seem* (1. 23/1,000 words) and *suggest* (1. 21/1,000 words) occupy respectively the third and fourth places of all hedging devices in terms of frequency. Whereas, in the NNS data, although *seem* and *suggest* are ranked top fifteen among all hedging devices, they have a noticeably lower frequency of occurrence (0. 43/1,000 words for *seem* and 0. 17/1,000 words for *suggest*). These figures illustrate that the NNS writers underuse the majority of the hedging lexical verbs in their assignments that express rhetorical functions at the heart of academic writing, and instead tend to limit their expression of hedging in the use of modal verbs and adverbs as stated in Chapter 2.

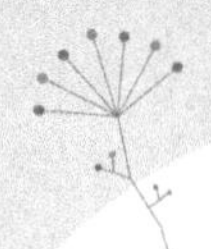

Table 17: Summary of Raw Occurrences and Normalised Frequencies of Lexical Verbs *Suggest* and *Seem* in Different Moves in Introduction and Discussion Sections

	NS-Introduction (110)			NS-Discussion (110)		
Moves	establishing a territory (110)	establishing a niche (22)	occupying a niche (56)	consolidating important points (110)	stating limitations (39)	making suggestions (54)
suggest	13/0.47	3/1.35	2/0.41	59/1.08	3/2.26	1/0.33
seem	13/0.47	13/5.86	0/0	94/1.71	1/0.75	0/0
	NNS-Introduction (110)			NNS-Discussion (110)		
Moves	establishing a territory (110)	establishing a niche (15)	occupying a niche (44)	consolidating important points (110)	stating limitations (19)	making suggestions (50)
suggest	9/0.13	0/0	1/0.11	3/0.06	1/1.64	0/0
seem	12/0.18	6/6.06	0/0	20/0.43	0/0	0/0

The differences between the two groups of writer in their overall use of hedging lexical verbs were also seen in the distribution of hedging lexical verb use across the different sections and different move types of their writing. Table 17 shows information on the Introduction and Discussion sections analysed in both the NS and the NNS corpora and summarises the results of occurrences of each selected lexical verb in the different move types. As we can see from the table, the Discussion section in the NS corpus was the one with a high relative incidence of *suggest* and *seem*, a finding to be expected on the basis of previous work by Salager-Meyer (1994) and Hyland (1998a). *Suggest* and *seem* were also frequently used in the Introduction sections of the NS corpus. As for the NNS group, since lexical verbs are not commonly used by the NNS writers to express hedging (accounting for 9.3% of the total), fewer examples of

suggest and *seem* were found in both the Introduction and Discussion sections of the NNS corpus. However, in the NS data, second only to the modal verbs, the realisation of the move 'establishing a territory' has found its reflection in the use of lexical verbs in Introduction sections of the NS students' writing.

In Table 17 we can see that the NS students used *suggest* more often in the realisation of the move 'establishing a niche' than they did in the realisation of the other two moves (Move 2 'establishing a niche' and Move 3 'occupying the niche'). On the contrary, in the NNS corpus, no incidence of *suggest* was found in Move 2 'establishing a niche' and the frequency of occurrence of *suggest* in Move 1 and Move 3 were quite low as well. Examples of *seem* in the NS and the NNS corpora were mainly distributed in Move 2 'establishing a niche', whereas no example was found to be used in Move 3 'occupying a niche'. As Table 17 shows, the NS and NNS students realised Move 4 'consolidating important points' and Move 5 'stating limitations' in the Discussion section of their writing the most by using hedging lexical verbs *suggest* and *seem*, whereas very few examples (none in the NNS corpus) of these two lexical verbs were found in Move 6 'making suggestions'. First of all, as stated by Hopkins & Dudley-Evans (1988), Move 5 'stating limitations' and Move 6 'making suggestions' are optional moves in the Discussion section, in the NS corpus these two moves occurred in less than half of the total NS students' assignments. So, in modifying statements and expressing present result in Move 4, we see the presence of reporting verb *suggest* and evidential verb *seem*. That is to say, the main rhetorical function of *suggest* and *seem* in Discussion sections is to tentatively state the findings and claims. The certain type of rhetorical function of *suggest* and *seem* could explain why these two lexical verbs were bonded to Move 4 and Move 5 rather than Move 6 in the NS

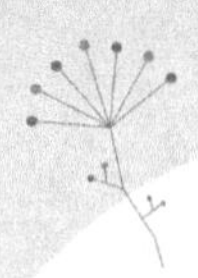

corpus. With a low frequency of occurrence of *seem* and *suggest* in Discussion sections of the NNS corpus, few examples of *seem* and *suggest* are found in realising all the three moves of Discussion sections of their writing, except for 20 occurrences of *seem* in Move 4 and a couple of examples of *suggest* in Move 4 and Move 5. This generalisation indicates the inadequacies of the NNS writers in their use of the lexical verbs *suggest* and *seem* to 'consolidate important points' of their studies. Section 5.4.2 presents detailed analyses of *suggest* and *seem* in Discussion sections of both the NS and the NNS corpora.

The frequency of the verb tense in each section and move is presented in Table 18. The data shows that in both the NS and the NNS corpora the Introduction section is characterised by a higher frequency of the present over the past tense. The preponderance of the present reflects the tendency in an Introduction for the writer to make background generalisations, establish the territory, and state the purpose of the work. The Discussion sections appear to conform broadly to the overall forms of verb use. There is, however, a noticeable rise in the use of present tense and co-occurrence of compound hedging (modal verb + hedging lexical verb) which appears in the rhetorical sections on Discussion. Here, the choice of verbs is influenced by the communicative functions: the simple present expresses generalisations and conclusions based on the results of research, and the modals help to qualify interpretations and conclusions (Edith & Akhta 1985). Examples from the corpora are 'These findings *suggest* that the development of social roles' (NS corpus: 6020b) and 'This *may suggest* that L is using a wider variety of bound morpheme... ' (NS corpus: 6206b). The use of qualified generalizations is a common feature of academic writing.

Table 18: Raw Occurrences of Verb Tense of *Suggest* and *Seem* in Different Moves in Introduction and Discussion Sections (110 Sample Assignments in Each Corpus)

	Native—Introduction (110)			Native—Discussion (110)			Non-native—Introduction (110)			Non-native—Discussion (110)		
Moves (occurrence of each move in 110 samples)	establishing a territory (110)	establishing a niche (14)	occupying a niche (31)	consolidating important points (110)	stating limitations (39)	making suggestions (54)	establishing a territory (110)	establishing a niche (15)	occupying a niche (14)	consolidating important points (110)	stating limitations (19)	making suggestions (50)
suggest	4	3	1	12	1	1	2	0	0	1	0	0
suggests	6	0	1	24	1	0	3	0	1	1	0	0
suggested	3	0	0	13	1	0	3	0	0	1	1	0
suggesting	0	0	0	10	0	0	1	0	0	0	0	0
seem	6	4	0	23	0	0	1	1	0	8	0	0
seems	7	7	0	62	1	0	5	3	0	11	0	0
seemed	0	2	0	5	0	0	4	1	0	0	0	0
seeming	0	0	0	4	0	0	2	0	0	1	0	0

* *Numbers in the row of 'moves' present how many assignments have each move listed in the table.*

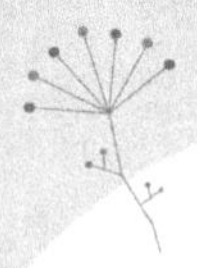

In the following section, linguistic features of lexical verbs *suggest* and *seem* and the rhetorical structure of the moves in the NS and NNS corpora are discussed and presented. The reporting verb *suggest* is studied to show how writers evaluate previous studies and present their own findings.

5.4.1 Lexical verb hedging realisation in Introduction sections

As stated in Chapter 2, Swales (1981, 1990, 2004) analyses the Introduction sections of academic writing in terms of moves. The move 'establishing the territory' is the one with the most occurrences of *suggest* and *seem*, followed by 'establishing a niche' with *seem* being used by both the NS and the NNS writers. The main focus of interest in his/her characterisation of this move is the main verbs which refer to the communicative, rather than the experimental, functions of the researchers.

5.4.1.1 Establishing a territory

According to Swales (1990, 2004), writers realise the first move of the Introduction sections of their academic writing 'establishing a territory' by sub-move steps 'claiming centrality' or/and 'making topic generalisations' or/and 'reviewing items of previous research'. In practice, in 'establishing a territory' we find the presentation of a situation within which a series of hypotheses will be studied based on the perception of certain phenomena. For this purpose, writers refer to the previous findings of experts in the field and establish the aims of the move 'establishing a territory'.

From the data, we can see that in the corpora, by using hedging lexical verbs *suggest* and *seem*, the first move is mainly realised through reviewing previous research. This step of 'establishing a territory' that gains attention from researchers is through the citation

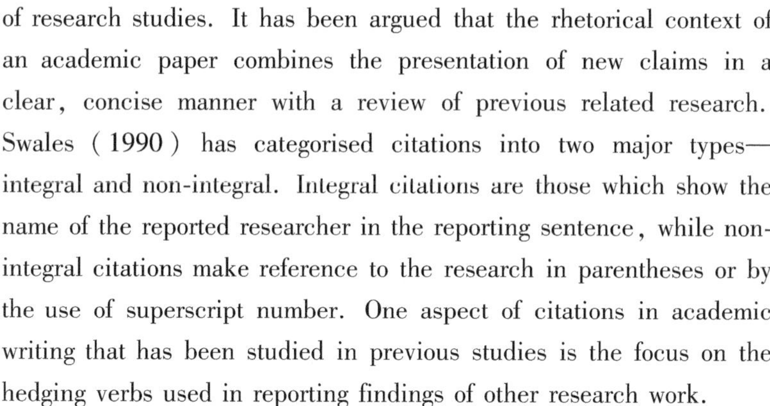

of research studies. It has been argued that the rhetorical context of an academic paper combines the presentation of new claims in a clear, concise manner with a review of previous related research. Swales (1990) has categorised citations into two major types—integral and non-integral. Integral citations are those which show the name of the reported researcher in the reporting sentence, while non-integral citations make reference to the research in parentheses or by the use of superscript number. One aspect of citations in academic writing that has been studied in previous studies is the focus on the hedging verbs used in reporting findings of other research work.

(1) Judgement reporting verb *suggest*

The category of reporting verbs includes many of the performative verbs mentioned by Perkins (1983:94) and Hyland (1998a: 120), so termed because they, in fact, 'perform, rather than describe, the acts they label' (Hyland ibid). What such verbs have in common with Varttala's research (2003) is that they can all be seen as tentative devices, useful in constructing reports of research by other scholars, or in tentatively describing writers' own work. Among different reporting verbs it is undeniable that *suggest* has received the most attention (Thompson & Yiyun 1991; Shaw 1992; Thomas & Hawes 1994; Hyland 1999; Charles 2006a, 2006b). The contextual analysis revealed two main functions of the reporting verb *suggest*: to cite previous research either by other researchers or by the same author or co-authors (Thomas & Hawes 1994); and to frame statements about the current research.

As for other author's research, 'author' as subject predominated. They accounted for most of the integral references. The results of concordance analysis reveal that the co-occurrence pattern 'authors' + *suggest* is largely used by both native and non-native English speaking students in reviewing items of previous

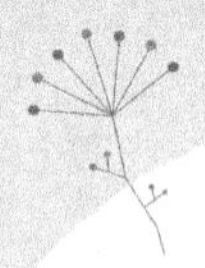

research to 'establish a territory' for their research. The left collocations such as 'authors' co-occur significantly with *suggest*, (e. g. *Lois Potter suggests that...*) downplaying the commitment of the writer to the truth value of the propositional information. This collocation can usually be considered as a sign of accuracy-oriented hedging in discourse. In the case of tentative *suggest*, the tentativeness could come from original or the reporting author.

Example (11) and example (12) are from the NS corpus and the NNS corpus respectively. They illustrate the use of *suggest* as an accuracy-oriented hedging device in Move 1 'establishing a territory' of an Introduction section. These two examples start with addressing the literature in order to assert those matters that are taken to be true for the purpose of the paper. The writers' reviews of previous studies provide background to their research which is assumed to be shared knowledge. The following two examples from academic writing written by the NS and NNS writers show how these two writers explore *suggest* for integral citation to acknowledge previous studies in order to 'establish a territory'.

> (11) However, <u>Lois Potter</u> <accuracy-oriented_M1> suggests </accuracy-oriented_M1> that the pressure of a heavily informed, divided nation even affected the creative output of capable writers as they sometimes rejected 'their theories about style and vocabulary when, abandoning them, they could score a point'. Both Wiseman and Randall agree that, while *The Famous Tragedie* is neither a dull nor weak play, it is heavily flawed as a piece of persuasive literature. Its strong, aggressive attack on the Reformation and abandonment of any 'degree of religio-political analysis' limits its readership only to 'those already hostile to parliament' (Wiseman, *Drama and Politics*,

p. 68). (NS corpus: 6998d)

(12) Third, Williams <accuracy-oriented_M1> suggests </accuracy-oriented_M1> that the absence of westerners proficient in Chinese was a major cause of much of the indifference and suspicion of the Chinese exhibited toward foreigners and, in this context, notes some of the difficulties attached to the learning of the Chinese language, including the lack of elementary books, grammars and vocabularies; the task of memorizing the characters (430). In addition, according to Williams, there was the easy accessibility to 'mixed' dialect. (NNS corpus: 013)

In examples (11) and (12), the writers use *suggest* to summarise the findings of Lois Potter's and Williams' research. By using the accuracy-oriented *suggest* in this example, the writers display their tentative stance in reviewing previous research, which aims to express the writer's desire to explicitly state the commitment to the knowledge.

The passive *suggest* and the active *suggest* with inanimate subjects are also found in the Introduction sections of the NS corpus, but not in the NNS corpus. These types of reference have similar functions. The choice of these forms, as opposed to author subjects, depends on both interpersonal and textual components (Halliday 1979). The depersonalised expression is required when authors evaluate previous work as they create their own 'research territory' in the Introduction (Swales 1990). As shown in the concordance analysis of hedging lexical verbs, integral reference prevents criticism from being interpreted as personal:

(13) Introduction

Establishing the territory

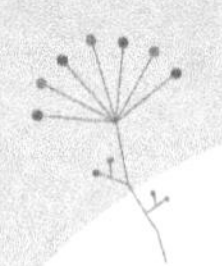

> It has been < writer-oriented_M1 > suggested </writer-oriented_M1 > that the current children's publishing market has reached another 'Golden Age'. Julia Eccleshare writes: "Children's books are now up front big sellers and the barriers to their success are tumbling down." An indicator of this might be the Harry Potter phenomenon, which has received enormous media coverage and is evident of the Television and film interest in children's fiction. A beginning point to this rise in status might be 2002 when Phillip Pullman won the Whitbread Book of the Year Award for *The Amber Spyglass*. Julia Eccleshare, 'A Fast Track for Children's Books', from *Publishers Weekly*, Special Report: British Publishing 2004, March 2004 (NS corpus: 3006i)

In example (13), the integral citation is used with the hedging lexical verb *suggest* which Swales (1990) defines as the category of verb employed to introduce past researchers and their findings. Since there is no named source associated with the attributed material in this example, the passive construction 'it has been *suggested*' has the effect of presenting the proposition as uncontentious, or less contentious, while giving credibility to the proposition as 'common knowledge', and therefore not worthy of referencing. The use of the passive construction indicates the absence of writer agentivity which is a distinctive characteristic of writer-oriented hedging (Hyland 1998a). *Suggest*, which has been rated inherently weak on the semantic scale (Howard 2004), used as a writer-oriented HD in the above example indicates that the writer aims to shield him/herself from the possible negative consequences in interpreting the results of previous research.

(2) Evidential verb *seem*

The group of evidential lexical verbs refers to apprehending or sensing (Hyland 1998a). *Seem*, which belongs to the category of evidential verb, is used in much the same way as the judgement reporting verb discussed, insofar as they express tentativeness concerning either the ideas put forth by the writer or those expressed in the sources referred to (Varttala 2001). In addition to the tentative reporting verb *suggest*, *seem* appeared to be the most frequently used hedge for the NS group. In reviewing previous research, writers rely on sensory evidence from the research literature, and the choice of the evidential verb *seem* can indicate their commitment to what is stated. In each of the following examples (14) (15) (16) and (17), we can see that the tentative evidential verb *seem* is employed to reduce assertiveness, implying limits as to the accuracy and applicability of the information presented.

(14) Introduction

Establishing the territory

A corpus-based description of English enables further insight into language beyond that which we gain from reference books and introspection of our own native language. The arrival and development of this approach in recent decades has led to much research into the behaviours of individual lexical items and phrases. Corpus analysis is concerned with patterns and frequencies and allows us to discover what is probable in language, by looking at statistical tendencies. Hunston and Francis have extended the application of the corpus based computer program to enable the studying of specific grammatical patterns. They played an important role in the creation of 'The Collins COBUILD Grammar Patterns Series' (Francisal 1996)

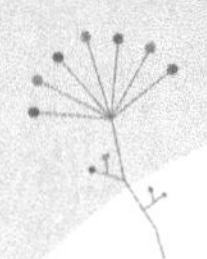

which was the first time that the comprehensive range of verb patterns were methodically organised. They investigate the following hypothesis: "that particular patterns will tend to be associated with lexical items that have particular meanings" (2000: 83). Halliday <accuracy-oriented_M1> seems </accuracy-oriented_M1> to follow this ideology, arguing that "grammar and vocabulary are not two different things" but instead refers to them as "the same thing seen by different observers" (1992b:63). (NS corpus: 6061c)

(15) Introduction

Establishing a territory

In this novel, Lawrence <accuracy-oriented_M1> seems </accuracy-oriented_M1> to show that man is the master of woman. There would be no harmony in the family if the woman did not bend to man's domination and woman's yielding to man might be the only way out of the distorted relationship. As some feminist critics pointed out, Lawrence showed strong male chauvinism in his works. The might support the idea. (NNS corpus: 085)

Example (14) and example (15) are from the NS and NNS corpus respectively. They illustrate the use of evidential stating verb *seem* as an accuracy-oriented hedging device in 'reviewing previous research' in Move 1 'establishing a territory' of an Introduction section. The pattern of *seem* in examples (14) and (15) is quite straightforward: 'author' + *seem*. The citations in these two examples were employed for acknowledgement as the authors Halliday and Lawrence were the writers of the citing statements cited. *Seem* in these two integral citations simply expresses the writers' perception and apprehension of Halliday and Lawrence's arguments with a

tentative standpoint.

Reviews of previous research usually invoke an evaluation of propositional truth. This could be considered as evidential argument, representing a seat of knowledge of previous studies. Evidential verb *seem* in the following two examples refers to this:

(16) Introduction

Establishing the territory

Lakoff did not carry out actual research but made basic assumptions and predictions and claimed that certain characteristics were abundant in women's language, to reflect their subordinate position in society. She identified "a number of linguistic features which were unified by their function of expressing a lack of confidence" (Holmes 2001:287) Lakoff felt that these characteristics, including such features as hedges, tag questions and 'superpolite' forms, all conveyed the impression of uncertainty and tentativeness. <u>Indefinite pronouns</u> <accuracy-oriented_M1>seem </accuracy-oriented_M1> to be a similar feature to those which Lakoff describes as they are those words which replace nouns without identifying exactly which nouns they are taking the place of. They generally refer to an unknown or undetermined person, place or thing and consequently, they are not gender specific. (NS corpus: 6120b)

(17) Introduction

Establishing a territory

In sharp contrast to *The Colossus*, <u>the publication of *Ariel* in 1965</u> <accuracy-oriented_M1> seems </accuracy-oriented_M1> to stun, astound, shock and excite the critics in various measures. Not published until two years after Plath's death and hailed as a 'major literary event', it is difficult to overestimate

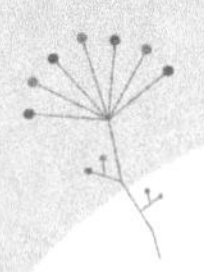

the impact and significance of *Ariel* in establishing Plath's reputation, and her place within the literary scene. (NNS corpus: 052)

In example (16), *indefinite pronouns* gives the impression of *having similar feature to those which Lakoff describes.* In this sense, *seem* was used to suggest in a cautious, guarded and tentative way, that this is a fact. In example (17), the NNS writer stated his/her impression of the *publication of Ariel in* 1965 as the NS writer did in example (16). The step of 'reviewing of previous research' is assumed to be shared knowledge in Move 1 'establishing a territory', the information is cited cautiously in order to build a foundation of substantiated facts upon which the argument to follow can be constructed.

5.4.1.2 Establishing a niche

According to Swales's (1990) CARS model, Move 2 of a research paper Introduction involves establishing a niche for the present research, principally by using one of the following strategies: 'counter claiming', 'indicating a gap', 'question raising' and 'continuing a tradition'. In this study, 14 and 15 out of 110 assignments contain Move 2 in the NS and NNS corpora respectively. In previous studies, 'indicating a gap' seems to be the predominant step of Move 2. Swales (1981) found 'indicating a gap' in 20 out of 48 Introductions in English from various disciplines, while Lopez (1982) found that it was used in 10 out of 21 Introductions in Spanish, and Najjar (1990) reported 7 cases out of 27 Move 2s in his Arabic research articles were employed to indicate a research gap. It is interesting to note that only a few of the indicating-a-gap steps found in this study offer an evaluation of the previous research while it is commonly found in English research articles (Swales 1981).

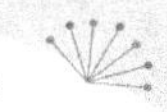

Instead, most NS and NNS assignments simply point to the insufficiency or the absence of research on the topic in the area of study. As can be seen from Table 18, few occurrences of *suggest* were found to be used in 'establishing a niche' by the NS and NNS writers, while the hedging lexical verb *seem* was largely used to realise this move. The following segments illustrate this phenomenon.

(18) Introduction

Establishing the niche

After a preliminary review of the data, it also <writer-oriented_M2> seems </writer-oriented_M2> evident that Nicaraguan Sign Language is not one homogenous system, but rather three manifestations of related but distinct communication systems resulting from the same social context (Kegl, Senghas, & Coppola 1999). Therefore, it <writer-oriented_M2> seems </writer-oriented_M2> prudent to expect that each of the three forms of Nicaraguan Sign Language will have formed from a different set of input. (NS corpus: 0032)

(19) Introduction

Establishing the niche

But it <writer-oriented_M2> seems </writer-oriented_M2> as if all above methods lack a bridge which is used to connect them perfectly. (NNS corpus: 032)

In the above examples (18) and (19), the strategy used to 'establish a niche' by the NS and NNS writers is to express a problem that needs to be addressed, as mentioned by Swales (1990). The writers elaborately identify and describe the potential problem phenomena before they move to Move 3 'occupying a niche', which offering a solution to the problem by announcing the present research. The hedging evidential verb *seem* in the above

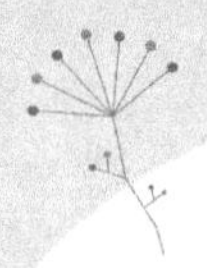

examples hedged the writers' arguments, however, the impersonal expression of *seem* in this ' Problem-raising strategy' (Swales 1990) indicated a writer-oriented hedge and a desire to guard against the possibility of error.

5.4.2 Lexical verb hedging realisation in Discussion sections

The Discussion sections present authors' research findings and their analysis of those findings. In an attempt to study the rhetorical purposes of lexical verbs expressed in the Discussion sections of assignments written by NS and NNS, the use of lexical verbs *suggest* and *seem* are examined in this section. As stated in the methodology chapter, the model used as the basis of analysis is Dudley-Evans (2000) for Discussion sections (see Chapter 3 for detail). The most frequent move of the Discussion sections of the NS and NNS corpora is Move 4 'consolidating important points', which is the core element of the Discussion sections. According to Dudley-Evans (2000), 'consolidating important points' is obligatory and the other two moves ('stating limitations' and 'making suggestions') are optional. The low occurrence of Move 5 and Move 6 could be explained due to the fact that, in the current study, the nominalised frequency of *suggest* in Move 5 is much higher than that of Move 4 and Move 6 in both the NS corpora and the NNS corpora, but the raw frequency of *suggest* is quite low in both corporing (3 and 1 in the NS and NNS corpora respectively).

The aim of Move 4 'consolidating important points' is to present and interpret the results of the research which has been carried out. There is a predominance of verbs of *suggest* and *seem* in this move in the NS corpus. This means that Discussion sections more often involve hedging lexical verbs to do with the 'consolidation of important points'. Propositions with these lexical verbs generally state

conclusions and/or claims arising from the data and results obtained from the work which was carried out. The tentative reporting verb *suggest* in Discussion/Conclusion sections can frame a comment on the significance of the results. In Discussion sections, such comments formed a bridge between the statement of a result and a generalisation (Hopkins & Dudley-Evans 1988). The choice of the verb *suggest* reflected the degree of author commitment. In their study, authors of clinical studies were generally more assertive and stressed the importance of the results whereas, in the academic writing of social science, *suggest* could lead to speculative argument. Compare:

> These findings <writer-oriented_M4> suggest </writer-oriented_M4>that the development of social roles [...] by this age. (NS corpus: 6020b)

and

> These findings confirm that the development of social roles [...] by this age.

Being a verb that can express evaluative meanings and writer judgment, *seem* in Discussion sections is generally like a propositional attitude verb. This is particularly evident in the examples with clausal complements. For example,

> It <writer-oriented_M4>seems </writer-oriented_M4> that even though the LSN model was incomplete, it was sufficient to activate whatever mechanism children possess for native language acquisition.

The choice of *seem* indicates the source of information (observation/inference/memory), and the writer's degree of certainty or commitment to the results/claims stated. In academic writing the generalisation and speculation that follow are often realised with

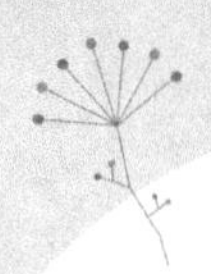

hedging lexical verbs *suggest* and *seem*. These verbs could introduce a local deduction for a specific result, and they often occupy a prominent summarising position in the Discussion sections (See examples below). Move 4 'consolidating important points' in Discussion sections (see Hopkins & Dudley-Evans 1988) is seen to correspond to a typical lexical choice in the NS and NNS corpora.

(1) tentative judgement verb *suggest*

With the construction 'abstract rhetors' + *suggest* and 'authors' + *suggest* and the present tense of *suggest*, the NS students stated their results and referred to previous research respectively in order to 'consolidate important points' of their research. However, different from the NS students, the NNS students hardly used *suggest* in Discussion sections to 'consolidate important points'. See extracts (20) and (21) as examples.

Example (20) is from a move of 'consolidating important points' of the NS corpus, *suggest* is categorised as a writer-oriented hedging device in this context. The purpose of using *suggest* in contexts as in example (20) was considered to generalise and state results of the research:

> (20) Discussion
>
> Consolidating the important points
>
> These findings <writer-oriented_M4> suggest </writer-oriented_M4> that the development of social roles although beginning before the age of five are not complete representations by this age. Instead development continues from the initial prosodic differences which mark social status (Clark 2003), and progresses to incorporate lexical and syntactic differences in determining social roles (Grunwell 1986). (NS corpus: 6020b)

In example (20), the writer expressed a tentative stance in stating his/her findings by using *suggest* with an epistemic possibility meaning in order to 'consolidate important points' of his/her study. The construction active verb *suggest* with 'abstract rhetor' *these findings* referred directly to the current research through deictic markers. Judgment reporting verb *suggest* introduced a result: 'These findings suggest that...'. In such cases care is taken to avoid assuming direct personal responsibility for a claim, principally by the author concealing him or herself behind the syntax through the use of 'abstract rhetors', which attributes claims to 'these findings'. '*These findings suggest*' in the above example suppresses writer agency in the evaluation of the findings.

In example (21), which is also from a move of 'consolidating important points' from the NS corpus, *suggest* is categorised as an accuracy-oriented hedging device in this context. The purpose of using *suggest* in the context used as in example (21) is considered to achieve the purposes of referring previous research in order to 'consolidate important points' of research.

> (21) Tallal's suggestion that integration deficits are a significant contributor to those diagnosed with SLI supports the evidence presented previously by Udwin and Yule (1983 as in Leonard, 2000: 121) in 2.1. <u>Whilst Kail</u> (1994) <accuracy-oriented_M4> suggests </accuracy-oriented_M4> that all verbal and non-verbal processes slow and therefore create the patterns of deficit that can be attached to SLI (as in Hill, 2001: 163), which would support the notion that children diagnosed as having SLI require more processing time and therefore are found to have deficits in auditory perception, hypothesis testing and analogical reasoning tasks. (NS corpus: 6206e)

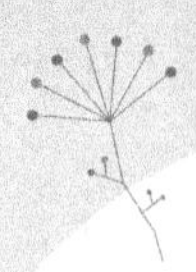

(2) Evidential verb *seem*

In academic writing the generalisation and speculation are often realised with *seem*. Although this verb could introduce a local deduction for a specific result, it often occupies a prominent summarising position in Discussion/Conclusion sections. The co-occurrence patterns 'abstract rhetors' + *seem* and 'it *seems* that' are largely used by both the NS and the NNS students in 'consolidating important points' to conclude their research.

'Abstract rhetors', which are used to attribute judgements to the research or the findings, frequently occur in Discussion sections. The impersonal construction contributes to blurring 'the relationship between a writer and a proposition when referring to speculative possibilities' (Hyland 1995: 35). As Hyland (1998a: 172) points out, expressions like 'these results' and 'the categories of agreement', which Hyland refers to as an expression of 'abstract rhetors', show there is evidence to support the claim. The use of *seem* in the following examples hedges the writer's attitude towards the claim which is expressed cautiously:

(22) Discussion

Consolidating the important points

Although the previously reported results were based on studies where the subjects were born four weeks gestational age prior to the subject of this study, <u>this result</u> <writer-oriented_M4> seems </writer-oriented_M4> to support the original hypothesis. (NS corpus: 6206b)

(23) Discussion

Consolidating the important points

So comes the sacred obligation of maturity the more sacred to Hester because it <writer-oriented_M4> seems </writer-

oriented_M4 > the only sacred thing left to her which restrains Hester from plunging recklessly into the abyss of overt degradation. (NNS corpus: 009)

The expression *it seems that* in examples (24) and (25) could be used to acknowledge the existence of viewpoints alternative to the one being contained in the information in the proposition. In this view, such expressions are inherently dialogic—they invite responses or reaction from dialogic respondents or acknowledge previously held viewpoints that may be different from the one being advanced in the current discourse (Cornillie 2009).

(24) Discussion

Consolidating the important points

From examining the research in these areas it <writer-oriented_M4>seems </writer-oriented_M4> that five marks a functional shift, for instance the function of discourse markers move from their use in constructing grammatical sentences to their role as cohesive devices within extended narratives (Karmiloff & Karmiloff-Smith 2002). (NS corpus: 6020b)

(25) Discussion

Consolidating the important points

From the evidence presented on non-verbal deficits in SLI it <writer-oriented_M4> seems </writer-oriented_M4> clear *that* the deficits children with SLI face are not exclusively related to language (Hill, 2001: 162), therefore causing speculation as to what the deficit does indeed entail. (NS corpus: 6206e)

Conclusion

This chapter presents concordance analysis and move analysis of hedging lexical verbs *suggest* and *seem* in academic writing written in

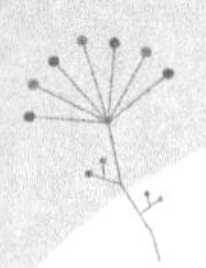

English by the NS and NNS students. Two main findings emerge from the concordance analysis. The first finding is that the NNS students significantly underuse the majority of 'academic verbs', i. e. the verbs *suggest* and *seem*, which express rhetorical functions at the heart of academic writing: they are used to quote and report what other scholars have written. However, when the NNS students use *suggest* and *seem*, they tend to use them in the same patterns as the NS students do, except that the NS students use more *suggest* and *seem* compound with other HDs. This could indicate that the NNS students have studied the uses of *suggest* and *seem* in different patterns, and, as a result, they are as familiar with these patterns as the NS students. On the other hand, the NNS students have not adopted how these two verbs can be used to express different hedging and rhetorical functions in academic writing. Therefore, assignments written by the NNS students do not completely conform to the conventions of their discourse community. As a result, explicit teaching of the use of hedging lexical verbs in academic writing seems essential.

With the basic information of co-occurrence patterns of *suggest* and *seem*, a move analysis of Introduction and Discussion sections written by the NS and NNS students is conducted. The rhetorical characteristics as well as linguistic features of *suggest* and *seem* of the Introduction and Discussion sections are examined using Swales's (1990) model for the Introduction sections and Dudley-Evan's (1988, 2000) model for the Discussion. The results of the move analysis indicate some similarities and differences in the use of *suggest* and *seem* in the generic structure of Introduction and Discussion sections written by NS and NNS students.

In Move 1, both the NS and the NNS students tend to use *suggest* and *seem* to 'review previous research' as a main strategy in 'establishing a territory'. In presenting the previous research,

students of both the NS and the NNS groups use *suggest* and *seem* frequently to cite integral citations. *Suggest* and *seem* allow the NS and NNS students to clearly convey the kind of activity reported and to precisely distinguish an attitude to that information, signalling whether the claims are to be taken as accepted or not.

In Move 2, both the NS and the NNS students mainly adopt the strategy of 'identifying potential problems' in 'establishing a niche' (Move 2). The incidences of *seem* are found to be found in this move by both the NS and the NNS students. Their use of the hedging lexical verb *seem* shows their avoidance of a bold claim. It seems that, with the great effort to save face and to respect a rigid system of seniority, both the NS and the NNS students find it inappropriate to criticise the works of their colleagues. Thus, they prefer to elaborate on the problem or the situation and leave it for their readers to evaluate and make their own decision.

In Move 4, *suggest* and *seem* are often used together with 'abstract rhetors' and in impersonal constructions by the NS students. The hedging function of *suggest* and *seem*, as a means of conveying a cautious approach to the statements being made, might be a strategy used by the students to gain acceptance for their work. Also, 'abstract rhetors' and impersonal construction suggest that the author is open to discussion or even open to being proven wrong. At the very least, it reduces the personal responsibility involved in making a statement, since it is impossible to be one hundred percent scientifically sure of something.

Comparisons of Introduction and Discussion sections in the two corpora reveal that students employ similar strategies in introducing and discussing their work. For example, impersonal constructions of *seem* are used by both the NS and the NNS students to express evaluative meanings and writer judgment. And the co-occurrence

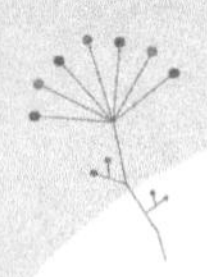

pattern 'authors' + *suggest* is largely used by both the NS and the NNS students in reviewing items of previous research. No major differences are found in the use of *suggest* and *seem* in the different move types between the NS and the NNS groups, except that the NS corpus contains the overwhelming majority of these two hedging lexical verbs.

The results suggest that the NNS students seem to have mastered the usage of *suggest* and *seem*, as they tend to use similar patterns of these two lexical verbs as the NS students do. Although the NNS students seem to know the constructions, they fail to use them enough in their academic writing. It seems that the NNS students are at an early stage in developing an academic style of writing. It is likely that the NNS students' educational background and their personality/stylistic choice seem to influence their stance. It is important for the NNS students to be aware of and follow the conventions of their discourse community, which necessitates rhetorical genre knowledge besides lexico-grammatical knowledge of English academic writing.

Chapter 6

Adjectives and Adverbs Hedging

Introduction

The remaining 5 terms of HDs used in the NS and the NNS corpora are *most*, *often*, *perhaps*, *usually* and *possible*. These adverbs and adjectives are referred to as the 'hedging adverbs/adjectives'. In academic writing, adjectives and adverbs play a prominent role in argumentation and have a strong impersonal dimension: they reveal much of a writer's attitude toward the textual content and are widely used to persuade readers that the topic under study is of interest and that the results are valuable. To put it simply, adjective and adverb hedging devices modify nouns and verbs, respectively. Adjectival hedging devices serve to reduce the force of noun meanings, and adverbial hedging devices have a similar effect on verb or sentence meanings (Quirk *et al.* 1985). Academic texts depend heavily on adjectives and adverbs in order to communicate the meaning effectively. This chapter starts with an overview of some examples of meanings of the selected adverbs and adjectives. In general terms, adverbs can be classified by their meanings, such as 'degree', 'frequency', 'probability', 'qualification' and 'quantification' (Section 6.1). These terms are introduced to describe the semantic types of the hedging adverbs and adjectives. Descriptions of the hedging adverbs/adjectives are on the basis of the hedges and the

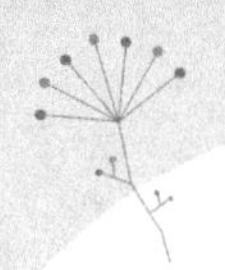

polypragmatic functions they share, according to the functional groups identified in the methodology chapter. In accordance with the modal verb hedges and lexical verb hedges, the contexts of adverb/adjective hedges are sufficient for the characterisation of polypragmatic functions. A combined approach of concordance analysis and genre analysis, as discussed in the methodology, are required. Section 6.1 presents the concordance analysis of hedging adverbs/adjectives and their polypragmatic functions with a closer look at concordance lines and local textual context. The genre analysis of the five selected hedging adverbs and adjectives is presented in Section 6.2. Genre analysis in this section focuses on how hedging adverbs/adjectives' active rhetorical features contribute to the persuasiveness of the students' academic writing. The conclusion section summarises the main results with regard to adverbs, determiners and adjectives as a group of hedging devices.

6.1 Concordance analysis of *most, often, usually, perhaps* and *possible*

6.1.1 An overview

As an indication of the relative frequencies of hedging adjectives and adverbs in academic writing, selected hedging adjectives and adverbs, namely *most*, *often*, *perhaps*, *usually* and *possible* are analysed. Using Hyland's (1998a) computations of word frequencies in the written components of the RAs as a rough comparison to give an idea of the behaviour of these words in general discourse, the same frequencies in the NS and the NNS corpora is calculated.

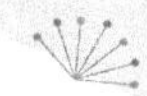

Table 19: Frequencies of Adverbs and Adjectives Used to Express Hedging in Various Corpora (per 1,000 Words)

	NS	NNS	Hyland's Research
most	1.05	1.49	0.23
possible	0.54	0.25	0.31
perhaps	0.52	<0.1	*
often	0.82	0.84	*
usually	<0.1	0.42	*

As can be seen from Table 19, there are some similarities and some differences in the relative frequencies of selected adverbs/adjectives. These involve similarities and differences between the NS corpus and the NNS corpus, and also between these and Hyland's computations. *Often*, *usually*, *possible* and *perhaps* show marked differences since *always* and *usually* are more than twice as frequent in the assignments of the NS corpus compared to the NNS corpus, while *possible* and *perhaps* in the NS corpus are almost twice as frequent as in the writing of the NNS corpus. The frequency result suggests that in the NS corpus *most* is almost as frequent as in the NNS corpus. We can see that in Hyland's study, half of the lexical hedges in the research articles are adjectives and adverbs. *Most* and *possible* are the two most frequent items shared by the NS and NNS corpora and Hyland's research articles. *Most* is much less frequent in Hyland's RAs than in either the NS corpus or the NNS corpus. *Possible* is used more frequently in Hyland's RAs than in the NNS corpus, but less than that in the NS corpus. As regards *perhaps*, *usually* and *often*, due to their low frequency in Hyland's RAs, it is not possible to make a significant comparison with the NS and the NNS corpora since Hyland does not present the occurrences of these items in his study.

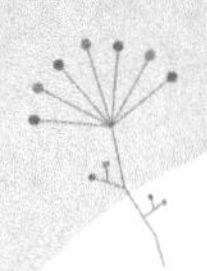

An examination of the corpora shows some evidence that the five selected adverbs/adjectives used in the extracts—*most*, *often*, *perhaps*, *usually* and *possible*—express a cline of students' academic statements and claims with these hedging adverbs/adjectives being more tentative. The selected adverbs belong to a wide range of different general terms of semantic types, as illustrated in example (1). *Most*, *often*, *perhaps*, *usually* and *possible*, since they belong to different categories, seem to collocate in quite different semantic fields.

(1)

a. *Always* (adverb of frequency)

—The play would *always* display a unity and wholeness... (NS corpus: 3005b)

Usually (adverb of frequency)

—Pre-determiners are *usually* the first type of determiner to be used. (NS corpus: 6048c)

b. *Perhaps* (adverb of probability)

—This indicates that personal style *perhaps* plays a role in hedging. (NS corpus: 0030)

c. *Most* as adverb (adverb of degree)

—... though her results can *most* likely be generalized... (NS corpus: 0030)

d. *Most* as determiner (determiner of quantification)

—... this would have been shocking to read as *most* people had not come to... (NS corpus: 3003a)

e. *Possible* (adjective of qualification)

—Therefore, aside from a *possible* lexical influence based on... (NS corpus: 0032)

Apart from the differences in relative frequencies of the chosen

hedging adverbs/adjectives, the corpus analysis carried out so far also shows a marked difference in types of usage. Concordances of the selected adverbs/adjectives are explored and mark the differences in both collocation and patterning. The patterns which are observed, however, apply to the specialised NS and NNS corpora which consist largely of student writings in disciplines with respect to the norms of the collection method (see Chapter 3), any generalisations must refer to the specific genre of student academic writing. This research takes into consideration the relation between the probability of the truth and the expression of degrees of certainty. While the statistical or truth aspect is rarely rendered explicit in the corpora, it is obvious that it is implied in many of the propositions the writers utter. This is illustrated in example (2) below where *usually* is chosen to indicate the statistical probability of an event taking place.

(2) The verb is *usually* used in reference to the suppression, curbing... (NS corpus: 3006f)

6.1.2 *Most*

The statistics in Table 19 show that the frequency of occurrence of the adverb *most* between the data in this study and Hyland's RAs differs significantly. As *most* can be a noun, pronoun, adjective or adverb depending on the context, this affects its frequency of occurrence as an HD. Hyland's (1998a) research considered the *most* function as an adjective as one of the most frequent adjectives expressing hedging. There is no discussion of the adverbial form of *most* being used as a HD in his RAs. All 17 examples of *most* out of 75,000 words (0.23 per 1,000 words, see Table 19) counted in Hyland's (1998a) study are adjectives. It seems that Hyland (1998a) may not have considered the adverbial form of *most* as a

hedging device or the frequency of occurrence of the adverbial form of *most* was too low to be noticed. However, in Hinkel's (2003) research on hedging, he states that the instruction of hedging may need to begin with lexically and syntactically accessible types of hedges, such as adverbs of frequency and degree. Hinkel (2003) explicitly indicates and exemplifies the adverbial form of *most* + adjective as a hedging construction to make writers' claims appear more tentative. As *most* in both adverbial and adjective forms can be used to express hedging, this study considers both forms of *most* rather than *most* as an adjective alone. And this could explain why there is a much higher frequency of occurrences of *most* than Hyland's research. Table 20 shows frequencies of *most* in adverbial and adjectival form in the NS and NNS corpora.

Table 20: Frequencies of Adverbial *Most* and Determiner *Most* in the NS and NNS Corpora

	Adverbial *Most*	Determiner *Most*
NS Corpus	78	22
NNS Corpus	68	32

Table 20 reveals that both the NS and the NNS writers employed *most* much more in adverbial form. Adverbial form of *most* is discussed in the following section and discussion on adjectival form of *most* is also presented.

Huang (1975: 21) defines adverbs of degree as follows:

> Degree adverbs express the degree or extent of a certain quality or state and presuppose an analysis of the grading properties in the semantics of, especially, adjectives. These adverbs either serve to indicate descriptively something about the degree, as in *She was very tall* or indicate the writer's reaction to the degree, as in *She was surprisingly tall*.

Biber *et al.* (1999: 554) say that 'they can be used to mark that the extent or degree is either greater or less than usual or than that of something else in the neighbouring discourse' and that 'they occur as both adverbials and modifiers'.

In the corpora of the current study, a large number of examples of *most* appeared in the adverbial form. As is evidenced in the corpora, students tend to prefer using it when writers seek to classify and comment on statements as accurately as possible. The examples of adverbial *most* mainly display two types of expressions: (1) the greatest or highest degree, which is often used with an adjective or adverb to form the superlative (e. g. the *most* appropriate choice); (2) a very great degree (e. g. this is *most* apparent in Wilde's indirect treatment). It would appear that *most* can be classified as an 'adverb of degree' as it is 'broadly concerned with the semantic category of degree' (Quirk *et al.* 1985: 589). As a grammatical form of superlative, *most* maximally intensifies the sense of an adjective. The adverb *most*, which expresses a very great degree, on the other hand, signifies less than maximal intensity. Concordance 19 is the first 25 examples of *most* sorted according to the first word to the right of the node word. Patterns that are invisible in the concordance are mainly patterns related to grammar. *Most* is to be found in the concordance in common patterns 'ADV adj n', and 'ADV adv/adj v'. It is also obvious to see the difference between the different meanings of *most* 'the greatest and highest degree' and 'a very great degree' on the basis of the concordance lines alone (see lines 15 and 3 in Concordance 19).

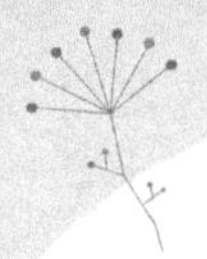

Concordance 19 25 examples of *most* in the NS corpus

1	life resonates with many of the novel's	most	crucial themes. Nicholas remain
2	eath that Nicholas makes his final and	most	enduring contribution to Levin's
3	han the others did, Levin felt that lie	most	painfully (456)) precedes Levin's
4	rs were also those responsible for the	most	daring and successful revolts in
5	there is a line, that when crossed, is	most	certainly evil. But one of Levi's
6	st certainly evil. But one of Levi's	most	crucial me ns- 24 rossed, is
7	s most crucial me ns- 24 rossed, is	most	certainly evil. But one of Levi's
8	st certainly evil. But one of Levi's	most	crucial me rossed, is most
9	of Levi's most crucial me rossed, is	most	certainly evil. But on ns- 25
10	But on ns- 25 vil. But one of Levi's	most	crucial me rossed, is most
11	ne of Levi's most crucial me rossed, is	most	certainly evil. But one of Levi'
12	st certainly evil. But one of Levi's	most	crucial me ns- 26 rossed, is
13	's most crucial me ns- 26 ossed, is	most	certainly evil. But one of Lev
14	ost certainly evil. But one of Levi's	most	crucial messages in The Drowned
15	under attack by Ras's mob. This is the	most	crucial moment of the narrator's
16	ational wealth among families), for the	most	part, it remains the connection.
17	the opposite, and is called the man	most	gracious and fair-minded, /
18	lives in the novel are also happy, but	most	have also gone though some sort
19	sition), Chaucer reserves some of his	most	outrageously immoral acts for
20	similar sins. The Pardoner is only the	most	obvious of the religious sinner
21	lity of the clergy to follow one of the	most	basic tenets of the Bible and
22	religious practice. This is borne out	most	fully by the reviled Pardoner
23	en Juani and Gina, because one of the	most	interesting parallels drawn in
24	o, Juani and Jimmy have arguably the	most	fractured and confused
25	ejas, 20), for Jimmy, his penis is the	most	significant defining

As we have seen, the adverb *most* shows a high frequency in the form of an adverb in both the NS and the NNS corpora; in addition *most* as an adverb to form a superlative has almost the same frequency as adverb *most* in expressing a very great degree; while it is used more often to modify an adjective to form a superlative in the NNS corpus.

Table 21 starts with a basic overview of the meaning distinctions and collocates that are based on the narrow context of the adverb of

the degree *most*. The table covers all 100 examples of adverbial *most*.

Table 21: Adverb of Degree *Most*—Overview of the 100 Examples in Each Corpus

most	Form of Superlative	A Very Great Degree
NS Corpus	N v-link *the most* ADV/ADJ (*commonly*, *heavily*, *significantly*, *etc.*) 5 the most ADJ N V (*significant*, *interesting*, *etc.*) 36	N v-link most ADV/ADJ (*certainly*, *apparently*, *etc.*) 7 N most ADV V (*likely*, *closely etc.*) 22
NNS Corpus	N v-link the most ADJ/ADV (*common*, *important etc.*) 11 the most ADJ N V (*difficult*, *important famous*, *frequently*, *etc.*) 41	N v-link most ADV/ADJ (*apparent*, *important*, *etc.*) 2 N most ADV V (*likely*, *important powerful etc.*) 5

The grammatical patterns of *most* used in the NS corpus and the NNS corpus follow almost the same trend. Examples of *most* are more often used to form a superlative adjective than to express a very great degree, and are in extensive use in the grammatical pattern 'the most ADJ N V'. Paradis (1997) suggests that gradable adjectives, such as *important* or *significant* mentioned in Table 21, which have comparative and superlative forms, can be modified by grading adverb *most*. This is clear in the examples, where *most* is used to indicate degree with respect to certain descriptive terms.

(3) Pattern of 'N v-link the most ADJ/ADV'

N	v-link	the most	ADJ	N
This act	is	the most	comprehensive	example of federal support

(4) Pattern of 'the most ADJ N V'

The most	ADJ	N	V	clause
The most	extensive	of these works	devoted	to...

(5) Pattern of 'N v-link most ADV/ADJ V'

N	v-link	most	ADV	V	clause
This phrase	is	most	often	found	in...

(6) Pattern of 'N most ADV V'

N	most	ADV	V	N
the term	most	usually	coupled with	history

In examples (3) and (4) there is the comparison of the noun with every other member of its group. In such examples, the adjective links *most* forming a superlative, and provides a background for the elements that express evaluative meanings. It is in this sense that the noun is considered by the writers in their work. While in examples (5) and (6) the degree of strength of adverbs or adjectives is modified by *most*. *Most* in such examples can be interchangeable with *very*.

The adverbs *most* as shown in examples (3) and (4) form a superlative to maximally intensify the sense of an adjective. In academic writing, such adverbs *most* are considered to mark exaggerations, and these examples could be considered as a maximiser rather than a HD.

6.1.3 Adverbs of frequency: *often* and *usually*

Adverbs of frequency are used to tell how often something happens. They often serve as hedging devices in written text and are employed in generalisations and evidential statements to reduce the writer's responsibility for the truth value of his/her proposition or

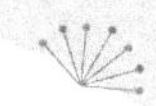

claim (Chafe 1986; Hinkel 2003). Based on the findings from her corpus data, Channell (1994) comments that the meanings of frequency adverbs are inherently vague and that they are used in similar contexts as other indefinite quantifiers. Following Swart (1991), *often* and *usually* are considered as frequency adverbs. This book refers to a sentence containing a frequency adverb as a frequency statement. Frequency statements with adverbs of frequency express probability judgments, and these, in turn, are interpreted as statements of hypothetical relative frequency. Frequency adverbs *usually* and *often* represent one of the most common and simple hedging devices. Adverbs of frequency are used to describe how often we do an activity. They normally precede the main verbs and if there is no main verb, then it comes after an auxiliary. Since these adverbs are lexically and syntactically simple, they can be accessible to most L2 learners, from those with intermediate to advanced L2 proficiency. In addition, due to their ubiquity, frequency adverbs can be employed to extend the meanings of verbs or whole sentences and can be easier to use in editing than other more complex types of hedge.

Apparently indicative of frequency, these adverbs allow the language user not to commit himself or herself to categorical assertions or exact figures when they cannot be obtained, if they are not categorically correct, or when numerical precision is not deemed necessary (Varttala 2001: 129). Varttala (2001) and Salager-Meyer (1994) have the same opinion that this kind of adverbs can be seen as typical, particularly in the language of science. It is for the inherent indefiniteness that these adverbs are always used to gain hedging purposes. The present book includes two such adverbs. By employing these adverbs of frequency, the writers give a roundabout indication of the degree to which the information applies, thus providing the possibility not to commit themselves to precise figures.

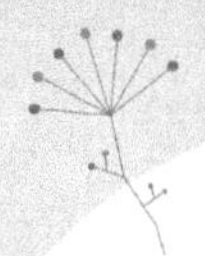

Before presenting the arguments for *often* and *usually*, the relation between truth conditions and probability should be considered. *Usually* carries an implicature to the effect that the probability is substantially greater than 80% (DeCapua, 2008). If the probability is lower than 80%, a sentence containing *usually* may be judged to be literally true but misleading. The probability of *often* is between 30% and 80% which is lower than *usually*. We assume that *usually* conveys a regular and predictable meaning. However, *often* is for something that happens or one does frequently, but not on a regular basis.

Often is recognised as the most common frequency adverb employed by both the NS and the NNS writers (0.82 and 0.84 per 1,000 words respectively). However, the occurrence of *usually* is relatively high in the NNS corpus. It is obvious that *usually* appears more often in the NNS corpus than in the NS corpus. That is to say, the NNS writers tend to overuse *usually* compared with the NS writers (0.11 per 1,000 words in the NS corpus vs 0.42 per 1,000 words in the NNS corpus). Occurrences of *often* and *usually* in the NNS corpus are in fact often, but not exclusively, used where a frequency statement is implied as the examples in Concordances 20 and 21 illustrate.

Concordance 20 The first 25 examples of *often* in the NS corpus

1 rals, and the morals it does convey are often conflicted. A Christian morality
2 d popular in England. Morality plays often involve characters that are
3 nd perhaps one or two college courses, often designated remedial. 6 It is
4 The phrase hither and thither is reused often throughout the remainder of the
5 , forcing him to confront difficult and often moribund topics that might not
6 tain the dream. Another well-known and often debated conflict between autonomy
7 then self-reliance is gone, and with it often goes the pride of men. Therefore,
8 he author utilizes the superlative form often in his descriptions of Beowulf.
9 9). When confronted with spring, autumn often seems pale in comparison. Anne

10 ent on a basic physical level. Satan is often flying around the universe, or
11 characters in the Canterbury Tales are often strained and criticism between
12 ned and criticism between characters is often somewhat dubious (easily attribu
13 gh language policy and education policy often has stated goals of helping
14 of America (Bush, Online News Hour), it often does nothing to actually provid
15 ion, language and education legislation often effectively bars immigrant stu
16 students, but the historical record has often shown that given their own way,
17 better services. State legislation has often sought to block immigrants from
18 y, Max no longer uses his German skills often and admits that they may have g
19 some contact with other languages will often also have difficulties because
20 f the time, and dative and genitive are often incorrect. This leads me to bel
21 4.2.1 Verb Placement Verb placement is often difficult for second language
22 new set of rules. In German, the verbs often occur in two different places in
23 had trouble finding the right word and often resorted to code-switching during
24 ed attention leaves unclear is just how often multiple hedging occurs, whether
25 attempts to answer the question of how often multiple hedging occurs) and a

Concordance 21 The first 25 examples of *usually* in the NS corpus

1 wever, is a repetition of the sermon he usually delivers to the masses, as far)
2 in German. Verbs using the to be form usually pertain to motion or movement
3 nal. In other words, the undergraduates usually chose double-hedged expressions
4 the person who utters the repair word (usually referred to hereafter as the
5 ith most of the repair phrases as well, usually when the original utterance has
6 ic so is used to indicate degree, which usually modifies an adjective or manner.
7 dicative complement. The antecedent is usually and AdjP but other categories
8 lture, and language, as the term most usually coupled with history and that
9 r of artifices and types of magic, acts usually assigned to women in these myth
10 ored. Anger boils to the surface of the usually collected Kip and Ondaatje brin
11 omething other, the verb 'knit' is not usually coined with the noun 'eye', wh
12 e understanding true love, but they are usually marginalized or dismissed for b
13 in debt. Algy talks of being "more than usually hard up" and hints at the unpaid
14 drum does not play itself. The verb is usually used in reference to the suppre
15 the adjective "native", which we might usually associate with "people". In line
16 drum does not play itself. The verb is usually used in reference to the suppre
17 'comparable moments of transition are usually recognitions of absence'. The

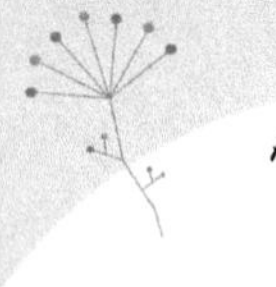

18 tmodern texts. To expand, postmodernism usually features ambiguity of the meani
19 onal thought and feelings but another, usually that of a famous character in
20 throughout most of the novel is the one usually taken upon the man of the house
21 off-spring from my brain". Offspring is usually a word to describe something th
22 ation of certain aesthetic principles, usually associated with the Imagistes.
23 tuation involving members of the elite, usually to do with sex, lies and politi
24 . and as lacking in all the attributes usually associated with ideal Victorian
25 ture, the formal properties of a work' usually refer to its structural design

Concordances 20 and 21 present the first 25 examples of *often* and *usually* in the NS corpus. Examples of *usually* illustrate a situation similar to that of *often*: patterns that are visible in the concordances are mainly patterns related to grammatical behaviour. They follow the general rules of adverb placement in a sentence:

a) Adv V: This pattern is regularly seen before the main verb, if the main sentence verb is not *be* (take lines 2, 3, 5, 7, 9, 13, 14, 16, 17, 22, 23, 24 and 25 in Concordance 20 as instances of *often*; take lines 1, 2, 3, 4, 5, 6, 8, 9, 10, 13, 15, 18, 19, 20, 22, 23, 24 and 25 in Concordance 21 as examples of *usually*).

b) be ADV, if the main sentence verb is be (see lines 1, 12, 20 and 21 in Concordance 20 and lines 17 and 21 as examples in Concordance 21).

c) In many cases, uses of frequency adverbs are accompanied by the present simple tense (see line 18 in Concordance 21 and line 14 in Concordance 20).

d) Sometimes, frequency adverbs are used in sentences in a passive voice (take lines 1 and 11 in Concordance 20 and lines 11,12,14,16 in Concordance 21 for instances).

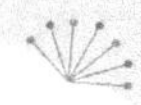

6.1.3.1 *Usually*

Although the frequency of occurrence varies a lot, basically the NS and NNS students use *usually* in a similar way. When used as a hedge, one of the most common grammatical patterns in which *usually* is found in the two corpora is the use of *usually* pre-verbally as a hedge. More than half occurrences of *usually* in the NS and NNS corpora showed this pattern.

One clear advantage of corpus data over intuitive data is that such collocates can be extensively documented. Collocates which occur as active or passive forms of verbs to the right of the node usually include:

associate, *use*, *refer*, *assign*, *choose*, *collect*, *compound*, *concentrate*, *couple*, *deliver*, *require* (from the NS corpus)

pay, *persuade*, *take*, *use*, *take*, *do*, *adopt*, *combine*, *keep*, *occur*, *say*, *show*, *accompany*, *apply*, *associate*, *avoid*, *carry*, *cause*, *compare*, *consider*, *describe*, *fall*, *gain*, *enjoy*, *imply*, *influence*, *keep*, *indicate*, *lead*, *make*, *name* (from the NNS corpus)

No particular verbs above occur more frequently with *usually* than the others. Most of these verbs, which are modified by the frequency adverb *usually*, are performative verbs. As Hyland (1998a) and Varttala (2001) discuss, due to its inherent indefiniteness, the frequency adverb *usually* may be seen as useful for hedging purposes, allowing language users, for example, to point out that what is stated *usually* applies. In Hyland's work, *usually* acts as 'downtoner' to lower the force of the verb they modify.

(7) The most serious mistakes in translating and interpreting are *usually* not the result of verbal inadequacy, but of wrong cultural assumptions.

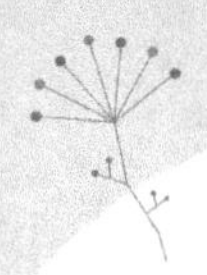

In example (7), *usually* conveys a certain qualification with regard to the degree of accuracy of the conclusion offered, indicating that what is said is 'true or accurate within certain limits' (Hyland 1998a: 187). As seen in example (7), the writer's claim is hesitant, based on logical inferences drawn from the analysis, and having no experimental data to support the accuracy, the writer chose to use the frequency adverb *usually* to make a categorical assertion of his/her statements. The example can thus be viewed as being marked by means of hedging so as to 'qualify the predicate intensity or the validity of the state of affairs expressed in the proposition' (Hyland 1998a: 166). In sum, the writer uses *usually* as an attribute hedging device to seek precision in expression, and example (7) encodes variability rather than the writer's perspective.

Several other grammatical patterns surrounding *usually* can be extracted from the NS and NNS corpora, in addition to the pattern ADV v. If we look at the left co-text of the pattern ADV v we find other co-selected features such as subjects expressed as concrete nouns which either could be subsumed under the semantic field of humans (*we*, *protagonist*, *they*, *Chinese people*, *politician*, *parents*, *the host*, *students*, *women*, *undergraduates*, *etc.*) or NPs characteristic of linguistic, literature or educational discourse (*the verb*, *infant's first words*, *indefinite article*, *the theme*, *minimal responses or back-channels*, *scientific and technical writing*, *brand names*, *terminology*, *the word 'greet'*, *etc.*).

6.1.3.2 *Often*

As the same kind of adverb, *often* expresses lower probability than *usually*, but it shows similar grammatical patterns to *usually*. The verbs which *often* modified in the NS and NNS corpora are as follows:

use, *strain*, *multiply*, *refer*, *find*, *wrap*, *accompany*, *have*, *alter*, *associate*, *cause*, *combine*, *conflict*, *debate*, *describe*, *engage*, *feel*, *find*, *offer*, *produce*, *question*, *seem*, *subject* (the NS corpus)

use, *talk*, *identify*, *translate*, *accuse*, *apply*, *ask*, *associate*, *begin*, *cause*, *choose*, *complain*, *consider*, *discuss*, *divide*, *help*, *identify*, *imagine*, *interact*, *label*, *mark*, *reduce*, *receive*, *relate* (the NNS corpus)

Lemmas of the verb *use* are by far the most frequent, while the others have only one or two tokens in the NS and NNS corpora.

In addition, if one looks to the left of the node word, *often* is found in colligations with gradability. The presence of gradability is hardly surprising in academic discourse where this form of comparative evaluation constitutes a major scientific/argumentative hedging. For example, events can be deemed more likely to happen than others, or people to do things rather than others, as can be seen from the Concordances 22 and 23. In both the NS and the NNS corpora, *more* and *most* are found to collocate with *often* although, of these, *more* is more frequent.

Concordance 22 Examples of *often* collocate with gradability in the NNS corpus

multiple hedging, which he refers to most often as double hedging (also mentioning trip
re Figure here Reductions are the most often used reformulations with this phrase,
e here Figure here This phrase is most often found in the context of expansions, to
e Figure here Expansions are found most often for this phrase, as would be expected,
ss amongst speakers. The word so is most often found at the beginning of a sentence
word lists show which words occur most often with a target word. For example the
t tends to occur in certain contexts more often than others and whether or not native
sumed that formal language is spoken more often by these speakers in these contexts.
ditions from my country, but later, more often, from your country (Ondaatje 283).
d we repeat ourselves in speech much more often than we do in writing." The contrast
lines are broken up by punctuation more often than elsewhere in the ' song' and

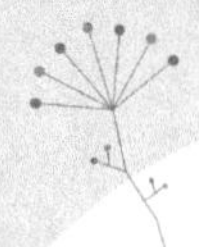

le doctors interrupted their patients more often than female doctors and used interru
le doctors were interrupted as often or more often by their patients than they themselves
use names and the pronouns you and we more often than men encouraging others to speak
a pattern to convey meaning and the more often it is used in a pattern the more distin
use the inclusive 'we' significantly more often in continuing the perception of solida
affective functions of an interaction more often than men do" (Holmes in Coates 1998:463
he idea 'the determining factor is more often the sex of the speaker, rather than
is was determined to be the case as more often than not stories of current interest

Concordance 23 Examples of *often* collocate with gradability in the NNS corpus

ohesion devices: References are used more often to achieve grammatical cohesion. Conjun
cts of AAVE have auxiliary deletion more often than urban varieties do. This shows th
example, black women were employed more often than white women as technicians, the
nd the accumulation of wealth. Far more often than whites, African Americans lived
rdy, and cut class about 30 percent more often than do students from intact homes. The
of the film. Foreign audiences are more often than not to comprehend the original fil
and better. Students will engage more often and more eagerly in behaviors related
of an ad, or in the middle of it, but more often they appear at the end of a commercial.
ess thing to serve as the subject much more often, so the passive voice is used. Therefor
anly. But Swedenians use eye language more often than Englishmen. And the French especia
fferent cultures communicate more and more often. We have more chance to exchange cultur
ghost towns for which the miners are more often remembered. With the curiosity of gold,
third elided in English. However, more often than not, it is reiterated in Chinese
necessary repetition. Thus, Chinese more often than not conforms to principle of b
3.5.3 Purple In China, purple is more often adopted by the feudal emperors and the
ver found its way into his talk but more often and loudly in the acts of his life"
season, while western festivals were more often named after the religious figures or
onsequently, the epistolary form is, more often than not, adopted as an ideal way to
icle clear and brief, abbreviations are more often used in headlines. In usual, abbrevi
hould be looked upon with suspicion: more often than not, an English text is better
o it can be dispensed with entirely; more often, they need to be retained but can be
oo of color in English culture and is most often used with negative connotation. Black
il in and of itself. These centers are most often, but not necessarily, circular. Jung
on. Mike has a terrible temper, which most often manifests itself during his extremely
n two or more different words and is most often used in poetry. The word "rhyme" may

ts should try their best to avoid the most often used writing skill; in stead they sho
influences of globalization that are most often condemned by the new nationalists and

6.1.4 Hedging adverb *perhaps*

Perhaps is another common adverb in the NS corpus. Adverbs in general tend to be involved in subjective evaluations (Nuyts 2001), and, as we have seen, the adverb *perhaps* shows a much higher frequency in the NS corpus compared to that in the NNS corpus (0.52 vs <0.1). Contrasting with that of *certainly*, *of course*, *clearly* and *obviously*, the use of *perhaps* displays an expression of probability. *Perhaps* is considered as a HD that mitigates the authors' evaluation of the likelihood of the event described in the proposition (Hyland 1998a). When it comes to academic discourse and to the analysis of this adverb as a qualifier of the standpoint, the degree of commitment of the source of evidence does not play a role in understanding the discourse effect that its use may have. The use of this hedging adverb *perhaps* has the discourse effect of emphasising the quality of the evidence that the protagonist is ready to forward be in support of the standpoint. In general, it is acknowledged that modal adverbs like *perhaps* indicate a weak degree of commitment to the truth of the proposition that is asserted in a sentence, and can thereby be used in order to downplay the effect that the asserted sentence has, or the expectations that it creates, for the audience (Holmes 1984; Sbisa 2001). Such a commitment is warranted on evidence the source or quality of which is not strong enough to justify a stronger degree of commitment.

Perhaps in example (8) signals lower levels of authorial commitment, leaving the information presented open to possible discussion:

(8) Though all poets age and inevitably die, *perhaps* only a

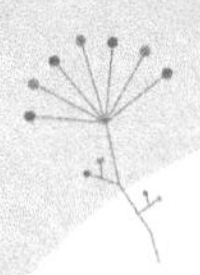

poet like Stevens, who started out on his poetic journey late in life, could write with such resonance and portent on the topic of death. (NS corpus: 0048)

In example (8), *perhaps* is used in the introductory section to the NS student's writing at a point where the writer states the focus of the paper which is precise to analyse Steven's poetry on the topic of death. The use of *perhaps* seeks to protect the writer's image by hedging a proposition in which he tries to justify investigating Steven's works. Its use allows him to gain the benevolence of the audience by trying to predispose them towards a positive reading of the paper. In this context and in terms of pragmatic effects, *perhaps* serves the purpose of minimising the risk of criticism against the authorial persona.

Like other adverbs, it is predictable that examples of *perhaps* were used to modify adjectives and verbs. Apart from this, another common behaviour in which *perhaps* is to be found in the NS corpus is that the hedging adverb *perhaps* is usually placed at the beginning of a sentence or before the subject of a clause. In these examples, in contrast to the adverb that modifies just adjectives and verbs, *perhaps* is used to comment on the entire sentence or clause and evaluate it. Compare the following examples.

(9) Similarly, the form and language of the poem is *perhaps* closer to prose than poetry, due to the absence of end rhyme and a regular metrical pattern. (NS corpus: 3066f)

(10) For any inexperienced teacher, classes of adolescents are *perhaps* the most daunting challenge. (NNS corpus: 022)

(11) *Perhaps* the most direct address of multiple hedges occurs in David Banks's (1994b) book *Writ in Water: Aspects of the Scientific Journal Article* and in his article 'Hedges and How to

Trim Them' (1994a). (NS corpus: 0030)

(12) *Perhaps* culture is one of the most difficult terms to define. (NNS corpus: 097)

In examples (9) and (10), the use of *perhaps* contrasts with that of *certainly*, *clearly* or *obviously*. *Perhaps* in these two examples are hedging devices that mitigate the writers' evaluation of the likelihood of the event described in the proposition: *closer to prose than poetry* in example (9) and *the most daunting challenge* in example (10). While, the HDs *perhaps* at the beginning of the sentences in example (11) and example (12) can be considered as attitudinal stance markers which convey the writers' attitudes or value judgments towards the whole propositional content. They all reveal the writers' affective attitude towards a given subject matter. For instance, the writer's desire that the argument *the most direct address of multiple hedges occurs in David Banks's* (1994b) *book* is not very sure as in example (11), or that a state of affairs *culture is one of the most difficult terms to define* contains some uncertainty as in example (12). *Perhaps* in these examples seems to play a prominent role in the rhetorical machinery of the student writing analysed in this book: they are not simply aimed at qualifying the information presented from the writers' point of view in various ways. Most importantly, they aim to create affective appeals or, in other words, appeals to the readers' emotions, inviting them to accept their discourse in the same way the authors entertain it. Writers use these types of hedging adverbials so as to guide their audience to intended interpretations.

6.1.5 Hedging determiner *most* and adjective *possible*

In academic writing, adjectives and determiners also play a prominent role in argumentation and have a strong interpersonal

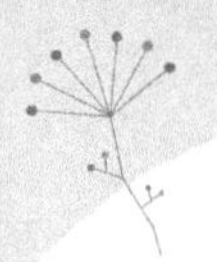

dimension: they reveal much of a speaker's/writer's attitude toward the textual content and are widely used to persuade the potential readers that the topic under study is of interest and that the demonstration and results are valuable. As reviewed in Chapter 2, recent studies by Hyland (1998a, 2005) and Fløttum *et al.* (2006) have shown that academic writing was not the neutral genre it was claimed to be, but that it was a highly dialogic genre where authorial presence and subjectivity were prevalent. Hedging adjectives and determiners are part of this authorial presence and a close examination of their use in academic writing can shed light on the rhetorical strategies used by the writer.

Hedging adjectives and determiners are a resource employed by writers to express their attitude, their evaluation of propositions, methods, results or points in the texts, and have been classified in several ways. For instance, Vande Kopple (1985) and Hyland (1999) refer to them as devices that express writers' attitude toward the propositional content and/or readers while taking a stance. Conrad and Biber (2000) regard them as part of stance, a cover term comprising both an epistemic and an attitudinal position for the expression of personal feelings and assessment. The evaluative value of the adjectives and determiners also have the function, as Francis *et al.* (1996) states, to facilitate the reader's interpretation of a text, since the skeleton of the structural scheme is reveals by signals that function as signposts, enabling the writer to organise the information and to form an intelligible picture of the relationship between any particular idea and the argument as a whole.

As mentioned, the frequency information reveals the most frequently used adjectives and determiners on which this author focuses and which represent a novelty compared to previous findings by other scholars. Cases in point are *possible* and *most*, which are also

in Hyland's top frequent list as the most frequent hedging adjectives and determiners in the NS corpus. The collocational patterning of the determiner *most* and the adjective form of *possible* reflects the way the NS and NNS students express claims in their texts, which is essential in helping the readers to understand the message.

6.1.5.1 Hedging determiner *most*

As mentioned in Section 6.1.2, *most* was also used by the NS and NNS writers as a determiner, but with lower frequency compared with the adverbial form *most*. The NNS corpus (17 out of 100 instances) included significantly lower rates of the determiner *most* than the NS corpus did (31 out of 100 instances). Although the determiner *most* occurs in the two sets of data at different frequencies, it was used in the same patterns as a quantifier (DET *of* def-n) or a determiner (DET pl-n) to refer to the majority of a group of things or people, or the largest part of something by both the two groups of writers.

Within the pattern DET pl-n, *most* is used to quantify a nonspecific group. That is to say, *most* is used when writers are speaking in general and do not have a specific group of people or things in mind. While, *most of* in pattern DET *of* def-n quantifies a specific group. The expression includes a phrase defining the number of a specific group. For example,

(13) The statement suggests collective denial, even though at the time this would have been shocking to read as *most* people had not come to this conclusion about Christianity. (NS corpus: 3003a)

(14) The study indicated that *most* students believed that it was very helpful to take the CBI courses (American geography, American culture and American history). (NNS corpus: 010)

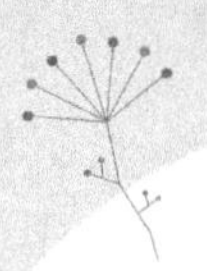

(15) Since I am focussing on language and gender from a sociolinguistic point of view, *most of* the research I am looking at is qualitative. (NS corpus: 6059a)

(16) Some students complain that *most of* the vocabularies learned in class can not be used in their daily life. Even those who have passed CET-6, TOEFL, or GRE have barriers in the communication with foreigners. (NNS corpus: 013)

In the above examples, *most* and *most of* are used to modify *people* in example (13), *students* in example (14), *the research* in example (15) and *the vocabularies* in example (16). They are applied to convey the expression of majority in order to make the statements explicit. In example (15) and example (16), the nouns being modified by *most of* are refined into specific groups, *the research* refers to *what I am looking at* and *vocabularies* are limited to those *learned in class*.

6.1.5.2 Hedging adjective *possible*

Like the determiner *most*, the hedging adjective *possible* was also found to combine with common nouns in the NS and the NNS corpora, which describe or presuppose a situation or entities: *possible points*, *possible cautions*, etc. The adjective *possible* is most frequent with academic observables (*points*, *causes*, *solution*, *consequences*). Examples of the adjective *possible* in the ADJ n pattern serve as HDs to reduce the force of the co-occurring noun meanings, and function as a marker of probability. In examples (17) and (18), *possible* is used by the NS and NNS writers to express probabilities of *linguistic transfer* and *reasons* being discussed in the propositions. The use of *possible* in these examples aims to indicate the degree of precision intended and convey the sense in which an idea may be held to be true.

(17) Several contrastive rhetoric studies have looked at hedging in different cultures (e. g. Mart & Burgess 2004) and the *possible* linguistic transfer that may result from attempts to hedge in the L2 (e. g. Clyne 1991; Hinkel 1997). (NS corpus: 0030)

(18) It is hoped, by a contrastive study of advertisements in both English and Chinese languages, similarities and differences of the two kinds of advertisements at different levels will be summarized and *possible* reasons will be given in the light of the meaning, and function of language, enabling English learners to better understand linguistic features of both English and Chinese advertisements, making them appreciate and experience the charm of advertising languages better, thereby improving their abilities of intercultural communication. (NNS corpus: 030)

The occurrences of *possible* in the NS corpus also match the patterns that Hunston and Sinclair (2003) suggest for a local grammar of evaluation from their analysis of the Cobuild Bank of English corpus. These patterns occur with *possible* obtained in the NS corpus, but rarely in the NNS corpus. The use of *possible* by the NNS writers is confined to attribute hedging. The two patterns are,

- *it* v-link ADJ (*possible*) *to*-inf clause
- *it* v-link ADJ (*possible*) *that* clause

Hunston and Sinclair (2003) considered these patterns are typically used to evaluate. Both patterns begin with an introductory or anticipatory *it*, followed by a link verb, an adjective, and a finite or non-finite clause (a *that*-clause, or *to*-infinitive clause). According to the local grammar of evaluation introduced by Hunston and Sinclair (2003: 84) the thing evaluated is located in the *to*-infinitive or *that*-

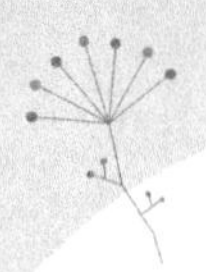

clause, whereas the evaluative category is realised by the adjective group, *possible* in this case. Here the *to*-infinitive or *that*-clause belongs to *possible*, in the pattern *it is possible to/that*, therefore there is also an association between *possible* and the clause that follows. The adjective *possible* indicates a validity situation, and is followed by the clause which indicates a proposition to be evaluated. To illustrate the first of these observations, consider the following two citations, which also serve to illustrate the two phraseological patterns that form the empirical focus of the present study.

(19) While hedging does occur very frequently and should, of course, be given some attention in any well-developed set of language teaching materials, *it is possible that* hedging does not receive more focus because it is not extraordinarily difficult for students to accomplish some base level of hedging, like the use of modal and lexical verbs, for example. It's likely that a relatively short amount of coverage would suffice. (NS corpus: 0030)

(20) In this case *it is possible to* guess at the intention of the poet if we take into account the volatile politics of the Elizabethan era, and the importance that the Queen herself placed on fostering the 'ideal of perfection to which she was wedded at the moment of her consecration.' (NS corpus: 3080f)

In the pattern '*it* v-link ADJ *that*-clause', the adjective *possible* is followed by a *that*-clause. The adjective *possible* in this pattern indicates someone's degree of certainty or awareness of something or attitude of talking about a state of affairs. As a result, this pattern of *possible* is most often used to attribute an evaluation of probability to the readers. It may be parsed as shown in the following examples. In

the pattern '*it* v-link ADJ *to*-inf clause', the adjective *possible* is followed by a *to*-infinitive clause. As can be seen, example (19) assesses the likelihood or validity of something, while example (20) assesses whether something is relatively easy or difficult to do.

However, clearly, this difference in meaning is not inherent in the word *possible* itself; neither is it completely context-dependent and thus only retrievable via the process of inferential pragmatics (Stubbs 2001). Rather, the claim is that the validity meaning is made by the pattern '*it* plus link verb, plus the adjective *possible*, plus a *that*-clause' (*it* v-link ADJ *that*), and the difficulty meaning is made by the pattern '*it* v-link ADJ *to*-inf clause' (*it* v-link ADJ *to*-inf). As Biber *et al.* (1999) point out, the '*it* v-link ADJ *that*' pattern is principally associated with validity (Biber *et al.* 1999: 675), while '*it* v-link ADJ *to*-inf' is more closely associated with importance, difficulty and desirability (Biber *et al.* 1999: 721). In addition, recent corpus-based work by Charles (2000, 2004) suggests that an even more fundamental form/meaning distinction can be made between these two patterns.

Charles (2000) argues that '*it* v-link ADJ *to*-inf' sequences are indeed rhetorically distinctive, in that they help to confer what Charles calls an 'appropriate academic persona' on the voice of the writer. The statement in example (20) *it is possible to guess at the intention of the poet* is less face-threatening than some alternatives, such as *we can guess at the intention of the poet*. Charles also finds that '*it* v-link ADJ *to*-inf' is far more frequently used to construct a positive aura around the writer-as-researcher, by exploiting the fact that, in this pattern, the adjective *possible* evaluates a *to*-infinitive clause, and thus by implication evaluates the performer of the action indexed by the *to*-infinitive verb itself. In example (20) above, it is the process of noting, as much as the proposition being noted, that is

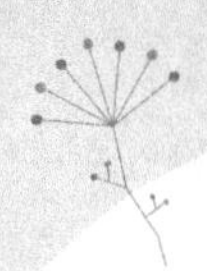

evaluated as 'possible', and, of course, it is the writer him/herself who is doing this noting, and is therefore seen as being possible at this point in his text. What Charles' work implies, then, is that a fundamental rhetorical distinction can plausibly be made between '*it* v-link ADJ *that*' as a pattern that evaluates propositions, and '*it* v-link ADJ *to*-inf' as a pattern that evaluates processes, and by extension the agents of these processes.

6.1.6 Polypragmatic functions of hedging adverbs and adjectives

From the above analyses, we can summarise that, consistent with Hyland's (1998a) study, hedging adverbs *most*, *often*, *usually* and *perhaps* and determiner *most* and adjective *possible* are used by both the NS and the NNS students as attribute hedges. As Hyland (1998a) states, adverbs and adjectives are mainly used to express accuracy-oriented hedging. Hedging adverbs or adjectives conveyed the frequency, the degree or the probability of the phenomena they modified within the propositions in order to express their statements accurately (*i. e.* *most* people; *perhaps* a bit too broadly; *possible* reason; *usually* closely or *often* incorrect).

In addition, this study also reveals that some patterns of hedging adverb *perhaps* and hedging adjective *possible* were used to make higher level claims by the NS and NNS students which indicate writer-oriented hedging. Their function is to put a distance between the statement and the writer, as illustrated in examples (11) (12) in Section 6.1.4 and in examples (19) (20) in Section 6.1.5.2.

Hedging devices in certain patterns, such as *it is* ADJ *to/that*, or being used as sentence adverbs like '*Perhaps* due to a rising middle class and exchange of goods an idea of reciprocity has entered Christianity.' (NS corpus: 0001), that indicate the writer's decision

to withhold complete commitment to a proposition, allow information to be presented as an opinion rather than accredited fact. Because all statements are evaluated and interpreted based on writers' assumptions, hedging devices like *perhaps* and *possible* are used to calculate what weight to give to an assertion, attesting to the degree of precision or reliability that they want it to carry, and perhaps to claim protection in the event of its eventually proving untruthful (Hyland 1998a).

Equally importantly, *possible* in 'it v-link ADJ *to/that* clause' and *perhaps* as a sentence hedging adverb also allow writers to open a discursive space where readers can dispute their interpretations. Claim-making is risky because it can contradict existing literature or challenge the research of one's readers, which means that arguments must accommodate readers' expectations that they will be allowed to participate in a dialogue and that their own views will be acknowledged in the discourse. By marking statements as provisional, hedging adverb *perhaps* and hedging adjective *possible* seek to involve readers as participants in their ratification, conveying deference, modesty, or respect for colleagues views (Hyland 1998a).

6.2 Move analysis of adverbs and adjectives hedging

Academic texts depend heavily on adjectives (which modify nouns and noun phrases) and adverbs (which modify verbs, adjectives and other adverbs) in order to communicate meaning effectively. As stated at the beginning of this chapter, adverbs and adjectives are most often employed to establish deictic references of relevant place, time, manner, or other parameters, which greatly affect how meanings in texts are conveyed and understood. In written academic discourse, adjectives and adverbs can perform a variety of rhetorical functions, many of which are discussed in some detail in

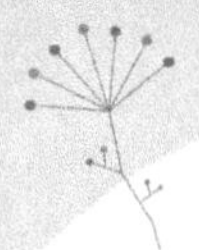

the genre analysis section of this chapter.

Academic writings are expected to be based on information obtained from published sources such as books, articles, reports, or print news. Thus following the thesis statement, the discourse frame moves to supporting information that takes the form of summaries, paraphrasing, or citation from sources (Swales 1990). Usually, in academic assignments, in addition to simply making summaries and paraphrasing information, students are expected to evaluate their sources and the opinions expressed in them critically. According to Swales and Feak (1994), for instance, in literature overviews and summaries, adjectives and adverbs represent an integral part of the writer's description of a work or source. That is to say, evaluations of the material obtained from sources necessitate uses of evaluative adjectives and adverbs. To this end, particularly in papers written for social sciences and humanities courses, after summarising the information, writers are expected to signal their own views on the topic, issue, or author's tone. The adjectives and adverbs are used to frame a writer's absolute judgements of certainty towards the propositions expressed. They indicate their complete confidence in the certainty of the state of affairs. Writers' confident voices as portrayed here by the use of these adjectives and adverbs do not seem to be simply the result of their intention to express an assured personal opinion. Contextual information indicates that these adverbs frame propositions which can be taken as conclusions of some logical reasoning where the premises involved are entertained with a high degree of confidence.

Hoye's (1997) substantial work on the meanings, functions, and roles of adverbs and adverbials with modals in spoken and written texts further underscores their importance and extraordinary diversity in corpora of English language data. Hoye specifies that adverbials

modify other sentence elements, such as adjectives, other adverbs, verbs and entire clauses. Although his study did not focus specifically on adverb classification, according to his findings, the diverse meanings of adverbials fall into several classes, the largest of which include adverbials of place, time, duration, frequency, cause, and manner, and the structure of adverbs can range from single words to adverb phrases to whole clauses.

The findings of the move analysis of selected hedging adverbs and adjectives are presented and discussed as follows: first, this author presents the overall distribution of the selected hedging adverbs and adjectives across the six organisational units and describe their preference uses/co-occurrence patterns. Next, this author moves on to the investigation of the specific location and rhetorical functions of the adverbs and adjectives in each move of the Introduction and Discussion sections in the NS and NNS corpora. The move analysis in the following section provides a rich linguistic context for, and facilitates the location and identification of the functions of the five selected hedging adverbs and adjectives in discourse. The analyses of the present study show how the selected adverbs and adjectives aid the writers in conveying their messages that serve different functions.

6.2.1 Distribution of hedging adverbs and adjectives across different rhetorical sections and rhetorical move types in the NS and NNS corpora

In this section of the study, this author takes a closer look at how the NS and NNS students instigated the use of hedging adverbs and adjectives in different sections and move types of their assignments. Table 22 presents the frequencies and co-occurrence patterns of hedging adverbs and adjectives under consideration in the different move types of Introduction and Discussion sections in the NS and NNS corpora.

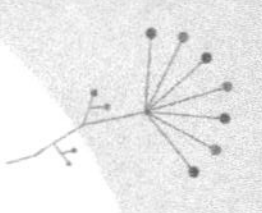

Table 22: Summary of Row Occurrences and Normalised Frequencies of *Often*, *Usually*, *Most*, *Perhaps* and *Possible* in Different Moves in Introduction and Discussion Sections

	NS—Introduction (110)			NS—Discussion (110)			NNS—Introduction (110)			NNS—Discussion (110)		
moves	establishing a territory (110)	establishing a niche (22)	occupying a niche (56)	consolidating important points (110)	stating limitations (39)	making suggestions (54)	establishing a territory (110)	establishing a niche (15)	occupying a niche (44)	consolidating important points (110)	stating limitations (19)	making suggestions (50)
often	26/0.94	20.90	3/0.62	37/0.67	3/2.26	0/0	39/0.58	1	0/0	17/0.36	0/0	1/0.47
usually	8/0.29	0/0	0/0	4/0.07	0/0	0/0	27/0.40	1	0/0	9/0.19	0/0	0/0
adverbial function of *most*	5/0.18	0/0	0/0	10/0.18	0/0	1/0.33	32/0.48	0	0/0	15/0.32	0/0	0/0
determiner *most*	5/0.18	0/0	0/0	29/0.53	0/0	0/0	20/0.30	0	0/0	4/0.09	0/0	0/0
perhaps	8/0.29	3/1.35	0/0	33/0.60	0/0	0/0	5/0.07	0	0/0	2/0.04	0/0	0/0
possible	18/0.65	2/0.90	4/0.82	37/0.67	0/0	0/0	9/0.13	3	2/0.23	8/0.17	0/0	2/0.93

* *Numbers in the row of 'moves' present how many assignments have each move listed in the table.*

* *The figures in the rows of 'would', 'may' and 'should' indicate the raw number/number per 1,000 words.*

Table 23: Hedging Adverbs and Adjectives and Their Co-occurrence Patterns in Each Move Type in the NS and NNS Corpora

	Move 1 (NS Corpus)	Move 4 (NS Corpus)	Move 1 (NNS Corpus)	Move 4 (NNS Corpus)
often	how *often* ADV v v-link ADV adv	ADV v v-link ADV adv/n	ADV v more *often* would *often* v-link ADV adv/n	more *often* ADV v v-link ADV adv/n
usually	v-link ADV adv ADV v	v-link ADV adv/n usually at initial position	usually at initial position v-link ADV adv ADV v	v-link ADV adv/n *usually* at initial position ADV v mod ADV
Adverbial function of *most*	ADV adj	ADV adj	*most* ADJ	*most* ADJ
determiner *most*	ADJ n	ADJ n	*most* n *most* of n in *most*	*most* n *most* of n
perhaps	v-link ADV adv/n *perhaps* at initial position	Perhaps at initial position v-link ADV n *that*-clause ADV	v-link ADV adv/n *that*-clause ADV	v-link ADV n
possible	It v-link ADJ to-inf It v-link ADJ that as adj as ADJ ADJ n	ADJ n *as* ADJ *as* adj *It* v-link ADJ *to-inf* *It* v-link ADJ *that*	*as* ADJ *as* adj ADJ n	*as* ADJ *as* adj ADJ n

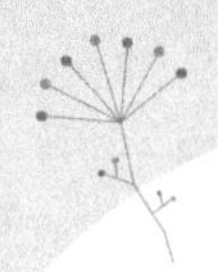

As has been stated in Section 6. 1, there are some similarities and differences between the NS and the NNS students in the use of hedging adverbs and adjectives. In the use of adverbs and adjectives to express hedging, the NS students seem to rely extensively on the frequency adverb *often*, adverb/adjective of degree *most*, probability adverb *perhaps*, and qualification adjective *possible* while in the NNS corpus, there is an overuse of the frequency adverb *usually*, but a low frequency of occurrence of *perhaps* and *possible* which are not popular used by the NNS students. Granger and Rayson (1998) discover that it is mainly the adverbs of frequency which are significantly overused by L2 English learners. Unlike the meanings and functions of various hedging devices, their contextual uses do not need to become very complicated. The uses of frequency adverbs are relatively easy for L2 writers to access.

These similarities and differences between the NS and the NNS groups in the overall use of hedging adverbs and adjectives were also seen in the distribution of hedging adverb and adjective use across the different move types of the Introduction and Discussion sections of their writing. Table 23 presents the moves in the Introduction and Discussion sections and summarises how the selected hedging adverbs and adjectives were used in each move.

As shown in Table 22, the distribution of selected hedging adverbs and adjectives in the NS and NNS corpus are not evenly distributed between the different rhetorical sections and rhetorical move types. As we can see from the table, while the NS writers used *often*, *perhaps* and *possible* the most in the Introduction sections of their writings, the NNS writers made frequent use of frequency adverbs *often*, *usually* and the adverbial form of *most* in the Introduction sections. All selected adverbs and the adjectives *often*, the adverbial form of *most*, *perhaps* and *possible*, except *usually* and

the determiner *most* were adopted most often by the NS writers in the Discussion sections. Whereas, except for *often* and determiner *most*, the other selected hedging adverbs and adjectives were hardly found in the Discussion sections of the NNS corpus. In consideration of these adverbs and adjectives in different move types, as shown in Table 22, two moves appear to be particularly salient with respect to the distribution of selected adverbs and adjectives: Move 1 'establishing a territory' and Move 4 'consolidating important points', which is consistent with the results of Gustilo's (2010) research on the uses of adverbs in Philippine English research articles. The move analysis of Gustilo's (ibid) research revealed that adverbs are extensively used in establishing the research territory, especially in reviewing previous studies. In the Discussion section, writers have a great need for adverbs in explaining/interpreting and reporting their findings. Adverbs played a role in establishing claims of knowledge associated with the Discussion section. Compared with hedging modal verbs and hedging lexical verbs, it is quite revealing that very few, or even no examples of adverbs or adjectives occurred in moves 'establishing a niche', 'occupying a niche', 'stating limitations' and 'making suggestions' in both the NS and the NNS corpora.

In Sections 6. 2. 2 and 6. 2. 3, the preferred co-occurrence patterns of the selected hedging adverbs and adjectives in each move as presented in Table 23 are discussed, and how they realised the rhetorical function of Move 1 and Move 4 are identified and interpreted in detail.

6. 2. 2 Hedging adverbs and adjectives in the move 'establishing a territory' of the Introduction sections

As underlined earlier, Move 1 'establishing a territory' was identified in all assignments of the NS and NNS corpora (see Table

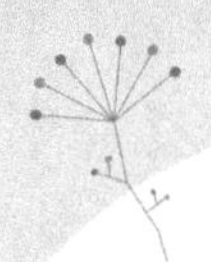

22), and it was often the opening move. The communicative function of the first move type is to introduce the topic of the study. As reviewed in Chapter 3, in order to show the originality of the research, the author needs to place the research in the context of existing knowledge in the field, which is done in the move 'establishing a territory'. The move 'establishing a territory' can be realised by claiming centrality, making topic generalisations and/or by reviewing, and usually evaluating, previous research (Swales 1990, 2004). It is observed that the Introduction sections include a relatively high number of the types of hedge that are typically linked to quantification, that is, adverbs and adjective hedges to do with indefinite frequency, indefinite degree, and approximation (Varttala 2001).

As Table 22 shows, both the NS and the NNS students use *often* the most and *perhaps* the least in this move type of their academic writings with varying percentages. However, they have different tendencies in the use of the other adverbs and adjectives. While the NS students use the hedging adjective *possible* the second most, the NNS students use the determiner *most* and the adverb *usually* with almost the same percentage the second most. It seems that the NNS students are in favour of using adverbs of frequency in expressing hedging in Move 1. In addition to the different frequencies of occurrence, these adverbs and adjectives are found to be used within different co-occurrence patterns to 'establish a territory' by the NS and NNS students.

6.2.2.1 Adverb of frequency *often* and *usually*

Adverbs of frequency ubiquitously function as hedges in written text. Based on Channell's (1994) findings of her corpus analysis, she specifies that the meaning of frequency adverbs is inherently vague and that they are used in similar contexts as other indefinite

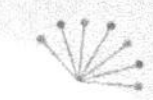

quantifiers or 'downtoners' (Hyland 1998a). They convey information about the frequency of events but do not provide either an exact absolute frequency (*this has occurred ten times*) or an exact relative frequency (*this occurs 10% of the time*). These items may be found 'when the language user, for one reason or another, does not want to or could not indicate the precise extent to which the information applies' (Varttala 2001: 128). Of significance is the prevalence of hedges expressing frequency (*usually* and *often*) in the move type 'establishing a territory' of the NNS writings in comparison with the NS corpus (*often*).

In Move 1, both the NS and the NNS students provide an introductory paragraph that serves to establish the 'research territory' (i. e. sharing background knowledge with their readers). Most of them 'claim centrality' of the topic by means of relevance adverbs of frequency (*often* and *usually*) in attributive positions as illustrated by the following instances:

> (21) In the past, during English courses, students are <accuracy-oriented_M1> often </accuracy-oriented_M1> uninterested in textbooks, and many of them feel that English classes are too difficult, uninteresting, useless, or impractical. To meet the students' needs, more and more schools begin to use multi-media equipment which can provide students a good environment for English study. At the same time, more people choose to study English on-line. There are also many schools set up courses on-line. Millions of English learners achieve benefits by the help of multi-media and network. (NNS corpus: 065)
>
> (22) Because of the culture differences between China and the West, especially those differences that relate to language, misunderstandings <accuracy-oriented_M1> often </accuracy-

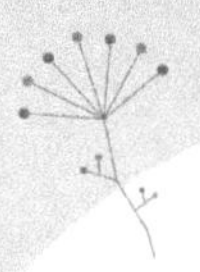

oriented_M1 > occur between Chinese and Westerners not simply because of grammatically inaccuracy or incorrect usage of vocabulary items, but also because of differences in customs and in the appropriacy of saying certain things in particular situation. (NNS corpus: 056)

(23) Tense is <accuracy-oriented_M1> often </accuracy-oriented_M1> viewed as a matter of time. It is used to describe time and therefore has the same qualities as time i. e. a past, a present and a future. In English, this expression of time is a property of a verb form. (NS corpus: 6059c)

(24) The term 'levels of language' refers to semantic, phonological, lexical and pragmatic development across language acquisition and use. Typical child language acquisition maps stages at which each of these 'levels' develop and become gradually more sophisticated, however, in atypical language development these 'levels' <accuracy-oriented_M1> often </accuracy-oriented_M1> appear impaired. (NS corpus: 6206d)

(25) A noun is a word used to name a person, animal, place, thing, and an abstract idea. Nouns are <accuracy-oriented_M1> usually </accuracy-oriented_M1> the first words which small children learn. A noun can function in a sentence as a subject, a direct object, an indirect object, a subject complement, an object, complement, an appositive, an adjective or an adverb. (NNS corpus: 009)

(26) Idioms are difficult to translate in that they are <accuracy-oriented_M1> often </accuracy-oriented_M1> of particular cultural origins. As an essential part of the language and culture of a society, idioms are characterized by their concise expressions, rich and vivid, involving geography, history,

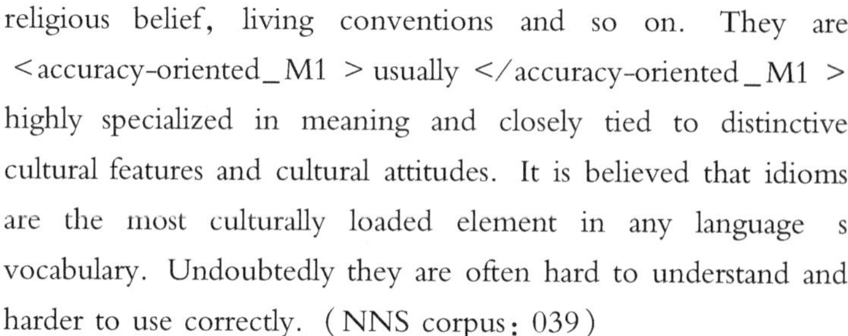

religious belief, living conventions and so on. They are <accuracy-oriented_M1 > usually </accuracy-oriented_M1 > highly specialized in meaning and closely tied to distinctive cultural features and cultural attitudes. It is believed that idioms are the most culturally loaded element in any language s vocabulary. Undoubtedly they are often hard to understand and harder to use correctly. (NNS corpus: 039)

In the above examples, the adverbs of frequency, whether *often* or *usually*, apparently convey a certain qualification with regard to the degree of accuracy of the proposition stated indicating that what is said is 'accurate within certain limits' (Hyland 1998a: 187). Syntactically, the adverbs *often* and *usually* frame verbs (*uninterest*, *occur*, *viewed*, *appear*, *learn* and *specialize* in above examples) by providing a sort of opinion or commentary. They provide modifying or additional meaning for the verbs that represent actions in writing, which helps to illustrate how often an action happens. The examples can thus be viewed as being marked by means of hedging so as to 'qualify the predicate intensity or the validity of the state of affairs expressed in the propositions' (op. cit.: 166). In sum, writers use the attribute hedges *often* and *usually* to seek precision in expression. The tentativeness and precision of expression in the step 'claiming centrality' of Move 1 enables the discourse community to accept the writer's view of the importance of doing research in the related area.

6.2.2.2 Adjective *possible*

The other frequently used hedging device to 'establish a territory' in the NS corpus is the probability adjective *possible*. As a familiar HD mentioned in Hyland's (1998a) study, one third of the examples of *possible* in the move 'establishing a territory' of the NS writing are used attributively with an apparently restricted, but

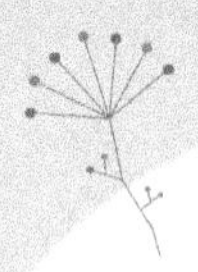

unspecified, range of nouns or noun phrases (such as *points*, *result*, *relationship*, *linguistic transfer* etc.). This data is substantially the same as that of Hyland's research (about 40% of the cases of *possible* occur in this syntactic environment).

> (27) Research has been undertaken on the pragmatics of hedging and its link to politeness, its social implications, and how it affects the negotiation of meaning between writer and reader (e. g. R. Lakoff 1972; Myers 1996; Salager-Meyer 1994). Several contrastive rhetoric studies have looked at hedging in different cultures (e. g. Mart & Burgess 2004) and the <accuracy-oriented_M1> possible </accuracy-oriented_M1> linguistic transfer that may result from attempts to hedge in the L2 (e. g. Clyne 1991; Hinkel 1997). (NS corpus: 0030)

In example (27), the writer uses *possible* to modify the noun phrase *linguistic transfer*. This noun phrase is the theme of the review of the previous research. The use of *possible* restricts the reference of the noun phrase *linguistic transfer* while still qualifying the writer's position. The use of *possible* in this context is epistemic, it does not refer to the physical objects in the real world, but to the states of affairs or abstract propositions which may or may not exist.

In sum, devices of these kinds can be used to express different extents of frequency (*often* and *usually*) or degrees of probability (*possible*) concerning the certainty or accuracy of what is being said, and they thus constitute typical groups of hedging devices. This view is supported by both Holmes (1988) and Hyland (1994), who suggest that adverbs of frequency and adjectives of probability occur rather frequently in academic writing. By using these hedging adverbs and adjectives as in the above examples, the writers display their tentative stance in claiming centrality or reviewing items of previous

studies to ‘establish a territory’ of their studies, which aims to indicate the writers' awareness of the fact that this part of the information is less certain. The attribution of information to a source constitutes an important feature of academic writing since it helps ‘writers to establish a persuasive epistemological and social framework for the acceptance of their arguments’ (Hyland 2004a: 22).

6.2.3 Hedging adverbs and adjectives in the move ‘consolidating important points’ of the Discussion sections

As can be seen from Table 22, selected hedging adverbs and adjectives were extensively used in the obligatory move ‘consolidating important points’ of the Discussion section. This move was identified in all the writings of the NS and NNS corpora (see Table 22). The move was realised by six steps, ‘giving background information’ and/or ‘stating results’, and/or ‘stating (un)expected outcomes’, and/or ‘referring to previous research’, and/or ‘making explanations’, and/or ‘making exemplifications’ (Hopkins & Dudley-Evans 1988; Dudley-Evans 2000). From the table we can see that the NS and NNS writers apply different strategies in their realisation of the move ‘consolidating important points’ by using different adverbs and adjectives. All selected hedging adverbs and adjectives, except *usually*, are heavily adopted by the NS students to ‘consolidate important points’ in their writings. However, only *often* and *most* are used by the NNS students. In addition, the NS and NNS students also show differences in their use of *most* to ‘consolidate important points’. The adverbial form of *most* is commonly used by the NS writers, while the NNS students favour the use of determiner *most* in this move.

In fact, regardless of adverb of frequency, adverb of probability, adverb of degree or adjective of probability, these adverbs and

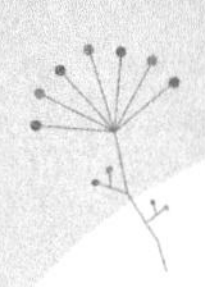

adjectives present similar functions. Adverbs of frequency, degree and probability are used to modify verbs and adjectives, and hedging adjectives are used to modify nouns and noun phrases in order to communicate meaning attributably. See extracts below for examples.

A) Adverb of frequency *often*

(28) In conclusion it is seen that time adds structure to a novel, conventionally, it is a factor that remains stable and constant. In comparison, dramas <accuracy-oriented_M4> often </accuracy-oriented_M4> use time in less conventional methods; this can make the plot more fantastic and dramatic. Due to the length of a novel, a lot of description can be conveyed to the reader. This allows the reader to internalise the characters and environment more intimately, which leads to a better understanding of the novel. (NS corpus: 3158b)

(29) Through analysis, we can find that: Most texts adopt simple Theme; Multiple and Clause Theme are rare; Marked Theme emphasizes circumstantial elements; Unmarked theme is <accuracy-oriented_M4>often </accuracy-oriented_M4> the same time the Simple Theme Simple Theme = Marked Theme + Unmarked Theme Register variable the sample cover letters Field: the specific job position the hunter is applying for Tenor: the job-seeker lowers interpersonal distance Mode: the applicant introduces himself Cohesion devices: References are used more <accuracy-oriented_M4>often </accuracy-oriented_M4> to achieve grammatical cohesion. Conjunction and repetition are frequently served as lexical cohesion devices. Substitution and ellipsis are rare in the cover letters. (NNS corpus: 001)

B) Adverbial form of *most* and determiner *most*

(30) To conclude, it would appear that what Dickens is

suggesting is that for those women who do not conform to the explicit and implicit expectations of society, instead choosing the reverse of their gender roles, the result is simply violence and chaos. This disorder is soon resolved when there is a return to the norm. In this respect it is possible to understand that amongst early Victorian society and literature, there was a very fixed understanding of how each gender should behave, and what positions in society are acceptable to them. Within the poetry of Browning these gender norms appear to be challenged, and perhaps confronted in order to raise awareness of the possibility of equality amongst men and women. Where Browning is aware of this possibility, Dickens seems very much convinced that the conception of the ' ideal woman' is there to guide those women in Victorian society to ensure they do not deviate, and experience the consequences deviation could incur. Barbara Bodichon <accuracy-oriented_M4 >most </accuracy-oriented_M4 > likely is reflecting an entirely accurate portrayal of how the Victorians perceived women and the attitude which was held against them. (NS corpus: 3129b)

(31) Findings of this study are mainly obtained through questionnaires and interviews. Major findings will be listed below. ... In the fourth year of the university, < accuracy-oriented_M4 > most </accuracy-oriented_M4 > students are busy with seeking job or making preparations for post graduate work. So they cannot finish 7 novels in the Selected Readings of Masterpieces. Therefore, some courses should be shortened or moved to a lower grade. (NNS corpus: 074)

C) Adverb of probability *perhaps*

(32) To sum up, the subject matter of the first three quatrains is mainly concrete. The poem mentions tangible objects

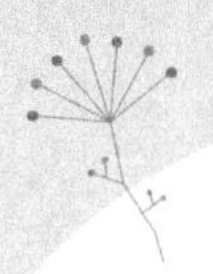

such as a room, a house, a fireplace and a page in a book, these are all concrete nouns. On the other hand, the focus of the last quatrain (age) is an abstract concept. Consequently, this stanza is more general. Unlike the others the thoughts expressed in it are not tied to a specific time and place. And <accuracy-oriented_M4>perhaps </accuracy-oriented_M4> <accuracy-oriented_M4>most </accuracy-oriented_M4> significantly, the immediate tense makes the action continuous and indefinite, rather like the daily routine of life itself. (NS corpus: 3066e)

(33) To conclude, it would appear that what Dickens is suggesting is that for those women who do not conform to the explicit and implicit expectations of society, instead choosing the reverse of their gender roles, the result is simply violence and chaos. This disorder is soon resolved when there is a return to the norm. In this respect it is possible to understand that amongst early Victorian society and literature, there was a very fixed understanding of how each gender should behave, and what positions in society are acceptable to them. Within the poetry of Browning these gender norms appear to be challenged, and <accuracy-oriented_M4>perhaps </accuracy-oriented_M4> confronted in order to raise awareness of the possibility of equality amongst men and women. (NS corpus: 3129b)

D) Adjective of probability *possible*

Possible is also frequently used by the NS writers in 'consolidating important points'. Like the use in the move 'establishing a territory' of the Introduction section, a large number of examples of *possible* are also found in the pattern of '*possible* N'. This use of *possible* is different from the way modal verbs and lexical verbs being were applied in 'consolidating important points' of the

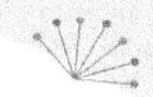

Discussion sections. As examples (34) and (35) illustrate, appearances of *possible* in the two examples attribute a possibility meaning to the modified nouns *combinations* and *reasons* without an evaluation of the writers' whole propositions. These instances of *possible* serve as attribute hedges to provide a more precise version of the propositions.

(34) In conclusion, it can be seen that there are many differing viewpoints on the area of tense in linguistics and this lack of certainty therefore makes it difficult to decide whether or not tense is a matter of syntax . All of these different <accuracy-oriented _ M4> possible </accuracy-oriented _ M4> combinations which can be used to refer to the future, therefore indicate that tense must be a matter of syntax as the correct arrangement of these words are essential in forming grammatically and linguistically correct sentences. (NS corpus: 6120c)

(35) This paper has analyzed the linguistic features of English and Chinese advertisements at lexical, syntactical, rhetorical and cultural levels, summarized similarities and differences of the two kinds of advertisements at different levels and gave <accuracy-oriented _ M4> possible </accuracy-oriented_M4> reasons. With the purpose of enabling English learners to better understand the linguistic features of both English and Chinese advertisements, better appreciate and experience the charm of advertising languages and improving their abilities of intercultural communication. (NNS corpus: 059)

The NNS students rely mainly on the use of *possible* combined with a noun within a very small number of occurrences of *possible* in their writings. However, the NS students also adopt *possible* in impersonal constructions '*it* v-link ADJ *to*-inf' (see Table 23).

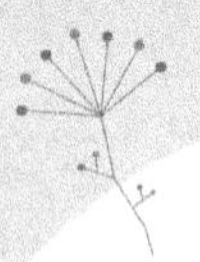

Charles (2000) argues that the pattern 'it v-link ADJ to-inf' such as examples (36) and (37) below is indeed rhetorically distinctive, in that they help to confer what she calls an 'appropriate academic persona' on the voice of the writer. The statement *it is possible to conclude that...* in example (36) is less face-threatening than its more confessional alternatives, such as *we conclude that...*. Charles also finds that '*it* v-link ADJ *to*-inf' is often used to construct a positive aura around the figure of the writer as a researcher, by exploiting the fact that, in this pattern, the adjective evaluates a to-infinitive clause, and thus by implication evaluates the performer of the action indexed by the to-infinitive verb itself. In example (36) below, it is the process of noting, as much as the proposition being noted, that is evaluated as 'possible', and, of course, it is the writer himself/herself who is doing this noting, and is therefore able to give such a claim at this point in his/her texts.

(36) It is <writer-oriented_M4> possible </writer-oriented_M4> to conclude that when determiners pre-modify the head of an NP, there are obligatory grammatical rules which mean they do so in a particular way depending on the type of determiner or the type of noun. English grammar handles combinations of determiners by application of grammatical rules like obligatory inclusion of preposition of for clusters of central determiners, and a general sequential rule taken from (Quirke, 1985). However, the requirement for agreement is applicable to other parts of speech which behave as pre-head modifiers. (NS corpus: 6048c)

(37) It seems that our language acquisition abilities have been evolutionarily programmed to allow us to acquire a socially constructed language from our parents. Nature also limits the

extent to which a child can create a language anew, a practical restriction which prevents the spontaneous creation of a new language by countless children born every day. It is <writer-oriented_M4>possible </writer-oriented_M4> for a group of children to create their own system of communication similar in complexity to LSN, but it is not <writer-oriented_M4> possible </writer-oriented_M4> for them to natively learn a unique and original language without input from the society around them. Perhaps this is nature's way of ensuring the transmission of language through the generations, so that grandparents can communicate with their grandchildren, and so that stories may be passed down from generation to generation. (NS corpus: 0032)

In the above two examples, important points are mainly consolidated by using impersonal constructions of *possible* '*it* v-link ADJ *to*-inf'. This enables the writers to have an evaluative stance in commenting on their findings with an epistemic possibility meaning.

Conclusion

In this chapter, it has been explored that the occurrence of selected hedging adverbs/adjectives and their rhetorical functions in the Introduction and Discussion sections of the NS and NNS student writing. It seems that the use of hedging adverbs and adjectives in the NS and NNS corpora has a twofold function: to interact with readers by evaluating the points and propositions in their texts and to promote the writers' claims by asserting that theirs is a correct interpretation of the topics. Hedging adverbs/adjectives seem to be present throughout the students' writing and with a major concentration in Introduction and Discussion parts where hedging plays a major role. The

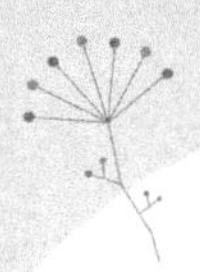

moderated attitude and comments on literature or findings expressed by hedging adverbs/adjectives are essential for the statements to be accepted by members of an academic community.

Quantitative analysis reveals that the NNSs students' use of hedging adverbs/adjectives is limited to the adverbs/adjectives *usually*, *often* and *most*, among which *usually* is largely overused. In contrast, the NS students seem to rely extensively on the probability adverb *perhaps* and the qualification adjective *possible*, which are neglected by the NNS students. The differences between the NS and the NNS groups may be due to the fact that the use of frequency adverbs is relatively easy to access by L2 writers, as argued by Granger and Rayson (1998).

In addition, concordance analysis shows that the NS and NNS groups use the selected hedging adverbs/adjectives in almost the same way (same co-occurrence patterns), except for one visible difference in the co-occurrence patterns of the hedging adjective *possible*. That is, the NNS students mainly use *possible* to modify nouns, while the NS students adopt *possible* in impersonal constructions 'it v-link ADJ to/that clause' in a large proportion. This difference directly impacts on the rhetorical function of *possible* in the Introduction and Discussion sections of the NS and NNS corpora. Move analysis of long extracts demonstrated that the pattern 'ADJ n' serves as attribute hedging in order to review previous studies accurately in the Introduction sections or to modify an aspect of a writer's claim without evaluating on the whole claim, in the Introduction or Discussion section. However, impersonal constructions of *possible* '*it* v-link ADJ *to/that* clause' are used to consolidate important points in Discussion sections. It enables the writers to have an evaluative stance in commenting on their findings with an epistemic possibility meaning.

The results of this chapter suggest that the NNS writers seem to

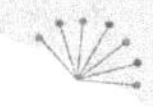

have mastered the usage of *usually*, *most*, *often* and *perhaps*, but they do not seem to use them appropriately in their writing. In the case of *possible*, it is likely that the NNS students have not mastered the use of *possible* in impersonal constructions to fulfil its rhetorical function in academic writing. It sounds sensible to remind the future teacher of the importance of paying attention to the different types of the use of *possible*.

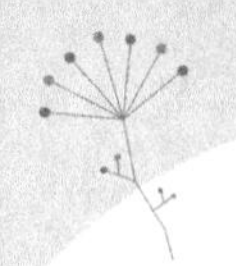

Chapter 7

Reconsidering the Role of Hedging in Academic Writing

Introduction

The use of HDs in students' writing can be viewed as a convention linked to the socially constructed expectation of the academic community, a convention with a variety of motivations (Hyland 1998a; Musa 2014). In inserting HDs into the different rhetorical moves of student assignments, writers can indicate that the information presented may not be categorically accurate or precise. It appears that in some cases HDs in student assignments may be viewed as a means of expressing caution. In brief, it can be seen from the analyses in Chapters 4 to 6, expressing caution may be seen as a strategy by which writers can, for instance, create research space in Introduction sections where HDs are employed to cautiously point toward limitations in earlier work, to present the value of their own contribution, and to put forward their own claims without presenting them as absolute. In the Discussion sections of student assignments, writers make use of HDs to delicately point toward the possible limitations of the research, to signal the uncertainties and inaccuracies potentially existing behind the results, or to bring out the tentative nature of the conclusions drawn and the generalisations

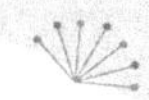

made. Since the data originated from one discipline, that is linguistic/English studies, naturally, it is necessary to make generalisations, cautiously concerning the expression of writer hedging using the ten selected HDs under discussion.

Chapters 4 to 6 characterise the ten selected HDs of the present study by relating frequency information to the description of forms and their meanings. The concordance analysis in these three chapters is based on the fact that meaning is observable through repeated patterns. The results of the concordance analysis relate the repeated patterns to the three categories of polypragmatic functions of HDs. The top-down corpus-based move analysis is based on a representative corpus of texts. The analyses of the rhetorical move types in Chapters 4 to 6 demonstrate the cumulative effect of hedging through a paper, and how students use different types of hedging to achieve different rhetorical purposes. By using different hedging forms, the NS and NNS students show that through presenting their claims with the precise degree of certainty, commitment and responsibility they wish to acknowledge, the NS and NNS students achieve academic accuracy, self-protection and deference to their audience in different move types to assist in fulfilling their rhetorical purposes. The analyses reveal the rhetorical impact of HDs.

This study has shown that the NS and NNS students have displayed, through the use of modal verbs, lexical verbs, adverbs and adjectives to express hedging, that they are aware of the fact that 'academic discourse is not just a mere collection of facts, unfolding in a direct and impersonal manner, and eventually leading to an inescapable truth' (Wishnoff 2000: 128). In the same vein, the NS and NNS students have demonstrated that they know the basic characteristics of HDs: to modify the writer's assertions, toning down uncertain or risky claims, emphasising what they believe to be true,

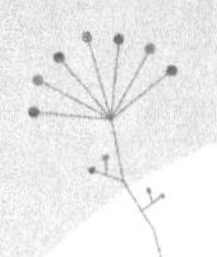

conveying appropriately collegial attitudes to potential readers and members of their discourse community and by protecting their reputation as researchers, avoiding absolute statements which might put themselves in an embarrassing situation (Hyland 1998a).

The previous chapters present the results of the study in three groups: hedging modal verbs, hedging lexical verbs and hedging adverbs and adjectives. The present section revisits the three aspects that the research aims address and explains how the current study identifies the main realisations of the ten selected HDs and brings together the results on the frequent collocations, colligations and polypragmatic functions (Section 7.1.1) and rhetorical features (Section 7.1.2) of these HDs in assignments written by the NS and NNS undergraduate students from English/linguistics departments.

7.1 Frequency

The frequency data, as the preliminary stage as discussed in Section 3.3, provides general information about the HDs evaluated in this study. The results of the frequency information show that the NS and NNS students display a difference in the overall use of different grammatical categories of lexical words to realise hedging. It is appropriate to discuss here how to compare the findings of this study with those of previous studies, so as to incorporate this study into the vast literature of hedging studies. First of all, when interpreting the findings of this study, readers must keep in mind the broad definition of 'hedging' and see the results as the effects of such an undertaking. For example, in this study the overall rate of HDs in the NS and NNS corpora is 18 and 14 per thousand words respectively (see p. 57). While the overall frequency of L2 HDs in Hyland & Milton's (1997) study is approximately 20 per thousand words and the overall frequency of HDs in the journal corpus (L1) is 20.9 per

thousand words in Hyland's (1998a) study. Can the findings from these studies be reconciled with each other? Before answering this question, it is necessary to review the definition of hedging and the nature of the data in Hyland (1998a) and Hyland & Milton's (1997) studies. It shows in Section 3.3.2 that the present study adopts a list of HDs from Hyland (2004), which Hyland compiles from the research literature on modality and his earlier work. Hyland (1998a) references published studies of epistemic or related notions in computer corpora, principally Holmes (1988) and Kennedy (1987). Hyland and Milton's (1997) research only includes the 75 most frequent epistemic expressions without covering any other categories. Obviously, their definition of hedging, which focuses on the expression of modality, is much narrower than the one in the present study. The broad definition of hedging given by Hyland (1998a) is adopted in this study. This covers several major categories of hedging: modal verbs, lexical verbs, adverbs, adjectives and nouns. Therefore, it seems reasonable to infer that the overall frequency of hedging in the NS corpus of this study could be equal to or greater than that in the two previous studies. However, the overall frequency of hedging in the NS corpus is 18 per thousand words which is slightly lower than the 20 per thousand words in Hyland and Milton's (1997) studies. In comparison with the NS group, the NNS corpus contains even fewer HDs. Another factor that needs to be considered is the corpora adopted in these studies. The Journal Corpus in Hyland's (1998a) study contains research articles in the field of cell and molecular biology. The corpora in Hyland and Milton's (1997) study are collections of essays written by Hong Kong and British pre-university students. Since the corpora in these studies contain papers in different disciplines and written by different levels of writers, the overall frequency information in these two previous studies can only

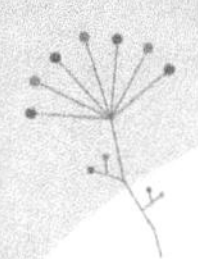

provide a general reference.

When considering HDs in different grammatical forms, modal verbs are the most frequent category of lexical HDs in both corpora in the present study, but the NS and NNS students behave differently in their use of hedging lexical verbs and adverbs. In the NS corpus, a wider range of hedging lexical verbs is used by the NS students and in a higher frequency than that in the NNS corpus. In the NNS corpus, students apply more hedging adverbs in terms of range and frequency than the NS students. Both groups use relatively few hedging adjectives and nouns, although the NS students use slightly more hedging adjectives and nouns than the NNS students. From the overview, we can see that the two corpora differ in a number of ways, but the most striking is the apparent overuse of hedging adverbs and the underuse of hedging lexical verbs in the NNS corpus. Since hedging adverbs are usually used to express 'degree', 'frequency', 'probability', 'qualification' and 'quantification', it could be argued that the NNS students express hedging to the extent of a certain quality or state in their assignments more often than the NS students. As discussed in Chapter 5, hedging lexical verbs *suggest* and *seem* are mainly used to report the findings of other researchers and at the same time express the degree of the writer's commitment to these findings. The low frequency and more limited choice of hedging lexical verbs in the NNS corpus show that the NNS students have problems in their use of lexical verbs to express hedging when presenting their findings and stating their claims. As mentioned in Chapter 5, this could indicate that the NNS students lack knowledge about how to use lexical verbs to hedge in student assignments.

From the frequency list in Chapter 3, we can also see that the NS and NNS students show similarities and differences across their assignments in the use of each single HD. For example, the use of

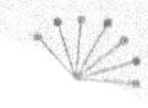

would in the NS corpus noticeably outnumbers other HDs. The NNS students employ *should* the most. As for the lexical verbs, *seem* and *suggest* are obvious in the NS corpus but virtually absent in the assignments written by the NNS students. The significant feature of the NNS data is the high presence of epistemic adverbs. However, the heavy reliance on the most frequent items—*most* and *often*—is found in both sets of data. The frequency statistics could indicate that being an NNS student makes a difference in the use of modal verbs, lexical verbs, adverbs and adjectives to express hedging in his/her writing. The results suggest that, in comparison with the NS students, the NNS students have a limited repertoire of lexical means to express uncertainty or tentativeness, and employed them with different frequency. However, as discussed in Chapter 3, the frequency information alone is not informative. The frequency information provides criteria for selecting HDs to be investigated in the present study, and it has to be interpreted in relation to the context provided by the texts. Ten HDs (three modal verbs, two lexical verbs and five adjectives and adverbs) are selected for a detailed concordance analysis and move analysis to understand HDs from the lexical and genre approaches.

7.2 Polypragmatic functions and co-occurrence patterns of HDs

Granted the above, the different uses of HDs can be seen as a performance of the NS and NNS students' adherence to the communally accepted rules of the academic community. It seems that in most of the cases in the NS and NNS corpora the rationale underlying hedging can be retraced to one or more of the motivations (e.g. hedges propositional content and/or hedges writer commitment and/or hedges assertiveness) categorised by Hyland's (1998a)

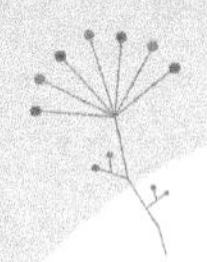

polypragmatic functions (accuracy-oriented, writer-oriented and reader-oriented hedging) discussed in Chapter 1.

The concordance interpretation in Chapters 4 to 6 provides a bottom-up point of view of the ten selected HDs. The concordance analysis is based on patterns in texts from the NS and NNS corpora. These co-occurrence patterns reveal relations between the forms of HDs and their polypragmatic functions in texts. The results of the study indicate that all of these HDs can fulfil functions in texts, where their meaning depends strongly on the combination with other text elements. The repeated patterns and the polypragmatic functions they shared reflect how meanings of HDs are characterised in texts. In Chapters 4 to 6, the findings are presented to illustrate the relation between the three polypragmatic functions and the common patterns used to express them.

Both the NS and the NNS students use the accuracy-oriented hedging function the most. There is no difference in the use of *would*, *may* and *should* to express accuracy-oriented hedging between the NS and the NNS groups. They show two common co-occurrence patterns 'MOD v' (performative verb in this case) and 'MOD adv' in conveying hedging to propositional content. These modal verbs express possibility, prediction or hypothesis to the action of the lexical action verbs or the adverbs precisely and tentatively signal the writer's interpretation to the propositional information in the text. As for lexical verbs, although lexical verb *suggest* has a low frequency in the NNS corpus, writers of both groups use it in roughly the same way to express accuracy-oriented hedging. When reviewing other researchers' work, 'author *suggests*' is the preferred co-occurrence pattern that both the NS and the NNS students use to express the writer's desire to explicitly state the commitment of knowledge. As argued by Varttala (2001) and Hyland (1998a), adverbs and

adjectives are among the more frequently identified HDs and the main source of accuracy-oriented hedging. Although the frequency of selected adverbs and adjectives varies (e. g. overuse of *usually* or underuse of *possible* by the NNS students compared with the NS students), generally the NS and NNS students use these adverbs and adjectives in a similar way to convey accuracy-oriented hedging. That is, hedging adverbs lower the force of the verb they modify and hedging adjectives express the frequency, degree or probability information of the phenomena they modify within the propositions.

In the writer-oriented hedging category, the major differences between the two groups with respect to the frequency and range of the use of HDs and hedging expressions, occurred in relation to modal verbs, lexical verbs and adjectives in impersonal constructions (co-occurring with 'abstract rhetors' or an empty subject). In general, the NS students use more writer-oriented hedging, and employ a wider range of expressions to mark writer-based strategy of hedging than the NNS students. The modal verbs *would* and *may* in impersonal constructions are main expressions for both the NS and the NNS students to perform writer-oriented hedging. Verbs, adverbs and adjectives are also employed to express writer-oriented hedging in some forms. In this study, the NNS students use substantially fewer examples of the lexical verb *suggest* than the NS students where a higher level claim with limited personal commitment is needed in academic writing. Such underuse indicates that the NNS students are having difficulties integrating their voice within the proposition itself. For adverbs, generally both the NS and the NNS students do not employ the selected adverbs *most*, *usually* and *often* as writer-oriented hedges. They place the adverb *perhaps* at the beginning of sentences to convey the writer's attitude or value judgment towards the whole propositional content. *Perhaps* with a probable meaning performs the

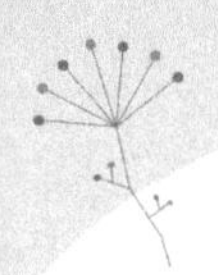

pragmatic function of hedging the writer's commitment to the content of the proposition, while leaving its truth value open. Moreover, the NS students use the adjective *possible* in the impersonal construction '*it* v-link ADJ *to/that* clause' to hedge the writer's commitment more than the NNS students.

In the reader-oriented hedging category, the NS students use a wider range of linguistic expressions than the NNS students as shown in Table 11 and Sections 5.2.1.1 and 6.1.5. The major differences occur with respect to modal verbs in attributing to a personal source, making recommendations or suggestions, referring to shared assumptions, and using hypothetical conditionals to suggest alternative interpretations or possibilities.

In making recommendations or suggestions, the preferred forms by the NS and NNS students are modal verbs rather than lexical verbs, adverbs or adjectives. Both groups express reader-oriented hedging mainly by specifying a personal source. The personal pronouns *we*, *our*, *I* and *my* are used to acknowledge the writer's personal views. Although there are no differences with regard to attributing a personal source, the NS and NNS students had different preferences in the use of the modal verbs *would* and *should* in this personal construction (cf. Sections 4.1.3.1.1 & 4.2.2.2). By generalising co-occurrence patterns from the concordance lines, an excessive use of *we should* is noticed in the NNS corpus, which is rarely seen in the NS corpus. As argued in Chapter 4, the diversity is likely to be due to the thinking and cultural differences in making arguments and suggestions in academic writing between the NS and the NNS students. Culture has a great influence on people's concept in spoken or written communication, especially for Chinese learners of English. They need to develop sensitivity to explicit and implicit western culture and its impact on communication (Zhu 2011). Both

EAP teachers and learners are expected to pay attention not only to the negative transfer but also to the fact that the cultural difference may raise great barriers to EAP learners.

'Addressing readers directly' (see Section 4. 1. 3. 1. 2) is another reader-oriented strategy to make recommendations or suggestions, but it is only found to be used by the NS students in the data of this study. Sometimes, writers wish to address readers directly, in order to accomplish the rhetorical goal of making suggestions and leave room for the potential readers to evaluate. As discussed in Chapter 4, the lack of use of the reader-oriented strategy of 'addressing readers directly' in making recommendations and suggestions could be due to the fact that the NNS students may have not been exposed to enough information about how and why to address readers in academic writing. Therefore, it is essential for the NNS students to receive guidance on how to address readers in academic writing to make reader-oriented suggestions, and they should be informed when this strategy is appropriate or inappropriate.

Furthermore, only the NS students suggest alternative interpretations or possibilities by using hypothetical conditionals in their assignments. Hypothetical conditionals are expressed by means of *if*-clauses in combination with the hedging model verb *would*. It would appear that the NNS students, in general, have difficulty in using *if*-clauses in combination with modal verbs in the past form. As explained in Section 4. 1. 3. 1. 3, this could be due to the construction being difficult for the NNS students to master or not enough information on hypothetical conditionals being given to them. It may, therefore, be necessary to show students how to express alternative interpretations or possibilities using *if*-clauses combined with a modal verb. In addition, because hypothetical conditionals are often stated in academic texts in ways that may not be obvious to NNS students, it

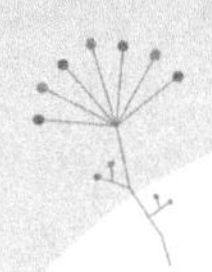

may be important to draw students' attention to the language that is used in formulating hypothetical conditionals and how this expression can be used to hedge.

7.3 Hedging as a textual feature in academic writing

Apart from being taken as a reflection of the uncertainties or inaccuracies encountered by researchers during the research process and of the intercommunal discretion expected in academic discourse, the strategy of hedging may be viewed from yet another perspective. Move analysis in Chapters 4 to 7 shows that HDs also have rhetorical functions which interact with other rhetorical features contributing to the persuasiveness of an academic paper.

As reviewed in Chapter 1, the rhetorical purposes of the Introduction sections are traditionally explained according to Swales's CARS model (1990): 'establishing a territory', 'establishing a niche' and 'occupying the niche'. Swales (1990) explains that the main function of the Introduction is to justify the reasons for the investigation and to make claims about statements from other research. This can be done by showing that the 'author's contribution to the discipline, whilst previously established as significant and reference-worthy, is as yet incomplete' (Swales 1990: 138). It seems natural that when academic writers are establishing a position for their work among those of other researchers, their language is cautious. The most useful strategy to make a cautious approach in introducing their views towards other studies is provided by hedging. HDs may be employed there in a variety of contexts, for instance when the writers point out the gap or shortcomings of the previous work or introduce their own research project and its importance (Varttala 2001: 159).

As can be seen from Tables 14 (Section 4.2.1), 17 (Section

5.4.1) and 22 (Section 6.2.1), hedging mostly takes the form of modal verbs, adverbs and adjectives in the Introduction sections of both the NS and the NNS corpora. Modal verbs *would* and *may*, adverb *often* and adjective *possible* are the most used HDs in the Introduction sections of the NS corpus. Hedging lexical verbs *suggest* and *seem* were also used by the NS students in Introduction sections, but with a much lower frequency of occurrence compared with other categories of HDs and with that in Discussion sections of the NS corpus while the modal verbs *should*, *may* and *would*, adverbs *often*, *usually*, *most* and determiner *most* and adjective *possible* are the most used HDs in the Introduction sections of the NNS corpus. In addition to the frequency differences of selected HDs between the two corpora, the NS and NNS students showed some similar different collocational preferences in the use of each HD to convey different rhetorical functions in the Introduction sections.

The patterns 'MOD v' (*would/may/should* + performative verb) and 'author *suggest*', identified in the Introduction sections in both corpora can be interpreted as accuracy-oriented hedging, which the writers employ to interpret or review the results of previous research in order to establish a territory for their own work. By claiming centrality, making topic generalisation and/or citing numerous studies to build an argument to support their own work, the patterns 'ADV v' and 'ADJ n' are also found in the NS and NNS corpora, but with a different choice of hedging adverb or adjective. The NNS students are found to overuse the adverb *usually* but underuse the adjective *possible* in conveying accuracy-oriented hedging through patterns like 'ADV v' (*usually*) and 'ADJ n' (*possible*). Both the NS and the NNS students realise the third move 'occupying the niche' by describing the purpose of their research with a preference in use for the hedging modal verb *would* as a reader-

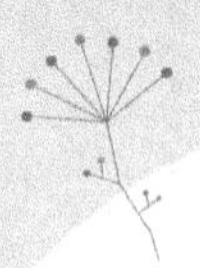

oriented hedging device (*we/I would*).

Discussion sections in this study turn out to be the most heavily hedged in both the NS and the NNS corpora, which corresponds with previous findings (Salager-Meyer 1994; Varttala 2001), and is linked to the kind of information presented in this part. The primary rhetorical function of this section is to make claims about the research findings, to summarise results, state conclusions and suggestions with reference to previous research and/or to the current work, to set further questions, sometimes with possible explanations, references and future developments and applications in the field of study. Thus, the very high frequency of HDs in this section, as compared to that observed in other sections is due to the fact that the claim is the core of the Discussion section. It is in this section of student assignments that writers speculate, argue, contrast the described results, and at the same time avoid stating results too conclusively so that readers can note that the writers are not claiming to have the final word on the subject. Hyland (1998a) expresses that for every explanation of the results, there might always be some alternative explanation somebody else might come up with. This explains why it is in this section of the NS corpus that compound hedges are most frequently used. By applying such expressions of hedging, researchers can avoid absolutes and thus indicate exactly the degree of certainty with which they present their discussion and also how strongly they want to align themselves with their claims. Room for disagreement is provided in this way. The presented examples in Chapters 4, 5 and 6 illustrate the fact that HDs are a consequence of the fact that research results are indicative rather than definitive.

In the Discussion sections, the NS students use a large number of modal verbs, among which *would* is the most frequent, followed by *may* and *should*. Hedging lexical verbs is another category of HDs

frequently used by the NS students in the Discussion sections of their writing. The NS students also have make extensive use of the frequency adverb *often*, the adverb/determiner of degree *most*, the probability adverb *perhaps*, and the qualification adjective *possible* in their Discussion sections. In contrast, in the Discussion sections of the NNS corpus, students are found using the hedging modal verb *should* the most frequently, followed by *may* and *would*. The adverb *often* and the adjectival form of *most* are also found in Discussion sections of the NNS corpus, but with a relatively lower frequency of occurrence compared with modal verbs. In comparison with the NS corpus, the biggest difference is that very few occurrences of lexical verbs *suggest* and *seem*, the adverb *perhaps* and the adjective *possible* are found in the Discussion sections of the NNS corpus. The use of impersonal expressions of modal verb *would* and *may* is a common feature shared by the NS and NNS data. However, the uses of impersonal expressions of the lexical verbs *suggest* and *seem* and the adjective *possible* as writer-oriented hedging show differences between the NS and the NNS data. This result indicates that Chinese students seem not to fully grasp the way to express their claims with a writer-oriented HD. There might be a risk that the claims of the findings of the NNS students turn out not be true and that they fail to gain acceptance from the potential reader. Moreover, there is an inappropriate use of the pattern *we should* by the NNS students to make suggestions in their Discussion sections. As analysed in Chapter 5, this abnormal use of the hedging modal verb *should* is most likely due to Chinese cultural transfer in foreign language use and may lead to difficulties in understanding.

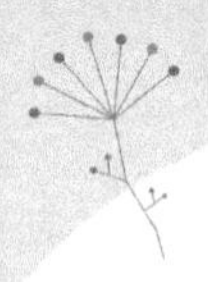

Chapter 8

Contributions of the Book

This book has made a significant contribution to the state of knowledge about HDs in Chinese undergraduate student assignments in English. In the present chapter, the major findings from the current study are highlighted and the significance of their contributions to the study of hedging in academic discourse are discussed. The findings have answered the research questions in this study and have helped to achieve the study's overall goals. The three main research questions set out in Chapter 3 are:

(1) What are the most frequent HDs in the NS and NNS corpora?

(2) What are the collocations or co-occurrence patterns of the use of HDs in the NS and the NNS corpora?

(3) How do HDs with different co-occurrence patterns or collocations interact with other rhetorical features in the move types of the Introduction and Discussion sections to perform particular communicative purposes?

These research questions are designed to characterise HDs in different aspects: frequency information, co-occurrence patterns and rhetorical features. They discuss how students from the NS and NNS groups seek to vary their expression of possibilities and manipulate their attitudes to the truth of statements through the combination and

concentrations of HDs. Reasons underlying the results have been investigated and the relationship between the results of the current study and previous studies reviewed in Chapter 1 has also been compared and discussed.

The contribution of the current study has been methodological and descriptive, rather than modification or extensions of current theories of hedging, since the analysis is based on an existing framework (Hyland 1998a). The methodological contribution has been the combined approach of corpus linguistics and move analysis to characterise the use of HDs in English student assignments written by Chinese undergraduate students. From the literature survey in Chapter 2, with respect to hedging in student assignments, it can be seen that very few attempts have been made to focus on the linguistic characteristics of HDs in rhetorical moves. Generally, studies have focused on frequency and distribution of HDs in academic writings. The descriptive aspect of the contribution of the current study is the fact that the ability to write papers in English is important for undergraduate English/linguistics students in China. The need for continuing research into student academic writing in English in China for the purposes of helping student writers develop authentic, critical voices as they feel their way into academic discourses is argued in Chapter 2. The descriptive contribution lies in providing a detailed account of the NNS students' academic writing, and indicating where the deficiencies lay with regard to the NS students' writing. The quantitative results and the qualitative description could be used to inform further hedging analyses, and in the teaching of hedging in academic writing, more specifically in assignments to students. Section 8.1 discusses the methodological effects which resulted from the corpus theoretical approach and corpus-based move analysis. The implications of results for teaching HDs in academic writing in L2

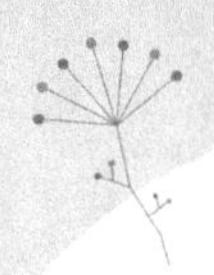

contexts are discussed in section 8.2.

8.1 The methodology of corpus study and genre study

The corpus linguistics methodology adopted in this study undertook linguistic description of HDs by examining collections of authentic data. The authentic data used in the current study are the NS and NNS corpora. One important achievement of this study is the fact that this author builds her own corpus (the NNS corpus) within the first year of her PhD programme. The corpus is compiled following the main criteria for building a corpus to the best of her knowledge. This corpus is unique, since it is especially designed for the current study, which contains 162 student assignments in English written by Chinese undergraduate students from English/Linguistics departments.

Various theoretical concepts and frameworks such as Hunston and Francis's (2000) Pattern Grammar, Hoey's (2005) concept of Lexical Priming or Sinclair's (1999) the Idiom Principle have emerged from corpus-linguistic approaches to language. Moreover, corpus linguistics has been shown to be particularly compatible with contemporary usage-based linguistic frameworks, including move analysis (Swales 1981, 1990). The present study suggests a link to a methodology that has been developed by Biber *et al.* (2007): the top-down corpus based move analysis. This method provides a comprehensive communicative and linguistic description of student assignments, uncovering the typical linguistic characteristics of HDs of each move type. The current corpus study is characterised by the relationship between the bottom-up concordance analysis and top-down corpus-based move analysis.

Frequency is the selection criterion of the HDs to be examined in the current study. It also provides basic information in the detailed

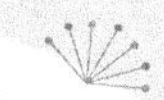

concordance analysis and move analysis. As the aim is to investigate co-occurrence patterns, polypragmatic functions and rhetorical functions of the HDs, the number of examples has to be limited to make the task manageable. By starting with basic frequency lists, the ten investigated HDs are the typical devices with hedging expression used by the NS and NNS students.

Concordance analysis in Chapters 5 to 7 observes a large number of linguistic features and polypragmatic functions of HDs which illustrate the relationship between the meaning and form of HDs. Move analysis in Chapters 5 to 7 associates these linguistic features and polypragmatic functions with the different communicative purposes of each move type. Chapters 5 to 7 and the discussion in Section 8.1 have shown how the results of corpus-based top-down move analysis and the bottom-up concordance analysis complement each other in describing HDs. The results of the study stress the importance of this combined approach to interpreting HDs in academic writing. In Chapter 3, it has been argued that corpus linguistic studies are generally considered to be used as a method to describe the use of linguistic forms in context. For example, in this study HDs are described in terms of their typical collocates. Grammatical variation is also described in terms of the HDs and grammatical structures that occur in the context. However, the bottom-up concordance analysis itself cannot fully describe how HDs are used in academic discourse (student assignments in this study), since HDs also interact with other rhetorical features to maintain the communicative purposes of rhetorical moves. Therefore, corpus-based move analysis is focusing on the study of linguistic variation, showing how linguistic choice of HDs is systematic and principled when considered in rhetorical moves. The study of discourse organisation is usually based on detailed analysis of a single text, resulting in a qualitative linguistic

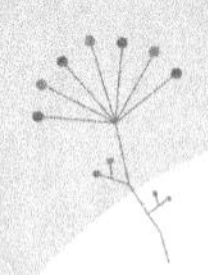

description of the textual organisation. In contrast, corpus studies are based on analysis of all texts in a corpus, utilising quantitative measures to identify the typical distributional patterns that occur across texts.

In conclusion, the combined method illustrates HDs in three aspects: frequency, linguistic choices, and rhetorical functions. Thus the study contributes to applying a corpus-based method to the description of discourse organisation. The integration of top-down corpus-based move analysis and bottom-up concordance analysis results in the identification of the linguistic features of HDs associated with each move type.

8.2 Implications for teaching of HDs in academic writing

The analysis of hedging undertaken in this book is a study of the written product. It is important to note that the teaching of writing is not the concern of this study. However, one of the most important implications of this study is the need to underline the significance of genre knowledge and purposes of the different rhetorical moves of student assignments and how they determine writer hedging for the NNS students who aspire to be able to address their global discourse community. It is essential for the NNS students to be aware of and follow the conventions of this discourse community, which necessitates pragmatic knowledge besides lexico-grammatical knowledge of HDs.

Another important implication of this study might be raising the awareness of English language tutors in Chinese universities of the significance of expressing writer hedging appropriately in academic writing. Some suggestions will be made regarding some implications of the present study for the teaching of hedging in academic writing to Chinese undergraduate students in the English/Linguistics

department, for whom academic writing in English is a qualification requirement. This author's suggestions for the teaching of academic writing are made in relation to the findings pertaining to the collocations and colligations of HDs, the three polypragmatic hedging functions and how the purposes of the different rhetorical moves in academic writing determine writer hedging. Overall, it should be remembered that, in comparison with the NNS student writers, the NS students not only use HDs and concomitant hedging functions to a much greater extent, but also employ a wider range of expressions in doing so.

The main differences exist in reader-oriented and writer-oriented categories of hedging. It is found that the NS students use not only more HDs, but also a wider range of linguistic expressions than the NNS students. In the reader-oriented category, the main differences regarding the extent of use occur with respect to modal verbs in making recommendations or suggestions, using personal attributions, referring to the reader directly, and using hypothetical conditionals to suggest alternative interpretations or possibilities. The NS students mainly resort to modal verbs *would*, *may* and *should* when making recommendations or suggestions. Only the NS students address potential readers directly and suggest alternative interpretations or possibilities. The absence of addressing potential readers directly and suggesting alternative interpretations or possibilities may be because students do not have the necessary background to do so (cf. Section 4.1.3.1). The overuse of the personal strategy *we should* in giving out recommendations and suggestions in the NNS students' writing may have something to do with their first language transfer (cf. Section 4.1.3.1). In the writer-oriented hedging category, the major difference between the two groups of students is in the use of the lexical verb *suggest*, adjective *possible* and adverb *perhaps* as writer-

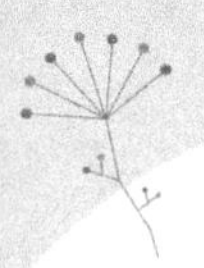

oriented HDs. Although the NNS students use the same patterns of *suggest* to express writer-oriented hedging as the NS students, the NS writers use the lexical verbs *suggest* to a far greater extent than the NNS students. Regarding *possible* and *perhaps*, it is found that the NNS students do have difficulty in using *possible* in the pattern '*it* v-link ADJ *to/that*' and *perhaps* as sentence hedging adverb to express writer-oriented hedging. Again, it is suggested that the NNS students be exposed to the different patterns of *possible* and *perhaps* that could be used as writer-oriented HDs.

In spite of these, though, it is important that undergraduate students, especially those for whom academic writing is a qualification requirement, be informed about reader-oriented HDs, and be shown the kinds of linguistic expressions that could be used in order to accomplish particular reader-oriented hedging functions. Various strategies could be used. For example, the students could analyse NS writers' academic writing in their field of study to see how professional writers express reader-oriented and writer-oriented functions. In addition to examining what kinds of expressions are used, students could examine more closely the kinds of expressions that professional writers use to state claims, generalise results, make recommendations, specify a personal source, refer directly to readers, and suggest alternative interpretations or possibilities. To teach specific linguistic patterns within a particular move, for example, how hypothetical conditionals are stated using *if*-clauses in combination with modal verbs, or how writer-oriented hedging is expressed by using *possible* in pattern 'it v-link ADJ to/that' and *perhaps* as a sentence HD exposure to these patterns could be beneficial. It may be necessary to give the students the opportunity to explore the use and the expressions of reader-oriented and writer-oriented hedging in both academic writing and professional papers. This, however, will take

time, and will require consistent and sufficiently detailed feedback from the tutor of the academic writing course. This, of course, applies to the other two hedging categories as well.

Another main implication of this book is the pressing need to underline the significance of the genre knowledge and the purposes of the different rhetorical sections of student assignments and how they determine writer-oriented hedging for the NNS academic writer who aspires to be able to address his/her global discourse community.

To conclude, the aim of the book is to examine the similarities and differences in linguistic and rhetorical features of HDs between the NS and the NNS corpora. With the similarities and differences observed in the data studied, this book has discussed the potential reasons for the similarities and differences and a number of possibilities of interpreting HDs in the different contexts. Despite the complexities, problems, and shortcomings that the present work no doubt includes, this book has not only presented useful information pertaining to the role of hedging in academic writing but also illustrated that there is still room for further research on HDs.

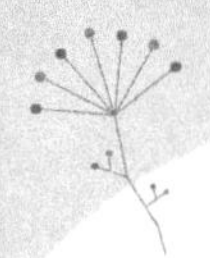

Appendices

A: Pattern Codes

Hunston & Francis's (2000:45) pattern codes, plus additional codes used in the present work.

v:	verb group
v-inf:	the base form of verb (infinitive)
v-s:	present form of verb
v-ing:	present participle form of verb
past pple:	past participle form of verb
n:	noun group
adj:	adjective group
adv:	adverb group
det:	determiner group
that:	clause introduced by *that* (realised or not)
-ing:	clause introduced by an '-ing' form
to-inf:	clause introduced by a *to*-infinitive form
wh:	clause introduced by a wh-word (including *how*)
with quote:	used with direct speech
to:	clause introduced by *to*
mod:	modal verb group
v-link:	link verb
per. v:	performative verb groups
JP:	adjective phrase
IP:	infinitive phrase
X:	intervening constituent

B: Hedging Functions and the Co-occurrence Patterns with Raw Occurrences of Modal Verbs Often Used to Express Them (100 Concordance Lines for Each Modal Verb)

	Reader-oriented		Writer-oriented		Accuracy-oriented			Reader-oriented		Writer-oriented		Accuracy-oriented	
NS Corpus	hedges assertiveness		hedges writer commitment		hedges propositional content		NNS Corpus	hedges assertiveness		hedges writer commitment		hedges propositional content	
	F	patterns	F		F	patterns		F	patterns	F	patterns	F	patterns
would	11	Hypothetical: would (3) personal attribution (7) addressing reader directly: one would (1)	11	empty subjects: it, this, there (9)	78	would performative verb/ adverb (71)	*would*	5	personal attribution: *I would* (5)	18	empty subject: *it*, *this*, *there* (13)	80	*would* performative verb/ adverb (72)
may	6	personal attribution (3) addressing reader directly: one may (2)	30	empty subjects: it, this, there (15)	64	may perfor-maitve verb/ adverb (63)	*may*	6	personal attribution: *we may* (6)	28	empty subject: *it*, *this*, *there* (17)	66	*may* perfor-maitve verb/ adverb (66)
should	37	make suggestion: *should be* + *past pple/ should be* (26)	0	N/A	63	should performative verb/ adverb (35)	*should*	58	personal attribution: *we should* (10) make suggestion: *should be* + *past pple/ should be* (44)	0	N/A	42	*should* performative verb/ adverb (31)

* *F*: *Frequency*

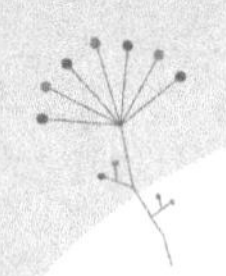

Bibliography

Aarts, J. & Granger, S. 1998. Tag sequences in learner corpora: A key to interlanguage grammar and discourse. In Granger, S. (ed.), *Learner English on computer*. London: Longman, 132 – 141.

Adams-Smith, D. E. 1984. Medical discourse: Aspects of author's comment. *The ESP Journal*, 3:25 – 36.

Adel, A. 2006. *Metadiscourse in L1 and L2 English*. Amsterdam: John Benjamins.

Ahmad, U. 1997. Research articles in Malay: Rhetoric in an emerging research community. In Duszak, A. (ed.), *Culture and styles of academic discourse*. Austin, TX: De Gruyter.

Allison, D. 1995. Why often isn't always. In Nunan, D., Berry, R. & Berry, V. (eds.), *Language awareness in language education*. Hong Kong: University of Hong Kong, Department of Curriculum Studies, 33 – 50.

Alsop, S. & Nesi, H. 2009. *The British academic written English (BAWE) corpus*. Coventry university, UK.

Anthony, L. 1999. Writing research articles introductions in software engineering: How accurate is a standard model? *IEEE Transactions on Professional Communication*, 42: 38 – 45.

Anthony, L. 2011. *AntConc (Version 3. 2. 2)* [Computer Software]. Tokyo: Waseda University. Available from http://www.antlab.sci.waseda.ac.jp/.

Arbor, A. 2009. *The Michigan corpus of upper-level student papers*. University of Michigan, USA.

Atai, M. & Sadr, L. 2006. A cross-cultural genre study on

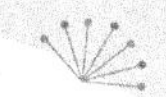

hedging devices in discussion section of applied linguistics research articles. Proceedings of the 11th Conference of Pan-pacific Association of Applied Linguistics, 42 – 57.

Atai, M. & Sadr, L. 2008. A cross-cultural genre study on hedging devices in discussion section of applied linguistic research articles. *Journal Teaching English Language and Literature Society of Iran*, 7(2): 42 – 57.

Austin, J. L. 1962. *How to do things with words*. Cambridge, MA: Harvard University Press.

Baker, P. 2006. *Using corpora in discourse analysis*. London: Continuum.

Barlow, M. 2005. Learner corpora. In Ellis, R. and Barkhuizen, G. (eds.), *Analyzing learner language*. Oxford: Oxford University Press.

Barnbrook, G. 1996. *Language and computers: A practical introduction to the computer analysis of language*. Edinburgh: Edinburgh University Press.

Bartsch, S. 2009. Patterns of verb colligation and collocation in scientific discourse. Corpus Linguistics Conference, Liverpool, UK.

Bazerman, C. 1988. *Shaping written knowledge*. Madison, WI: University of Wisconsin Press.

Bernhardt, S. A. 1985. The writer, the reader, and the scientific text. *Journal of Technical Writing Communication*, 15(2): 163 – 174.

Bhatia V. K. 1993. *Analysing genre. Language use in professional settings*. London & New York: Longman.

Biber, D. 2006. Stance in spoken and written university registers. *Journal of English for Academic Purposes*, 5: 97 – 116.

Biber, D., Conard, S. & Leech, G. 2002. *Longman student grammar of spoken and written English*. Washington, DC: Author.

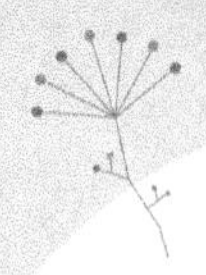

Biber, D., Conard, S. & Reppen, R. 1998. *Corpus linguistics: Investigating structure and use*. Cambridge: Cambridge University Press.

Biber, D., Connor, U. & Upton, T. 2007. *Discourse on the move: Using corpus analysis to describe discourse structure*. Amsterdam: John Benjamins.

Biber, D., Johansson, S., Leech, G., Conrad, S. & Finegan, E. 1999. *Longman grammar of spoken and written English*. Essex: Longman.

Bird, S., Klein, E. & Loper, E. 2009. *Natural language processing with Python: Analyzing text with the natural language toolkit*. Sebastopol, California: O'Reilly Media.

Bisenbach-Lucas, S. 1994. A comparative genre analysis: The research article and its popularization. Unpublished doctoral dissertation, Georgetown University.

Blankenship, K. L. & Holtgraves, T. 2005. The role of different markers of linguistic powerlessness in persuasion. *Journal of Language and Social Psychology*, 24: 3 – 24.

Bloor, M. & Bloor, T. 1991. Cultural expectations and socio-pragmatic failure in academic writing. In Adams, P., Heaton, B. & Howarth, P. (eds.), *Socio-cultural issues in English for academic purposes*. London: Macmillan.

Bloor, M. & Bloor, T. 1993. How economists modify propositions. In Willie, H., Tony, D. & Roger, B. (eds.), *Economics and language*. London/New York: Routledge.

Brown, G. & Levinson, S. 1978. Universals in language usage: Politeness phenomena. In Goody, E. N. (ed.), *Questions and politeness*. Cambridge: Cambridge University Press, 56 – 310.

Brown, G. & Levinson, S. 1987. *Politeness: Some universals in language usage*. Cambridge: Cambridge University Press.

Butler, C. 1990. Qualifications in science: Modal meanings in scientific texts. In Nash, W. (ed.), *The writing scholar: Studies in academic discourse.* Newbury Park, CA: Sage.

Bybee, J., Perkins, R. & Pagliuca, W. 1994. *The evolution of grammar: Tense, aspect and modality in the languages of the world.* Chicago: University of Chicago Press.

Channell, J. 1994. *Vague language.* Oxford: Oxford University Press.

Chafe, W. L. 1986. Evidentiality in English conversation and academic writing. In Chafe, W. L. & Nichols, J. (eds.), *Evidentiality: The linguistic coding of epistemology.* Norwood, N. J.: Ablex, 261 – 272.

Charles, M. 2000. The role of an introductory it pattern in constructing an appropriate academic persona. In Thompson, P. (ed.), *Patterns and perspectives: Insights into EAP writing practice.* Reading: The University of Reading, CALS.

Charles, M. 2004. The construction of stance: A corpus-based investigation of two contrasting disciplines. Unpublished doctoral dissertation. Birmingham, UK: University of Birmingham.

Charles, M. 2006a. Phraseological patterns in reporting clauses used in citation: A corpus-based study of theses in two disciplines. *English for Specific Purposes*, 25: 310 – 331.

Charles, M. 2006b. The construction of stance in reporting clauses: A cross disciplinary study of theses. *Applied Linguistics*, 27: 492 – 518.

Chen, Y. 2009. Lexical bundles across learner writing development. Unpublished doctoral dissertation, Lancaster, UK: Lancaster University.

Chen, Y. & Baker, P. 2010. Lexical bundles in L1 and L2 academic writing. *Language Learning and Technology*, 14: 30 – 49.

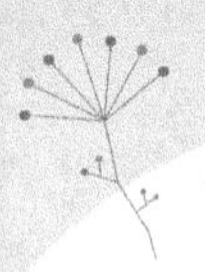

Cheng, W., Greaves, C. & Warren, M. 2006. From n-gram to skipgram to concgram. *International Journal of Corpus Linguistics*, 11 (4): 411 – 433.

Cherry, R. 1988. Politeness in written persuasion. *Journal of Pragmatics*, 12: 63 – 81.

Chief, L. C., Huang, C. R., Chen, K. J., Tsai, M. C. & Chang L. L. 2000. What can near synonyms tell us? *Computational Linguistics and Chinese Language Processing*, 5(1): 47 – 60.

Clyne, M. 1991. The sociolinguistic dimension: The dilemma of the German-speaking Scholar. In Schroder, H. (ed.), *Subject-oriented texts*. Berlin/New York: Walter de Gruyter.

Coates, J. 1983. *The semantics of modal auxiliaries*. London: Croom Helm.

Cohen, A. 1999. Generics, frequency adverbs and probability. *Linguistics and Philosophy*, 22(3): 221 – 253.

Collins, 2009. *Collins COBUILD Advanced Dictionary*. 6th ed. Boston, MA: Heinle Cengage Learning.

Connor, U., Davis, K. & De Rycker, T. 1995. Correctness and clarity in applying for overseas jobs: A cross-cultural analysis of U.S. and Flemish applications. *Text*, 15 (4): 457 – 476.

Connor, U. & Mauranen, A. 1999. Linguistic analysis of grant proposals: European Union research grants. *English for Specific Purposes*, 18(1): 47 – 62.

Connor, U., Precht, K. & Upton, T. 2002. Business English: Learner data from Belgium, Finland, and the US. In Granger, S., Hung, J. & Precht, S. (eds.), *Computer learner corpora, second language acquisition, and foreign language teaching*. Amsterdam: Benjamins.

Conrad, S. & Biber, D. 2000. Adverbial marking of stance in speech and writing. In Hunston, S. & Thompson, G. (eds.),

Evaluation in text: Authorial stance and the construction of discourse. Oxford: Oxford University Press, 57 – 73.

Cornillie, B. 2009. Evidentiality and epistemic modality: On the close relationship of two different categories. *Functions of Language*, 16 (1): 32 – 44.

Crompton, P. 1997. Hedging in academic writing: Some theoretical aspects. *English for Specific Purposes*, 16: 271 – 289.

DeCapua, A. 2008. *Grammar for teachers: A guide to American English for native and non-native speakers.* New York: Springer Science & Business Media.

Dudley-Evans, T. 1991. English for Specific Purposes: International in scope, specific in purpose. *TESOL Quaterly*, 25: 297 – 314.

Dudley-Evans, T. 2000. Genre analysis: A key to a theory of ESP. URL: www.uv.es.aelfe/webRAs/RA_2_Dudley.pdf.

Dudley-Evans, A. & St. John, M. J. 1998. *Developments in English for Specific Purposes.* Cambridge: Cambridge University Press.

Durik, A. M., Britt, M. A., Reynolds, R. & Storey, J. 2008. The effects of hedges in persuasive arguments. *Journal of Language and Social Psychology*, 27(3): 217 – 234.

Edith, A. S. & Akhta, K. 1985. Verbs form and rhetorical function in Science writing: A Study of M. S. theses in biology, chemistry, and physics. *The ESP Journal*, 4(1): 49 – 58.

Falahati, R. 2004. A contrastive study of hedging in English and Farsi academic discourse. Unpublished MA thesis. Tehran: University of Tehran, Department of Linguistics.

Falahati, R. 2005. The use of hedging across different disciplines and rhetorical sections of research articles. Unpublished PhD thesis, University of Ottawa.

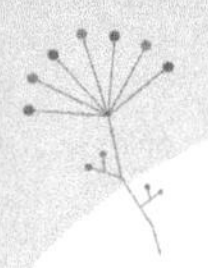

Firth, J. R. 1957. Modes of meanings. *Papers in linguistics 1934 – 1951*. London: Oxford University Press.

Fløttum, K., Dahl, T. & Kinn, T. 2006. *Academic voices across languages and disciplines*. Amsterdam/Philadelphia: John Benjamins.

Francis, G., Hunston, S. & Manning, E. 1996. *Verbs*. London: Harper Collins/Cobuild.

Francis, G., Hunston, S. & Manning, E. 1997. *Collins cobuild grammar patterns 1: Verbs*. London: HarperCollins.

Francis, G., Hunston, S. & Manning, E. 1998. *Collins cobuild grammar patterns 2: Nouns and Adjectives*. London: HarperCollins.

Fraser, B. 1975. Hedged performatives. In Cole, P. & Morgan, J. L. (eds.), *Syntax and semantics*. New York: Academic Press, 3, 187 – 210.

Fraser, B. 2010. Pragmatic competence: The case of hedging. In Kaltenbock, G., Mihatsch, W. & Schneider, S. (eds.), *Studies in Pragmatics 9: New Approaches to Hedging*. Bingley: Emerald Group Publishing Ltd.

Gabrielatos, C. & McEnery, T. 2005. Epistemic modality in MA dissertations. In Fuertes-Olivera, P. A. (ed.), *Lengua y socieded: Investigaciones recientes en lingüística aplicada*, Lingüística y Filologia no. 61. Valladolid: Universidad de Valladolid, 311 – 331.

Gao, Q. 2012. Interpersonal functions of epistemic modality in academic English writing. *Chinese Journal of Applied Linguistics*, 35 (3): 352 – 344.

Gilbert, G. N. & Mulkay, M. 1991. Replication and Mere Replication. In Mulkay, M. (ed.), *Sociology of science: A sociological pilgrimage*. PA: Open University Press.

Gillett, A. 2006. Features of academic writing—hedging. *Using English for academic purposes* [*Online*]. Retrieved 14 Nov, 2010 from: www.uefap.com/writing/feature/hedge.htm.

Grabe, W. & Kaplan, R. B. 1996. *Theory and practice of writing: An applied linguistic perspective.* New York: Longman.

Granger, S. 1998. *Learner English on computer.* London: Addison Wesley Longman.

Granger, S. & Paquot, M. 2005. The phraseology of EFL academic writing: Methodological issues and research findings. Paper presented at AAACL6 & ICAME 26, 12 – 15 May 2005, Ann Arbor, Michigan.

Granger, S. & Paquot, M. 2009. Lexical verbs in academic discourse: A corpus-driven study of learner use. In Charles, M., Pecorari, D. & Hunston, S. (eds.), *Academic writing: At the interface of corpus and discourse.* London and New York: Continuum.

Granger, S. & Rayson, P. 1998. Automatic profiling of learner texts. In Granger, S. (ed.), *Learner English on computer.* London: Longman.

Gustilo, L. E. 2010. '*Although if* is more frequent than *whether...*' An analysis of the uses of adverbial clauses in Philippine English research articles. *Philippine ESL Journal*, 4: 24 – 44.

Hallilday, M. A. K. 1979. *Language as a social semiotic.* London: Edward Arnold.

Halliday, M. A. K. & Martin, J. R. 1993. *Writing science: Literacy and discursive power.* London: Falmer Press.

Halmari, H. & Virtanen, T. 2005. *Persuasion across genres: A linguistic approach.* Amsterdam: John Benjamins.

Hanania, E. A. S. & Akhtar, K. 1985. Verb form and rhetorical function in science writing: A study of M. S. theses in biology, chemistry, and physics. *The ESP Journal*, 4: 49 – 58.

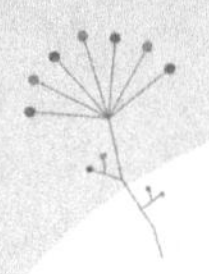

Harwood, N. 2003. Person markers and interpersonal medadiscourse in academic writing: A multidisciplinary corpus-based study of expert and student texts. Unpublished doctoral thesis, Canterbury Christ Church University College.

Harwood, N. 2005. 'We do not seem to have a theory ... The theory I present here attempts to fill this gap': Inclusive and exclusive pronouns in academic writing. *Applied Linguistics*, 26 (3): 343 – 375.

Herslund, M. 2005. Subjective and objective modality. *Office of Scientific & Technical Information Technical Reports*, 51(13): 33 – 51.

Hinkel, E. 1995. The use of modal verbs as a reflection of cultural values. *TESOL Quarterly*, 29 (2), summer: 325 – 341.

Hinkel, E. 1997. Indirectness in L1 and L2 academic writing. *Journal of Pragmatics*, 27: 361 – 386.

Hinkel, E. 2003. Adverbial markers and tone in L1 and L2 students' writing. *Journal of Pragmatics*, 35: 1049 – 1068.

Hinkel, E. 2004. Teaching academic ESL writing: Practical techniques in vocabulary and grammar. *The Keiai Journal of International Studies*, 16: 115 – 119.

Hoey, M. 1997. From concordance to text structure: New uses for computer corpora. In Lewandowska-Tomaszczyk, B. & Melia, P. J. (eds.), *PALC' 97: Practical Applications in Language Corpora*. Porland: Lodz University Press, 223.

Hoey, M. 2000. A world beyond collocation: New perspectives on vocabulary teaching. In Lewis, M. (ed.), *Teaching Collocations*. Hove, UK: Language Teaching Publications.

Hoey, M. 2005. *Lexical priming: A new theory of words and language*. London: Routledge.

Hoey, M., Mahlberg, M., Stubbs, M. & Teubert, W. 2007. *Text, discourse and corpora: Theory and analysis*. London:

Continuum.

Hoey, M. & O'Donnel, M. B. 2008. Lexicography, grammar, and textual position. *International Journal of Lexicography*, 21 (3): 293 – 309.

Holmes, J. 1982. Expressing doubt and certainty in English. *RELC Journal*, 13: 9 – 28.

Holmes, J. 1984. Modifying illocutionary force. *Journal of Pragmatics*, 8: 345 – 365.

Holmes, J. 1988. Doubt and certainty in ESL textbooks. *Applied Linguistics*, 9(1): 21 – 44.

Hopkins, A. & Dudley-Evans, T. 1988. A genre-based investigation of the discussion sections in articles and dissertations. *English for Specific Purposes*, 7: 113 – 121.

Hosman, L. A. 1989. The evaluative consequences of hedges, hesitation, and intensifiers: Powerful and powerless speech-styles. *Human Communication Research*, 15: 383 – 406.

Howard, W. 2004. Lexical frames and reported speech. *ELT Journal*, 58(2): 247 – 257.

Hoye, L. 1997. *Adverbs and modality in English*. Essex: Longman.

Hu, Z., Brown, D. & Brown, L. 1982. Some linguistic differences in the written English of Chinese and Australian students. *Language Learning and Communication*, 1: 39 – 49.

Huang, S. 1975. *A Study of Adverbs*. Berlin/New York: Mouton de Gruyter.

Huddleston, R. & Pullum, G. K. 2002. *The Cambridge grammar of the English language*. Cambridge: Cambridge University Press.

Hunston, S. 2002. *Corpora in applied linguistics*. Cambridge: Cambridge University Press.

Hunston, S. 2007. Semantic prosody revisited. *International Journal of Corpus Linguistics*, 12(2): 249 –268.

Hunston, S. 2008. Starting with the small words: Patterns, lexis and semantic sequences. *International Journal of Corpus Linguistics*, 13 (3): 271 –295.

Hunston, S. & Francis, G. 1998. Verbs observed: A corpus-driven pedagogic grammar. *Applied Linguistics*,19(1): 45 –72.

Hunston, S. & Francis, G. 2000. *Pattern grammar: A corpus-driven approach to the lexical grammar of English.* Amsterdam and Philadelphia: John Benjamins.

Hunston, S. & Sinclair, J. 2003. A local grammar of evaluation. In Hunston, S. & Thompson, G. (eds.), *Evaluation in text: Authorial stance and the construction of discourse*. Oxford: Oxford University Press, 74 –101.

Hunston, S., Francis, G. & Manning, E. 1997. Grammar and vocabulary: Showing the connections. *ELT Journal*, 51(3): 208 –216.

Hwang, L., Ze Vang, M. & Dyer, J. 2010. A corpus-based analysis of citation practices of Generation 1. 5 and international student writers. *Poster presentation at the UROP Spring Research Symposium*. The University of Michigan, Ann Arbor, MI.

Hyland, K. 1994. Hedging in academic writing and EAP textbooks. *English for Specific Purposes*, 13: 239 –256.

Hyland, K. 1995. The author in the text: hedging scientific writing. *Hong Kong Papers in Linguistics and Language Teaching*, 18: 33 –42.

Hyland, K. 1996a. Talking to academy: Forms of hedging in science research articles. *Written Communication*, 13: 251 –281.

Hyland, K. 1996b. Writing without conviction? Hedging in science research articles. *Applied Linguistics*, 17: 433 –454.

Hyland, K. 1997. Scientific claims and community values: articulating an academic culture. *Language & Communication*, 17: 19 – 31.

Hyland, K. 1998a. *Hedging in scientific research articles*. Amsterdam/Philadelphia: John Benjamins Publishing Company.

Hyland, K. 1998b. Boosting, hedging and the negotiation of academic knowledge. *Text*, 18: 349 – 382.

Hyland, K. 1999. Talking to students: Metadiscourse in introductory course books. *English for Specific Purposes*, 18: 3 – 26.

Hyland, K. 2000. *Disciplinary discourses: Social interactions in academic writing*. Harlow: Longman.

Hyland, K. 2001. Humble servants of the discipline? Self-mention in research articles. *English for Specific Purposes*, 20: 207 – 226.

Hyland, K. 2002. Authority and invisibility: Authorial identify in academic writing. *Journal of Pragmatics*, 34: 1091 – 1112.

Hyland, K. 2004. Metadiscourse in academic writing: A reappraisal. *Applied Linguistics*, 25: 77 – 156.

Hyland, K. 2005. *Metadiscourse: Exploring interaction in writing, continuum discourse series*. New York: Continuum.

Hyland, K. 2008. As can be seen: Lexical bundles and disciplinary variation. *English for Specific Purposes*, 27 (1): 4 – 21.

Hyland, K. & Milton, J. 1997. Qualification and certainty in L1 and L2 students' writing. *Journal of Second Language Writing*, 6: 183 – 205.

Hyland, K. & Tse, P. 2007. Is there an 'Academic Vocabulary'? *TESOL Quarterly*, 41(2): 235 – 253.

Ivanic, R. 1998. *Writing and identity: The discoursal construction of identify in academic writing*. Amsterdam/Philadelphia: John Benjamins.

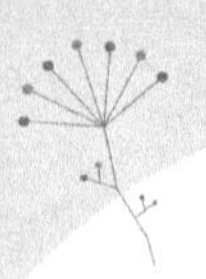

Jogthong, C. 2001. Research article introductions in Thai: Genre analysis of academic writing. Unpublished doctoral dissertation, West Virginia University.

Jordan, R. R. 1997. *English for academic purposes. A guide and resource book for teachers*. Cambridge: Cambridge University Press.

Kachru, B. B. 1985. Standards, codification and sociolinguistic realism: The English language in the Outer Circle. In Quirk, R. & Widdowson, H. (eds.), *English in the world: Teaching and learning the language and literatures*. Cambridge: Cambridge University Press.

Kennedy, G. 1987. Expressing temporal frequency in academic English. *TESOL Quarterly*, 21: 69 – 86.

Kennedy, G. 2002. Variation in the distribution of modal verbs in the British National Corpus. In Reppen, R., Fitzmaurice, S. M. & Biber, D. (eds.), *Using corpora to explore linguistic variation*. Amsterdam/Philadelphia: John Benjamins Publishing Co.

Kuo, C. H. 1999. The use of personal pronouns: Role relationships in scientific journal articles. *English for Specific Purposes*, 18(2): 121 – 138.

Kwachka, P. B. & Basham, C. 1990. Literacy acts and cultural artifacts: On extensions of English modals. *Journal of Pragmatics*, 14: 413 – 429.

Lakoff, G. 1972. Hedges: A study in meaning criteria and the logic of fuzzy concepts. *Chicago Linguistic Society Papers*, 8: 183 – 228.

Leech, G. 1987. *Meaning and the English verb* (1st ed.). London: Longman.

Leech, G. 1991. The state of the art in Corpus Linguistics. In Aijmer, K. & Altenberg, B. (eds.), *English Corpus Linguistics*.

London: Longman.

Leech, G. 1992. Corpora and theories of linguistic performance. In Startvik, J. (ed.), *Directions in corpus linguistics*. Berlin: Mouton de Gruyter.

Leech, G. 1998. Learner corpora: What they are and what can be done with them. In Granger, S. (ed.), *Learner English on Computer*. London: Longman.

Leech, G. 2004. *Meaning and the English verb* (2nd ed.). London: Longman.

Leech, G. 2005. *Meaning and the English verb* (3rd ed.). London: Longman.

Levelt, W. 1989. *Speaking: From intention to articulation*. Cambridge, MA: MIT Press.

Lewin, B. A. 2005. Hedging: An exploratory study of authors' and readers' identification of 'toning down' in scientific texts. *English for Specific Purposes*, 4: 163 – 178.

Lopez, G. S. 1982. Article introduction in Spanish: A study of comparative rhetoric. Unpublished doctoral dissertation, University of Aston at Birmingham, UK.

Lorenz, G. 1999. Adjective intensification—learners versus native speakers. A corpus study of argumentative writing. *Language and computers: Studies in practical linguistics 27*. Amsterdam & Atlanta: Rodopi.

Low, G. 1996. Intensifiers and hedges in questionnaire items and the lexical invisibility hypothesis. *Applied Linguistics*, 17: 1 – 37.

Luukka, M. & Markkanen, R. 1997. Impersonalization as a form of hedging. In Markkanen, R. & Schroder, H. (eds.), *Hedging and discourse: Approaches to the analysis of a pragmatic phenomenon*. Berlin: Walter de Gruyter.

Lyons, J. *Semantics* (Vol. 2). Cambridge: Cambridge University.

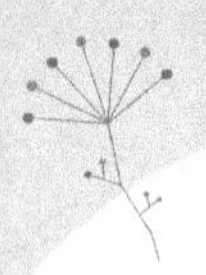

Mahlberg, M. 2009. Local textual functions of 'move' in newspaper story patterns. In Römer, U. & Schulze, R. (eds.), *Exploring the lexis-grammar interface.* Amsterdam: John Benjamins Publishing Company, 265 – 287.

Mahlberg, M. & O'Donnell, M. B. 2008. A fresh view of the structure of hard news stories. In Neumann, S. & Steiner, E. (eds.), *Online proceedings of the 19th European Systemic Functional Linguistics Conference and Workshop*, Saarbrücken, 23 – 25 July 2007. http://scidok.sulb.uni-saarland.de/volltexte/2008/1700/.

Malcolm, L. 1987. What rules govern tense usage in scientific articles? *English for Specific Purposes*, 6: 31 – 43.

Marco, C. & Mercer, R. E. 2004. *Hedging in scientific articles as a means of classifying citations.* Paper delivered at AAAI (American Association for Artificial Intelligence) Spring Symposium on Exploring Attitude & Affect in Text: Theories and Applications, Stanford University.

Markkanen, R. & Schroder, H. 1989. Hedging as a translation problem in scientific text. In Lauren, C. & Nordman, M. (eds.), *Special languages: From human thinking to thinking machines.* London: Multilingual Matters.

Markkanen, R. & Schroder, H. 1992. Hedging and its linguistic realization in English. In Nordman, M. (ed.), *German and Finnish philosophical texts: A case study*. Frankfurt: Peter Lang.

Markkanen, R. & Schroder, H. 1997. Hedging: A challenge for pragmatics and discourse analysis. In Markkanen, R. & Schroder, H. (eds.), *Hedging and discourse: Approaches to the analysis of a pragmatic phenomenon in academic texts.* Berlin/New York: Walter de Gruyter.

McEnery, T. & Wilson, A. 2001. *Corpus linguistics* (2nd ed.). Edinburgh: Edinburgh University Press.

McEnery, T., Xiao, R. & Tono, Y. 2006. *Corpus-based language studies*. London and New York: Routledge.

Meyer, C. F. 2002. *English corpus linguistics*. Cambridge: Cambridge University Press.

Meyer, P. G. 1997. Hedging strategies in written academic discourse: Strengthening the argument by weakening the claim. In Markkanen, R. & Schroder, H. (eds.), *Hedging and discourse: Approaches to the analysis of a pragmatic phenomenon in academic texts*. Berlin/New York: Walter de Gruyter.

Mindt, D. 1995. *An empirical grammar of the English verb: modal verbs*. Berlin: Cornelsen.

Moltmann, F. 2003. Propositional attitudes without propositions. *Synthese: An International Journal for Epistemology, Methodology and Philosophy of Science*, 135: 77 118.

Müller, C. & Strube, M. 2006. Multi-Level Annotation of Linguistic Data with MMAX2. In Braun, S., Kohn, K. & Mukherjee, J. (eds.), *Corpus technology and language pedagogy: New resources, new tools, new methods*. Frankfurt: Peter Lang.

Musa, A. 2014. Hedging in academic writing: A pragmatic analysis of English and Chemistry masters' theses in a Ghanaian University. *English for Specific Purposes World*, 42(15): 1 – 26.

Myers, G. 1989. The pragmatics of politeness in scientific articles. *Applied Linguistics*, 10: 1 – 35.

Myers, G. 1990. *Writing biology: Texts in the social construction of science*. Madison WI: Madison University Press.

Najjar, H. 1990. Arabic as a research language: The case of the agricultural sciences. Unpublished doctoral dissertation, University of Michigan.

Narvaez-Berthelemot, N. & Russell, J. 2001. World distribution of social science journals: A view from the periphery.

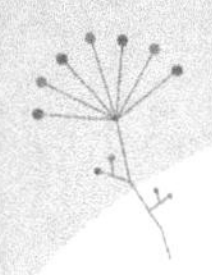

Scientometrics, 51(1): 223 – 239.

Nuyts, J. 2001. *Epistemic modality, language and conceptualization: A cognitive-pragmatic perspective*. Amsterdam and Philadelphia: John Benjamins.

Nwogu, K. N. 1997. The medical research paper: Structure and functions. *English for Specific Purposes*, 16: 119 – 138.

Oakey, D. J. 2005. Academic vocabulary in academic discourse: The phraseological behaviour of EVALUATION in economics research articles. In Tognini-Bonelli, E. & Del Lungo Camiciotti, G. (eds.), *Strategies in academic discourse*. Amsterdam: Benjamins, 169 – 183.

O'Donnell, M., Scott, M., Mahlberg, M. & Hoey, M. 2012. Exploring text-initial words, clusters and concgrams in a newspaper corpus. *Corpus Linguistics and Linguistic Theory*, 8(1):73 – 111.

Palmer, F. R. 1990. *Modality and the English modals* (2nd ed.). London: Longman.

Palmer, F. R. 2001. *Mood and modality* (2nd ed.). Cambridge: Cambridge University Press.

Paradis, C. 1997. Degree modifiers of adjectives in spoken British English. *Lund Studies in English 92*. Lund: Lund University Press.

Perkins, M. R. 1983. *Modal Expressions in English*. London: Pinter.

Pindi, M. & Bloor, T. 1986. Playing safe with predictions: Hedging, attribution and conditions in economic forecasting. *Written Language*. BAAL. 2 CILT.

Precht, K. 2003. Stance moods in spoken English: Evidentiality and affect in British and American conversation. *Text*. 23: 239 – 257.

Quirk, R., Greenbaum, S., Leech, G. & Svartvik, J. 1985.

A comprehensive grammar of the English language. London: Longman.

Römer, U. & Wulff, S. 2010. Applying corpus methods to writing research: Explorations of MICUSP. *Journal of Writing Research*, 2(2): 99 - 127.

Rounds, P. 1982. Hedging in written academic discourse: Precision and flexibility. Mimeo, The University of Michigan.

Salager-Meyer, F. 1991. Medical English abstracts: How well structured are they? *Journal of the American Society for Information Science*, 42 (7): 528 - 531.

Salager-Meyer, F. 1992. A text-type and move analysis study of verb, tense and modality distribution in medical English abstracts. *English for Specific Purposes*, 11: 93 - 113.

Salager-Meyer, F. 1994. Hedges and textual communicative function in medical English written discourse. *English for Specific Purposes*, 13: 149 - 170.

Salager-Meyer, F. 1995. I think that perhaps you should: A study of hedges in written scientific discourse. *Journal of TESOL*, 2: 127 - 143.

Sbisa, M. 2001. Illocutionary force and degrees of strength in language use. *Journal of Pragmatics*, 33: 1791 - 1814.

Schiffer, S. 2008. Propositional content. In Lepore, E. & Smith, B. C. (eds.), *The Oxford handbook of philosophy of language*. Oxford: Oxford University Press.

Schiffrin, D., Tannen, D. & Hamilton, H. 2001. *The handbook of discourse analysis*. Oxford: Blackwell.

Schütz, R. 2005. *English—The international language*. Retrieved December 20, 2006. http://www. sk. com. br/sk-ingl. html

Scollon, R. S. & Scollon, S. 2001. *Intercultural communication*

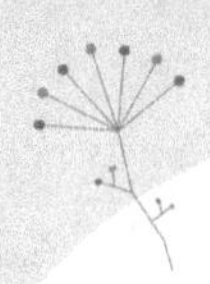

(2nd ed.). Oxford: Blackwell.

Scott, M. 1999. *WordSmith tools help manual* (Version 3.0). Oxford: Oxford University Press.

Šeškauskien, I. 2008. Hedging in ESL: A case study of Lithuanian learners. *Studies About Languates*, 13:6.

Shaw, P. 1992. Reasons for the correlation of voice, tense and sentence function in reporting verbs. *Applied Linguistics*, 13: 302 - 319.

Simpson, P. 1990. Modality in literary-critical discourse. In Nash, W. (ed.), *The writing scholar: Studies in academic discourse*. Newbury Park: Sage Publications.

Sinclair, J. M. 1991. *Corpus, concordance, collocation*. Oxford: Oxford University Press.

Sinclair, J. M. 1996. The search for units of meaning. *Texts*, IX: 75 - 106.

Sinclair, J. M. 1999. A way with common words. In Hasselgard, H. & Oksefjell, S. (eds.), *Out of corpora: A study in honour of Stig Johansson*. Amsterdam: Rodopi, 157 - 175.

Sinclair, J. M. 2004. *Trust the text: Language, corpus and discourse*. London: Routledge.

Skelton, J. 1998. The care and maintenance of hedges. *ELT Journal*, 42: 37 - 43.

Stubbs, M. 2001. On inference theories and code theories: Corpus evidence for semantic schemas. *Text*, 21: 437 - 465.

Sun, W. 2004. Yingyu zhuanye xueshi lunwen xiezuo xianzhuang fenxi [The problems in thesis writing of undergraduate students majoring in English in China]. *Foreign Language World*, 3: 59 - 64.

Swales, J. M. 1981. Aspects of article introductions. *Aston ESP research reports No. 1*. Birmingham, UK: Aston University,

Language Studies Unit.

Swales, J. M. 1990. *Genre analysis: English in academic and research setting.* Cambridge: Cambridge University Press.

Swales, J. M. 2004. *Research genres: Exploration and applications.* Cambridge: Cambridge University Press.

Swales, J. M. & Feak, C. 1994. *Academic writing for graduate students.* Michigan: The University of Michigan Press.

Swart, H. D. 1991. Adverbs of quantification: A generalized quantifier approach. Groningen University dissertation. Also published 1993, New York: Garland.

Tang, R. & John, S. 1999. The 'I' identity: Exploring writer identity in student academic writing through the first person pronoun. *English for Specific Purposes*, 18: S23 – S39.

Taylor, J. R. 1995. *Linguistic categorization: Prototypes in linguistic theory.* Oxford: Clarendon Press.

Thomas, S. & Hawes, T. P. 1994. Reporting verbs in medical journals. English for Specific Purposes, 13: 129 – 148.

Thompson, P. 2001. A pedagogically-motivated corpus-based examination of PhD theses: Macrostructure, citation practices and uses of modal verbs. Unpublished PhD thesis, University of Reading.

Thompson, G. & Yiyun, Y. 1991. Evaluation in the reporting verbs used in academic papers. *Applied Linguistics*, 12 (4): 365 – 382.

Tognini-Bonelli, E. 2001. *Corpus linguistics at work. Studies in Corpus Linguistic*, 6. Amsterdam: John Benjamins.

Upton, T. & Connor, U. 2001. Using computerized corpus analysis to investigate the textlinguistic discourse moves of a genre. *English for Specific Purposes*, 20: 313 – 329.

Vande Kopple, W. 1985. Some exploratory discourse on metadiscourse. *College Composition Commun.*, 36 (1): 82 – 93.

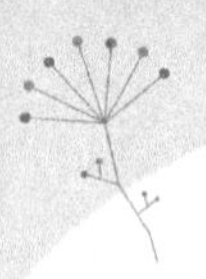

Varttala, T. 2001. Hedging in scientifically oriented discourse: Exploring variation according to discipline and intended audience. (Doctoral dissertation, University of Tampere). Retrieved Nov 20, 2010. https://tampub.uta.fi/bitstream/handle/10024/67148/951-44-5195-3.pdf? sequence=1.

Varttala, T. 2003. Hedging in scientific research articles: A cross-disciplinary study. In Cortese, G. & Riley, P. (eds.), *Domain-specific English: Textual practices across communities and classrooms*. New York: Peter Lang.

Vassileva, I. 1998. Who am I/who are we in academic writing?: A contrastive analysis of authorial presence in English, German, French, Russian and Bulgarian. *International Journal of Applied Linguistics*, 8 (2): 163-190.

Vassileva, I. 2001. Commitment and detachment in English and Bulgarian academic writing. *English for Specific Purposes*, 20: 83-102.

Ventola, E. & Mauranen, A. 1990. *Tutkijat ja englanniksi kirjoittaminen*. Helsinki: Helsiniki University Press.

Verschueren, J. 1980. *On speech act verbs*. Amsterdam: John Benjamins B. V.

Wang, H. 2010. *The end of the revolution: China and the limits of modernity*. London: Verso.

West, G. K. 1980. That-nominal construction in traditional rhetorical divisions of scientific research papers. *TESOL Quarterly*, 14 (4): 483-488.

Widdowson, H. G. 1984. *Explorations in applied linguistics 2*. Oxford: Oxford University Press.

Wingard, P. 1981. Some verb forms and functions in six medical texts. In Selinker, L., Tarone, E. & Hanzelli, V. (eds.), *English for academic and technical purposes: Studies in honor of Louis*

Trimble. Rowley, MA: Newbury House Publishers Inc.

Winkler, A. C. & McCeuen, J. R. 1989. *Writing the research paper: A handbook with both the MLA and APA documentation styles.* San Diego: Harcourt Brace Jovanovich.

Wishnoff, J. R. 2000. Hedging your bets: L2 learners' acquisition of pragmatic device in academic writing and computer-mediated discourse. *Second Language Studies*, 19: 119 – 148.

Xu, L. L. 2005. A genre-based approach to the writing of the introduction section of an ESL/EFL academic paper. *Sino-US English Teaching*, 2: 22 – 26.

Yang, R. & Allison, D. 2004. Research articles in applied linguistics: Structures from a functional perspective. *English for Specific Purposes*, 23(3): 264 – 279.

Zhang, Y. 2005. Interpersonal meanings of hedges in academic discourse. *Journal of Literature, History and Philosophy*, 6: 100 – 106.

Zhu, H. 2011. A probe into Chinese learners' negative cultural transfer in EFL. *Journal of Language Teaching and Research*, 2: 212 – 215.

Zuck, J. G. & Zuck, L. V. 1986. Hedging in news writing. In Cornu, A. M., Van, J., Ddlahaye, P. M. & Baten, L. (eds.), *Beads or bracelets? How do we approach LSP*, *Selected papers form the fifth European symposium on LSP.* Oxford: Oxford University Press.

Zuck, J. G. & Zuck, L. V. 1987. Hedging in newswriting. In Cornu, A., Vanparijs, J., Delahaye, M. & Baten, L. (eds.), *Selected papers from the fifth European symposiums on LSP.* Oxford: Oxford University Press.